Breaking Barriers, Shaping Worlds

Edited by Jill Campbell-Miller,
Greg Donaghy, and Stacey Barker

Breaking Barriers, Shaping Worlds
Canadian Women and the Search for Global Order

© UBC Press 2021

All rights reserved. No part of this publication may be reproduced, stored in a retrieval system, or transmitted, in any form or by any means, without prior written permission of the publisher, or, in Canada, in the case of photocopying or other reprographic copying, a licence from Access Copyright, www.accesscopyright.ca.

30 29 28 27 26 25 24 23 22 21   5 4 3 2 1

Printed in Canada on FSC-certified ancient-forest-free paper (100% post-consumer recycled) that is processed chlorine- and acid-free.

Library and Archives Canada Cataloguing in Publication

Title: Breaking barriers, shaping worlds : Canadian women and the search for global order / edited by Jill Campbell-Miller, Greg Donaghy, and Stacey Barker.
Names: Campbell-Miller, Jill, editor. | Donaghy, Greg, editor. | Barker, Stacey, 1973- editor.
Description: Includes bibliographical references and index.
Identifiers: Canadiana (print) 20210290846 | Canadiana (ebook) 20210290978 | ISBN 9780774866408 (hardcover) | ISBN 9780774866415 (paperback) | ISBN 9780774866422 (PDF) | ISBN 9780774866439 (EPUB)
Subjects: LCSH: Women in development—Canada. | LCSH: Women—Political activity—Canada. | LCSH: Women diplomats—Canada. | LCSH: Canada—Foreign relations—1945-
Classification: LCC HQ1240.5.C3 B74 2021 | DDC 327.0820971—dc23

Canada

UBC Press gratefully acknowledges the financial support for our publishing program of the Government of Canada (through the Canada Book Fund), the Canada Council for the Arts, and the British Columbia Arts Council.

This book has been published with the help of a grant from the Canadian Federation for the Humanities and Social Sciences, through the Awards to Scholarly Publications Program, using funds provided by the Social Sciences and Humanities Research Council of Canada.

Printed and bound in Canada by Friesens
Set in Myriad and Garamond by Artegraphica Design Co.
Copy editor: Robyn So
Proofreader: Alison Strobel
Cover designer: David Drummond

UBC Press
The University of British Columbia
2029 West Mall
Vancouver, BC V6T 1Z2
www.ubcpress.ca

*To Greg, for your guidance and mentorship.
We hope we have made you proud.*

Contents

Acknowledgments / ix

Introduction: "Where Are the Women?" / 3
Jill Campbell-Miller and Greg Donaghy

Part 1: Women in Missions, Aid, and Development

1 Quietly Contesting Patriarchy: Dr. Jessie MacBean's
  Medical Work in South China, 1925–35 / 21
  Kim Girouard

2 A Mission for Modernity: Canadian Women in Medical
  and Nursing Education in India, 1946–66 / 39
  Jill Campbell-Miller

3 Life Stories, Wife Stories: Women Advisors on Economic
  Development / 63
  David Webster

Part 2: Women in International Resistance

4 Historically Invisible: The Women's International League for Peace and Freedom, 1914–29 / 93
   Sharon Anne Cook and Lorna McLean

5 Collecting Teeth for Peace: The Voice of Women, the Baby Tooth Survey, and the Search for Security in the Atomic Age / 116
   Susan Colbourn

6 Marie Smallface-Marule: An Indigenous Internationalist / 135
   Jonathan Crossen

Part 3: Women in Diplomacy

7 P.K. Page and the Art of Diplomacy: An Ambassadorial Wife in Brazil / 161
   Eric Fillion

8 Jean Casselman Wadds: Patriation, Dinner Party Wars, and a Political Diplomat / 183
   Steve Marti and Francine McKenzie

9 Flora MacDonald: Secretary of State for External Affairs, 1979–80 / 205
   Joe Clark

Conclusion: Breaking Historiographic Barriers / 212
   Dominique Marshall

Greg Donaghy: An Appreciation / 222
   Patricia E. Roy

Bibliography / 226

Contributors / 246

Index / 248

Acknowledgments

Thanks go first to the Donaghy family, especially Mary, who reached out to ensure the book's continued success after Greg's death. We are grateful.

This volume would not have been possible without the support of many individuals and organizations. A special and devoted thanks goes to Randy Schmidt, our extremely patient representative at UBC Press, for his guidance through a difficult time. We owe you a great debt of gratitude. Thank you also to the anonymous peer reviewers for their insights and suggestions, which strengthened the manuscript.

We must also thank Patricia E. Roy, who stepped in to write the epilogue under a time pressure. Thank you for your insights. We acknowledge David Webster's advice and encouragement following Greg's passing, as well as all the authors for their patience in seeing this project to its completion.

We are grateful to Global Affairs Canada, who helped fund a public conference on the topic of women in Canadian foreign policy in March of 2019. We would like to thank retired members of the civil service who shared their personal insights into the topic. We would like to particularly thank Elissa Golberg, who delivered the opening remarks, and Jillian Stirk, Deborah Chatsis, Adèle Dion, Sandelle Scrimshaw, and Senator Julie Miville-Dechêne, who chaired the sessions.

Jill Campbell-Miller owes many thanks to her mother, Charlotte Campbell, and her mother-in-law, Marguerite Miller, who looked after children, washed dishes, swept floors, and travelled during a pandemic so that Jill could finish the manuscript during her parental leave. She also would like to thank her husband, David, who took vacation days from work for the same reason. This volume would have been severely delayed without their support. Stacey Barker would like to thank many, but especially Roxanne Thomas, for her unfailing support and constant encouragement.

Breaking Barriers, Shaping Worlds

Introduction
"Where Are the Women?"

Jill Campbell-Miller and Greg Donaghy

IN 1994, POLITICAL SCIENTIST Deborah Stienstra asked, "Can the silence be broken?"[1] Stienstra referred to the silence surrounding gender in the analysis of foreign policy within Canadian political science. It was not enough, for her, to merely tackle "women as a subject."[2] Rather, it was imperative to analyze the underlying gender relations on which the whole field was constructed. Stienstra, along with her colleagues Heather A. Smith and Claire Turenne Sjolander, coedited a book titled *Feminist Perspectives on Canadian Foreign Policy* nearly a decade later, in 2003. In the preface to that volume, they noted that their reports, based on two roundtables on gender and Canadian foreign policy "attracted much interest, but also some hostility, from policy makers."[3] In the introduction to their book, they asked "why there might still be reluctance to integrate feminist critiques and to address gendered analysis in the analysis of Canadian foreign policy and foreign policy more generally."[4]

Much has changed. For example, by 2019 some of the top positions at Global Affairs Canada (GAC), including foreign minister, deputy minister, and assistant deputy minister of strategic policy, were filled by women (though significantly, all white women). The department itself had reoriented to focus on issues applicable to gender and women, particularly in the arena of international development. In 2017 the department renamed Canada's foreign aid program the Feminist International Assistance Policy. Though skeptics remain guarded about the concrete outcomes of this female-forward reorientation within GAC, the difficult questions posed by scholars such as Stienstra in the 1990s and early 2000s helped make such a change possible.

Canadian historians of diplomacy and foreign policy can be less sanguine about their field's achievements. With a few notable exceptions, the silence surrounding women and gender relations in histories that investigate Canada and the world has been profound. Despite the changing nature of Canadian international history over the last twenty years, women still rarely feature as central characters. In striking contrast to recent US historiography, there is little scholarship investigating the participation of Canadian women in global affairs as diplomats, aid workers, or members of non-state transnational networks. When reviewing the present state of Canadian international historiography, one can still easily ask, as political scientist Cynthia Enloe did of US international relations history in 1990, "Where are the women?"[5]

This book offers a concise answer: they are everywhere. Though often hidden, forgotten, or ignored, wherever Canada's global influence has been felt in the past century, Canadian women were there. Whether as activists working at home to change Canada's foreign policy, through nascent efforts in humanitarianism and international development, or in the arena of formal diplomacy, women's paid or unpaid work was consequential in shaping the trajectory of Canada's relationship with the world in the twentieth century. This book is the first edited collection to specifically examine women who shaped Canada's international history.

The chapters within this volume break barriers, taking seriously the role of women in a variety of contexts, whether it be within the domestic sphere or as official agents of the state. More often, as these chapters show, women's work occupied the liminal space between these two extremes and thus remained hidden; their so-called domestic activities greased the wheels of officialdom, while their paid work often operated in gendered spaces considered worthwhile yet unremarkable. This collection not only makes visible these usually hidden or downplayed efforts, it also treats them with the same analytic rigour that traditional diplomatic history is granted. The authors do not seek to make new heroes, or to celebrate women who operated in the same complicated, imperialist, and racialized spaces as men. Rather, they aim to fill out a fuller and more comprehensive picture of Canada's global past.

Canada's New International History

As such, this book fits in with historiographical efforts already under way in Canada. For decades, Canadian international history unfolded as the story of Canada's diplomatic and trade relations with a small set of countries managed by a small set of actors. Generations of historians tracked prime ministers and foreign ministers, all white and mostly male, as they toiled alongside a similar group of ministers, diplomats, and bureaucrats. Diligently, historians documented Ottawa's pursuit of the national interest within the narrow confines of John Bartlet Brebner's "North Atlantic triangle," even as they debated the relevance of his phrase, primarily interested in the outsized role that London and Washington played in defining Canada's domestic and international histories.[6] The best work was meticulously researched, solidly grounded in archives and interviews, and elegantly written. It illuminated the profound ways that global events have shaped Canada's national history and, in turn, how Canada has influenced world affairs.

Over the past two decades, international history in Canada has changed dramatically. Inspired by the emergence of transnational history in the United States and Europe, historians interested in Canada's international past have broadened their outlook and subject matter considerably. As editors Asa McKercher and Philip Van Huizen explain in the introduction to their 2019 collection, *Undiplomatic History: The New Study of Canada and the World,* the "goal is to move away from an exclusive focus on diplomatic history, viewed (rightly, in certain ways) as hidebound, elitist, and overly concerned with the state and the small group of white males who dominated it."[7] Instead, by expanding their scope of analysis, McKercher and Van Huizen aim to situate past diplomacy in its broadest domestic and external contexts, incorporating the approaches of transnational and global history into the study of Canada's international history.[8] In the introduction to their earlier collection, *Dominion of Race: Rethinking Canada's International History,* Laura Madokoro and Francine McKenzie succinctly summarize this shift as an expansion in the field's "subject, geography, and methodology."[9]

These changes are especially evident in three ways. First, historians are more curious than ever about *who* is relevant to Canada's international past. Here, historians of Canadian foreign policy have gained inspiration from other historical approaches. For example, primarily since the 1980s, historians have begun to study traditionally marginalized immigrant and refugee groups, expanding their interest beyond those hailing from the British Isles and considerably broadening our understanding of Canada's domestic political and social histories.[10] Yet it is only recently that historians of international relations and diplomacy have begun to understand how previously overlooked populations are relevant to Canada's role in the world, and to employ new methodologies to examine these groups.

Transnational methodologies extract Canada and its peoples from their singular state and relocate them within a global context of interconnected empires and communities, ideas, and relationships. As the chapters in the 2015 collection *Within and Without the Nation: Canadian History as Transnational History* demonstrate, important domestic policies surrounding colonialism and assimilation, immigration, or even health care are thrown into new light when connected to ideologies and movements extending beyond Canada's borders.[11] Such methodologies are also useful for excavating the histories of Canadians who reached out globally to find inspiration and drive change at home or abroad outside the confines of government institutions. Reframing who is of interest in Canada's international history allows for an expanded view of what constitutes influence and power.

Second, historians have broadened *where* they are looking for global connections in Canada's international past. Just as studies of migration highlight an expanded geography in understanding Canada's domestic past, looking beyond the United States and Great Britain yields fascinating insights into Canada's connections with the world. Though relations with countries in Asia, Africa, or Latin America may rarely have been at the centre of the Department of External Affairs' political map, these geographies nevertheless generate important stories about events and activities central to Canada's self-image and place in the world. Some recently published edited collections focusing largely on topics that look beyond North America and Europe, including *Canada and the Third World: Overlapping Histories*, edited by Karen Dubinsky, Sean Mills, and Scott Rutherford, and *A Samaritan State Revisited: Historical Perspectives on Canadian Foreign Aid*, edited by Greg Donaghy and David Webster, exemplify this interest.[12]

Third, historians have broadened their view of *what* is relevant to Canada's international history. As historians look beyond formal diplomatic relationships for deeper insights into Canada's global engagement, they have exploited innovative theoretical and methodological approaches to raise new and sometimes difficult questions about this history. Indigenous history and postcolonial theory have been particularly influential. While Canada's own position as a colony preoccupied early generations of historians interested in international relations, relatively little thought had been given to Canada's own history as a colonial and imperial actor. However, newer scholarship examining interactions between the British and French Crowns and sovereign Indigenous nations between the sixteenth and nineteenth centuries allows for a fuller understanding of the significance of 1867.[13] This appreciation provokes and troubles previously held assumptions about Canada's "domestic" history, something that many Indigenous leaders have long understood, and as Jonathan Crossen points out in Chapter 6. Seeing Indigenous peoples as nations acting within an international context of transnational empire brings new, complex dimensions to the study of Canada and the world.

Despite the many original contributions made in recent years to Canada's international history, there has been an omission. In the five edited collections mentioned above, only seven chapters of sixty have focused exclusively on women or gender.[14] Similarly, almost every academic paper on women and gender published in the *International Journal: Canada's Journal of Global Policy Analysis* has been written by political scientists about contemporary issues.[15] This collection offers a starting point for scholars interested in rectifying women's absence in Canada's international history.

Finding Women in the Historiography

Though it explores a new dimension of Canadian historiography, this book naturally builds on the shoulders of other historians who have written about women on the global stage. Much of this work has occurred outside of Canada. As well as a growing number of biographies and memoirs, scholars have focused on the work of European, British, and American women abroad, for example, by examining women who have been unofficial partners in diplomacy.[16] The journal *Diplomatic History* has often been a venue for writing about the history of women in international relations in the United States.

In Canada, there is a small historiography on women in global affairs. There is very little, for instance, on women diplomats and diplomatic partners. Yet to understand the history of Canadian diplomacy and the Department of External Affairs, it is necessary to look beyond those formally employed by it. This is a point made by Christine Hantel-Fraser, who recorded her own experiences and interviewed others about their lives as "diplomatic wives."[17] Journalist Margaret Weiers' *Envoys Extraordinary: Women of the Canadian Foreign Service,* published in 1995, profiled pioneers and individual women working in the Department of External Affairs and its successor departments.[18] Claire Turenne Sjolander also wrote about one of Canada's most important female diplomats, Margaret Meagher, in an edited collection about the department published in 2009.[19] Unfortunately, as British scholar Vivien Hughes lamented over a decade ago, there are still no memoirs by significant Canadian career women diplomats.[20]

Canadian scholars have focused on women's role in the peace movements of the late nineteenth and early twentieth centuries and on international meetings that brought women together to pursue political action.[21] They have also looked at women's roles within international organizations, such as the Red Cross and the Girl Guides.[22] Tarah Brookfield, for instance, has examined the careers of women who worked for international agencies such as the United Nations Relief and Rehabilitation Administration, as well as the varied experiences of women's activism in Canada on international issues related to child welfare throughout the Cold War.[23] Traditionally, such gendered efforts were seen as beyond formal state-to-state relations and, therefore, of less importance. Yet as Brookfield demonstrates, they played crucial roles in the creation of durable international and transnational networks between people and organizations. These types of networks fostered conditions that allowed for the formation of a rules-based global international order among Western nations after the devastating ruptures of the Great Depression and the Second World War. Women's work, invisible or visible, helped form the backbone of postwar male-led international organizations, societies, and regimes.

Two other overlapping areas have received particular attention from Canadian and international scholars interested in women and their relationship with global movements: missionary history and the history of medicine and nursing. While much older writing about missionaries amounted to little more than hagiographies, recent scholarship has found new ways to understand the work and roles of missionaries within the context of imperialism.[24] Like the "modern women" doctors that Ruth Compton Brouwer studies in her work, medical missionaries often displayed an unyielding commitment to their scientific professions while maintaining strong beliefs surrounding their Christian faiths.[25] Likewise, nurses who travelled abroad to work played a role in shaping perceptions about the role of women in public life and institutions. Karen Flynn's scholarship shows that Caribbean nurses who worked abroad not only filled an important need in newly developing public health systems in the UK and Canada, but also engaged in international nursing organizations that built networks between professional women living in different countries.[26] Understanding the stories of working women in global professional environments adds a new dimension to Canada's role in the twentieth century, moving the conversation beyond government-sponsored actions.

Breaking Barriers, Shaping Worlds

The chapters in this book explore three major themes associated with the role of Canadian women on the world stage during the twentieth century. The first three chapters explore the role of Canadian women in the fields of foreign aid, international development, and global humanitarian work. They went first as missionaries, but by the second half of the twentieth century, they were volunteering abroad through international non-governmental organizations. Though some Canadian women, such as Lotta Hitschmanova, the founder of USC Canada, rose to public prominence for their work, most laboured in obscurity. This was certainly true of Jessie MacBean, the subject of the book's opening chapter, by Kim Girouard. It examines an important precedent to women's work in the postwar international development field – the role of medical missionaries abroad. Though the work of such women is controversial, given the association between mission work and "Anglo-Saxon" imperialism, it was nonetheless meaningful and important. MacBean played a leading part in the organization of the first preventive health services for mothers and infants in South China at the Hackett Medical College for Women in Guangzhou (Canton) between 1925 and 1935. A parallel theme in Girouard's work is the opportunity granted to MacBean to rise above the restrictions based on gender in place for women in medicine in her own country.

This theme is echoed in Jill Campbell-Miller's chapter on the work of two Canadian women in India as medical educators during the two decades immediately after India's independence: Edith Buchanan and Florence Nichols. In this era so close to India's recent imperial past, these two white Canadians were granted privileges based on their connections to this history. Yet, their undoubted medical expertise was acknowledged and valued as institutions in India worked hard to modernize and create an independent postcolonial state. Both women were educational leaders at historically significant nursing and medical colleges in India. Their work illuminates India's post-independence ambitions and the role that these professional women played in the context of the newly developing field of international development.

Women played other vital yet overlooked roles in shaping Canada's postwar relations with an emerging Global South. Historian Susanna Erlandsson reminds us that traditional diplomatic historians have misunderstood the crucial role of gender and women's work in the diplomatic field, which often blended the domestic and public spheres and, as a result, have produced factually incorrect scholarship.[27] Both David Webster and, later in the book, Eric Fillion explore this overlap and the crucial role that Canadian women have played in shaping their spouses' diplomatic postings.

Wives, Webster insists, were often diplomatic assets necessary for the success of development work in the middle decades of the twentieth century. His chapter on the wives of technical assistance advisors explores four "wife stories" that offer insights into the forgotten role of women's labour in this field. Barbara Cadbury, Beatrice Keyfitz, and Beatrice Harding were women married to so-called experts employed to live and work abroad as technical advisors. Eleanor Hinder's case diverges from the other three in that she was legally and socially unable to marry her long-term partner, a woman who worked in the US foreign service. Taking UN posts working in technical assistance allowed Hinder to remain close to her life partner. Regardless of their sexual orientation or their roles "behind the scenes" or as professionals in their own right, the women in Webster's piece demonstrate the intertwined nature of the professional and personal in diplomacy, highlighting the role that women played in "caring labour" and social duties in an international context.

The second section of the book profiles women who acted internationally or who became politically active on issues and in networks of international significance. Sharon Anne Cook and Lorna McLean survey the range of women's peace-based organizations before and during the First World War, resulting in the founding of the Women's International League for Peace and Freedom (WILPF), in 1915. Their chapter profiles six prominent women from the United States, Canada, and the United Kingdom who were recognized as global leaders in peace ideology. Despite their influence on important public figures of the day, most of these women have received little public or scholarly attention. Why, Cook and McLean pointedly ask, is there such public amnesia around women peace activists during the First World War and interwar period, even as organizations such as the League of Nations remain firmly within public and historical memory? Their answer is complex. They describe women who upended prevailing gender norms, arguing for peace from an academic rather than maternalist position. Yet, as Cook and McLean show, they were also self-effacing, adhering to gendered expectations that valued their silence, modesty, and submission. They were sadly complicit, this chapter points out, in erasing their social and political contributions.

Women were also written out of later histories of Canadian peace activism. This is true, for instance, of the national debates over nuclear weapons policy in the late 1950s, usually depicted as a confrontation between Progressive Conservative prime minister John Diefenbaker and his male ministers. Susan Colbourn's chapter on the women's peace movement in this era examines a generation of women activists who fiercely opposed atomic weapons testing programs, restoring women to the larger story. Focusing on the Voice of Women/la Voix des Femmes, a Canadian women's peace organization founded in 1960, Colbourn explores the strategies that this group employed in opposing nuclear testing, including making use of women's gendered roles as child care providers to enlist their participation in baby teeth research. She examines how the Voice of Women/la Voix des Femmes shaped the public conversation around militarization and nuclear weapons testing, arguing that they "blended personal, national, and global understandings of security."

The final chapter in this section, written by Jonathan Crossen, examines Indigenous internationalism through a profile of Marie Smallface-Marule. Born to the Indigenous Káínai community near Lethbridge, Alberta, Smallface-Marule developed an interest in both First Nations politics and international politics while studying at the University of Alberta in the 1960s. After encountering pan-Africanist ideas during volunteer stints with the international development organization Canadian University Service Overseas (CUSO) in Zambia, Smallface-Marule came to understand Indigenous oppression within its full global imperial and colonial context, tapping into a rich vein of intellectual and political power that could be mobilized for change. As a founding staff member of the World Council of Indigenous Peoples, she helped push Indigenous activism beyond domestic politics and onto the global stage.

The final part of the book examines women who acted in the formal realm of diplomacy. Eric Fillion tackles the diplomatic journey of P.K. Page, the poet, author, and wife of Canadian diplomat W. Arthur Irwin. Irwin and Page spent much of the 1950s in Brazil, where he was posted as Canada's ambassador. Though Page did little public writing during this time, she was, as Fillion writes, "neither silent nor invisible." Her independent status as an "artist-ambassadress" gave her access to a uniquely cultivated cultural capital and made her an effective cultural representative of Canada in Brazil. Fillion's description of Page's journey through the field of cultural diplomacy adds another dimension to Canadian international history that has gone largely unexamined, though it has been a subject of interest outside of Canada for some time.[28] Studies of cultural diplomacy allow for another way of finding women's contributions to international history outside of the confines of the embassy.[29]

Both Fillion and Webster's chapters name these women as diplomats, even though they were not officially recognized that way. Yet by the late twentieth century, it was increasingly common for women to be appointed as diplomats by the Canadian government, a theme explored in the book's third section. Steve Marti and Francine McKenzie examine the life and work of one high-ranking diplomat, Jean Casselman Wadds, the first Canadian woman appointed high commissioner to the United Kingdom. Though Casselman Wadds became high commissioner during a particularly sensitive time in Anglo-Canadian relations, as negotiations were under way to repatriate the Canadian constitution, her role has been diminished in historical memory and her mission minimized as just a "dinner party war." Marti and McKenzie challenge that view. Though Casselman Wadds downplayed her gender as irrelevant to her work, it profoundly shaped her diplomatic and strategic choices. Cultivating a "civil, refined, and charming" professional persona, Casselman Wadds emerged as an outstanding and effective high commissioner. Yet, Marti and McKenzie also point to Casselman Wadds' position as a privileged political insider, allowing her to navigate the gendered terrain of international affairs without fundamentally challenging or questioning the sexist barriers in place for other women.

Our final chapter stands apart from the rest. It offers a memoir and personal reflection on Canada's first woman secretary of state for external affairs, Flora MacDonald, the long-time Progressive Conservative politician. Authored by her former boss and colleague, Joe Clark, the prime minister who appointed her to his cabinet in 1979, it is a candid reflection on the barriers to women's advancement in Ottawa. Most important, it is a forthright account of both MacDonald's shortcomings and accomplishments as foreign minister. More women have found homes within the arena of formal diplomacy in recent years. For example, as already alluded to, in 2019, Marta Morgan became the first female deputy minister of foreign affairs. In 2020, Kirsten Hillman became the first ambassador to the United States, and as in that same year women were serving as ambassadors to both the UK and France, all considered prestige postings. Yet by 2020, only three women had ever held the position of minister of foreign affairs, suggesting that Canadian federal politics remains one of the most regressive professional spaces for women in the country.

Conclusion

Historians of Canada's international history must confront the silences embedded into our writing. As this book demonstrates, women's work has been consistently ignored, overlooked, or forgotten. However, more than that, this book also invites others to continue the work of uncovering how gender shaped Canada's presence in the world. In the past, Canada's search for a global order was limited by its adherence to strict gender roles that constrained its ability to solve diplomatic problems, increase trade, and address poverty. Finding women and other groups marginalized by traditional concepts of gender, including 2SLGBTQQIA (two-spirit, lesbian, gay, bisexual, transgender, queer, questioning, intersex, and asexual) people is an increasingly important task for historians of Canada's international history.

Several common themes emerge from these chapters. The first is the importance of biography and, as David Webster points out, prosopography (the collective biography of a linked group) to examining the history of women in international affairs. As many of these chapters show, the presence of Canadian women working and living abroad in the twentieth century, or working on political issues of international concern, was usually tied to very particular and personal life trajectories that set them apart from the dominant culture in which they lived. Whether they were staying within social boundaries as missionaries or wives, or contesting them as activists, understanding their unique life histories is important to placing them within their own social and historical context.

Related to this theme is the presence of women on the margins of political power. The cases of Barbara Cadbury and P.K. Page, or those profiled by

Sharon Anne Cook and Lorna McLean, are especially instructive. Despite Cadbury's vital role in shaping her husband's views and expertise on family planning (and the fundamental importance of women in the history of that often problematic transnational movement), Webster is the first historian to highlight Cadbury's own body of work as influential. P.K. Page seemed to fall silent while in Brazil, yet, as Fillion shows, measured by a different metric she was a sustained voice for Canada while in the country. Similarly, the women leaders of the Women's International League for Peace and Freedom, such as Canadian Julia Grace Wales, interacted with prominent politicians of the day, including Woodrow Wilson. Yet as Cook and McLean demonstrate, these activists' role as promoters of peace during an era very much concerned with international stability has been consistently forgotten, even if their ideas had currency among decision makers of the day.

The women who Cook and McLean discuss, as with Marie Smallface-Marule or those in the Voice of Women/la Voix des Femmes, found intellectual and physical homes in countercultural spaces as academics and activists. Sometimes, exclusion from political power allowed for a certain type of freedom. Unlike Jean Casselman Wadds or Flora MacDonald, who remained circumscribed by the political structures within which they worked, such women were free to speak truth to power. These were women who may have found themselves marginalized based on their gender (and race, in the case of Smallface-Marule), but that hardly prevented them from agitating on behalf of the issues that motivated them.

Yet even those women that stayed within the acceptable boundaries of their gender had to push against the dominant trends of their societies. For women like Jessie MacBean or Florence Nichols, simply to obtain their professional credentials was a major achievement in an era when few women joined the ranks of professional medicine. Though becoming Protestant missionaries as unmarried women was the height of propriety, as women with careers they used overseas positions to pursue professional achievement denied them in Canada, an act of rebellion cloaked in respectability. Similarly, as politicians and diplomats, Jean Casselman Wadds and Flora MacDonald were engaged in an act of feminism even if they rarely applied that label. Their willingness to shoulder these roles spoke to an inner belief in their equality with men, not to mention a steely determination that by its very nature countered sexist stereotypes.

The common element among all the women in this book, named or unnamed, high profile or invisible, remembered or forgotten, is an implicit refusal to be confined within a space determined solely by predetermined gender roles. This is not to valorize them, as for the most part this book represents upper- or middle-class, educated, and white women with opportunities that others in their societies did not have. It is not the historian's job to find or make heroes to celebrate. At the most basic level, what the historians writing in this book do show is that *women were there*, that they are part of the story of Canada's place in the twentieth-century world, and that they influenced the societies within which they worked and lived, in sometimes immeasurable ways. Most profoundly, they show that as Canadian governments sought to construct a global order that allowed the country to remain secure and prosperous, women were assuredly and assertively part of that search, whether they stood within the diplomatic corps or, more often, beside and outside of it.

Notes

1 Deborah Stienstra, "Can the Silence Be Broken? Gender and Canadian Foreign Policy," *International Journal* 50, 1 (1994–95): 103.
2 Stienstra, "Can the Silence Be Broken?" 104.
3 Deborah Stienstra, Claire Turenne Sjolander, and Heather A. Smith, "The Genesis and Journey of This Volume," in *Feminist Perspectives on Canadian Foreign Policy*, eds. Claire Turenne Sjolander, Heather A. Smith, and Deborah Stienstra (Toronto: Oxford University Press, 2003), xii.
4 Stienstra, Turenna Sjolander, and Smith, "Taking Up and Throwing Down the Gauntlet: Feminists, Gender, and Canadian Foreign Policy," in *Feminist Perspectives on Canadian Foreign Policy*, 2.
5 Cynthia Enloe, *Bananas, Beaches, and Bases: Making Feminist Sense of International Politics*, 2nd ed. (Berkeley: University of California Press, 2014), 1. The phrase was also used as the title in Rosemary Foot's review of Enloe's book: Rosemary Foot, "Where Are the Women? The Gender Dimension in the Study of International Relations," *Diplomatic History* 14, 4 (Fall 1990): 615–22.
6 For a recent historiographical review of past works of Canadian international history, see David Meren, "The Tragedies of Canadian International History," *Canadian Historical Review* 96, 4 (Winter 2015): 534–66.
7 Asa McKercher and Philip Van Huizen, "Introduction – Undiplomatic History: Rethinking Canada and the World," in *Undiplomatic History: The New Study of Canada and the World*, ed. Asa McKercher and Philip Van Huizen (Montreal/Kingston: McGill-Queen's University Press, 2019), 5.
8 McKercher and Van Huizen, "Introduction," 3.
9 Laura Madokoro and Francine McKenzie, "Introduction: Writing Race into Canada's International History," in *Dominion of Race: Rethinking Canada's International History*, ed. Laura Madokoro, Francine McKenzie, and David Meren (Vancouver: UBC Press, 2017), 5.
10 For summaries of this trend and relevant historiographies, see booklets produced in the Canadian Historical Association's Immigration and Ethnicity in Canada Series, for example, Marlene Epp, *Refugees in Canada: A Brief History*, Immigration and Ethnicity in Canada

Series 35 (Ottawa, ON: The Canadian Historical Association, 2017), https://cha-shc.ca/_uploads/5c374fb005cf0.pdf.
11 Karen Dubinsky, Adele Perry, and Henry Yu, eds., *Within and Without the Nation: Canadian History as Transnational History* (Toronto: University of Toronto Press, 2015).
12 Karen Dubinsky, Sean Mills, and Scott Rutherford, eds., *Canada and the Third World: Overlapping Histories* (Toronto: University of Toronto Press, 2016); Greg Donaghy and David Webster, *A Samaritan State Revisited: Historical Perspectives on Canadian Foreign Aid* (Calgary, AB: University of Calgary Press, 2019).
13 For example, J.R. Miller, *Compact, Contact, Covenant: Aboriginal Treaty-Making in Canada* (Toronto: University of Toronto Press, 2009). See also scholarship by Peter Cook, e.g. "Onontio Gives Birth: How the French in Canada Became Fathers to Their Indigenous Allies, 1645–73," *Canadian Historical Review* 96, 2 (2015): 165–93.
14 This count excludes the introductions and conclusions of each volume. Whitney Wood, "Spreading the Gospel of Natural Birth: Canadian Contributions to an International Medical Movement, 1945–1960," in McKercher and Van Huizen, *Undiplomatic History*, 137–60; Amanda Ricci, "Making Global Citizens? Canadian Women at the World Conference of the International Women's Year, Mexico City 1975," in McKercher and Van Huizen, *Undiplomatic History*, 206–29; P. Whitney Lackenbauer, "Race, Gender and International 'Relations': African Americans and Aboriginal People on the Margins of Canada's North, 1942–48," in Madokoro, McKenzie, and Meren, *Dominion of Race*, 112–38; Karen Flynn, "'She Cannot be Confined to Her Own Region': Nursing and Nurses in the Caribbean, Canada, and the UK," in Dubinsky, Perry, and Yu, *Within and Without the Nation*, 228–49; Kristine Alexander, "Canadian Girls, Imperial Girls, Global Girls: Race, Nation, and Transnationalism in the Interwar Girl Guide Movement," in Yu, Perry, and Dubinsky, *Within and Without the Nation*, 276–92; Bettina Bradbury, "'In England a Man Can Do as He Likes with His Property': Migration, Family Fortunes, and the Law in Nineteenth Century Quebec and the Cape Colony," in Yu, Perry, and Dubinsky, *Within and Without the Nation*, 145–67; and Laura Ishiguro, "'How I Wish I Might Be Near': Distance and the Epistolary Family in Late-Nineteenth-Century Condolence Letters," in Yu, Perry, and Dubinsky, *Within and Without the Nation*, 212–27.
15 There are exceptions. Historian Janice Cavell offers an analysis of the highly gendered nature of the historiography about Canadian foreign policy in "Like Any Good Wife: Gender and Perceptions of Canadian Foreign Policy, 1945–75," *International Journal* 63, 2 (Spring 2008), 385–403.
16 See, for example, Susanna Erlandsson, "Off the Record: Margaret Van Kleffens and the Gendered History of Dutch World War II Diplomacy," *International Feminist Journal of Politics* 21, 1 (2019): 35–37; Dana Cooper, *Informal Ambassadors: American Women, Transatlantic Marriages, and Anglo-American Relations, 1865–1945* (Kent, OH: Kent State University Press, 2014); Helen McCarthy, "Women, Marriage and Work in the British Diplomatic Service," *Women's History Review* 23, 6 (2014): 853–73; Molly Wood, "'Commanding Beauty' and 'Gentle Charm': American Women and Gender in the Early Twentieth-Century Foreign Service," *Diplomatic History* 31, 3 (June 2007): 505–30; and Molly Wood, "Diplomatic Wives: The Politics of Domesticity and the 'Social Game' in the U.S. Foreign Service, 1905–1941," *Journal of Women's History* 17, 2 (Summer 2005): 142–65.
17 See Sondra Gotlieb, *Wife of ... An Irreverent Account of Life in Washington* (Halifax, NS: Formac, 1987); and Christine Hantel-Fraser, *No Fixed Address: Life in the Foreign Service* (Toronto: University of Toronto Press, 1993). Other writings by "diplomatic wives" include Rae Hardy, *Distaff Diplomacy, or, My Elegant Life as a Diplomat's Wife* (Victoria, BC: Trafford on demand, 2001); Landon Pearson, *Letters from Moscow* (Newcastle, ON: Penumbra Press, 2003); and Tova Clark, *Compartments* (Newcastle, ON: Penumbra Press, 2005).

18 Margaret K. Weiers, *Envoys Extraordinary: Women of the Canadian Foreign Service* (Toronto: Dundurn Press, 1995).
19 Claire Turenne Sjolander, "Margaret Meagher and the Role of Women in the Foreign Service: Groundbreaking or Housekeeping?" in *Architects and Innovators: Building the Department of Foreign Affairs and International Trade, 1909–2009*, eds. Greg Donaghy and Kim Richard Nossal (Montreal/Kingston: McGill-Queen's University Press, 2009), 223–36.
20 Vivien Hughes, "Women, Gender, and Canadian Foreign Policy, 1909–2009," *British Journal of Canadian Foreign Studies* 23, 2 (2010): 172.
21 Mary Jane Woodward Bean, *Julie Grace Wales: Canada's Hidden Heroine and the Quest for Peace, 1914–1918* (Ottawa: Borealis Press, 2005); Mary Kinnear, *Woman of the World: Mary McGeachy and International Cooperation* (Toronto: University of Toronto Press, 2004); Ricci, "Making Global Citizens?"
22 Kristine Alexander, "Canadian Girls, Imperial Girls, Global Girls: Race, Nation, and Transnationalism in the Interwar Girl Guide Movement," in Yu, Perry, and Dubinsky, *Within and Without the Nation*, 276–92; Kristine Alexander, *Guiding Modern Girls: Girlhood, Empire, and Internationalism in the 1920s and 1930s* (Vancouver: UBC Press, 2017); Sarah Glassford, *Mobilizing Mercy: A History of the Canadian Red Cross* (Montreal/Kingston: McGill-Queen's University Press, 2017).
23 Tarah Brookfield, *Cold War Comforts: Canadian Women, Child Safety, and Global Insecurity* (Waterloo, ON: Wilfrid Laurier University Press, 2012).
24 See the recent issue of *Diplomatic History* on missionaries, and especially Laura R. Prietao, "Introduction: Women and Missionary Encounters with Foreign Nationalism in the 1920s," *Diplomatic History* 43, 2 (2019), 238.
25 Ruth Compton Brouwer, *Modern Women Modernizing Men: The Changing Missions of Three Professional Women in Asia and Africa, 1902–69* (Vancouver: UBC Press, 2002).
26 Karen Flynn, *Moving beyond Borders: A History of Black Caribbean and Caribbean Women in the Diaspora* (Toronto: University of Toronto Press, 2011); Karen Flynn, "'She Cannot Be Confined to Her Own Region': Nursing and Nurses in the Caribbean, Canada, and the UK," in Yu, Perry, and Dubinsky, *Within and Without the Nation* 228–49.
27 Erlandsson, "Off the Record," 38.
28 For example, Frank A. Ninkovich, *The Diplomacy of Ideas: U.S. Foreign Policy and Cultural Relations 1938–1950* (Cambridge University Press, 1981); and Akira Iriye, *Cultural Internationalism and World Order* (Baltimore: John Hopkins University Press, 1997). Kailey Hansson offers a Canadian perspective on this field in "Dancing into Hearts and Minds: Canadian Ballet Exchanges with the Communist World, 1956–76," in McKercher and Van Huizen, *Undiplomatic History*, 233–52.
29 For example, see Ashley Brown, "Swinging for the State Department: American Women Tennis Players in Diplomatic Goodwill Tours, 1941–59," *Journal of Sport History* 42, 3 (Fall 2015): 289–309.

PART I
Women in Missions, Aid, and Development

1

Quietly Contesting Patriarchy
Dr. Jessie MacBean's Medical Work in South China, 1925–35

Kim Girouard

WHEN I PRESENT my findings on Dr. Jessie MacBean and the work she pursued in South China at the beginning of the twentieth century, there are always several people in the audience who point out that MacBean's journey in China is reminiscent of that of Norman Bethune. Indeed, their stories show some similarities. They were both Canadian doctors, driven by humanism, who practised medicine in China during an eventful period with the aim of relieving suffering and improving the lives of the local populations. Yet, their paths, their personalities, and their legacies could not be more different. In fact, their respective experiences in China provide a striking contrast, showing how Canada's international past, as well its historiography, is profoundly shaped by gender.

Bethune's life and career embodied gendered masculine norms. His sincere commitment to the welfare of the most vulnerable took the form of innovative thoracic surgeries and unprecedented war medical procedures, as well as loud social activism. His political convictions notably led him to organize medical services for Mao Zedong's Eighth Route Army in the remote area of Yan'an (known as Yenan by foreigners at the time) in North-Central China, during the First Sino-Japanese War in 1938. He died dramatically on site a year and a half later by cutting his finger and contracting septicemia while he was operating bare-handed on a wounded soldier. Often described as provocative, abrasive, and temperamental, Bethune had the reputation of having a difficult personality. Today he is celebrated as a revolutionary, a war hero, and an outstanding humanitarian in Canada as well as in China.

In both countries, statues were erected in his effigy, and public places, universities, schools, and hospitals were named in his honour. He was the subject of many biographical books, films, and television series, and inspired several novels and movies. With reason, Bethune also caught the attention of historians and other scholars, who published books and articles that analyze the significance of his professional achievements, unconventional life, and impressive legacy.[1]

MacBean embodied the acceptable career woman who stayed within the boundaries of femininity. Her genuine concern for the spiritual and physical well-being of non-Christian women led her to become an unmarried missionary physician specializing in obstetrics. Deeply committed to her faith, her colleagues, students, and patients, she made her life and whole career in South China. Arriving in the southern Chinese province of Guangdong in 1906, MacBean was first stationed at the Canadian Presbyterian Mission in Jiangmen (known as Kongmoon by foreigners at the time), a small market town located in the Pearl River Delta. Three years after having pursued itinerate medical work in the town and its surroundings, MacBean was named chief of the newly built women's hospital, the Marion Barclay Hospital. Between 1925 and 1935, she pursued her work in the provincial capital, Guangzhou (known as Canton by foreigners at the time), where she was appointed chair of obstetrics at the Hackett Medical College for Women, a prominent institution established in 1899 by Dr. Mary H. Fulton under the auspices of the American Presbyterian Mission.[2] A recognized pioneer of mother and infant health care services in South China, MacBean was known to be a pragmatic, efficient, and hard worker. Her colleagues also acknowledged her patience, her tender and cheerful character, as well as her gracious social skills. MacBean retired on account of ill health in 1935 and died nine years later in her home in Toronto. Unsurprisingly, her professional achievements, personal life, and legacy have, until now, barely emerged from dusty mission archives.[3]

Taking an unconventional approach to power and using MacBean as a case study, this chapter aims to show that Canada's medical and humanitarian leadership in early-twentieth-century China took forms that went beyond the contours of Bethune's legendary contribution. Although MacBean had a more subdued style than Bethune, she nonetheless dedicated herself to improving the health and living conditions of the Chinese population, making a discernible impact on their daily lives. In particular, during her time at Hackett, she not only provided quality care and preventive health services for Chinese mothers and children, but also contributed to the empowerment of Chinese women by training them in medicine. In the process, she reached a level of professional achievement which would probably have been out of reach for her in Canada and likely far beyond what she had envisioned for herself as a young woman. The peculiar conditions she encountered in South China, which favoured her as a white missionary, were conducive to the development of women's medical practice and education; this enabled her to contest medical patriarchy in her own quiet way and to position herself as a medical authority alongside her male colleagues.

There is a relatively large historiography that addresses the medical work of the various Christian missions established in China in the middle of the nineteenth century.[4] Yet, very few historians have examined Canadian case studies and their relevance to women's history.[5] Sociologist Yuet-Wah Cheung's book is the only one to focus on the Canadian Presbyterian South China Mission in Jiangmen, where MacBean was first stationed between 1906 and 1925.[6] Since Cheung focused on the work of the mission's male doctors, who were more numerous and whose work was considered more valuable by the mission board, MacBean appears as a very marginal figure. Historians Sara W. Tucker and Guangqiu Xu have also explored the history of the Hackett Medical College for Women, but only the latter has looked at the late development of the institution, and neither devotes even a few words to the work undertaken by MacBean.[7] Yet in the archives she consistently appears as a prominent figure at Hackett in the late 1920s and early 1930s.

MacBean's overlooked experience is by no means exceptional. While Canadian women's and gender history is considered a mature and extensive field, women are still marginalized within many fields of Canada's domestic history.[8] When it comes to Canada's international history, which long remained male, white, and confined to the North Atlantic World, women have usually been completely ignored. Recently, several historians added new regions to our understanding of Canada's international role in the past.[9] Others offered new perspectives on race that further complicated the portrait.[10] Still, as David Meren pointed out in 2017, this history lacks women's experiences and few historians offer a gendered analysis in their scholarship.[11] Like the other trajectories presented in this book, MacBean's case study helps to fill this gap. It is a basic but necessary reminder that Canadian women, although generally connected to China through the

Protestant missions and the British and American empires, were active medical and humanitarian workers on Chinese soil at the beginning of the twentieth century. This case study is also an example of the subtle ways Canadian women navigated the international system produced by the interplay of empire and race, and patriarchy and gender, in order to exert their own version of leadership.

The Privileged Missionary

When MacBean graduated from the Ontario Women's Medical College in 1905, she was eager to join the Canadian Presbyterian missionary community. Profoundly influenced by missionary literature, she was convinced that India was her calling. She already envisioned herself saving the bodies and souls of her Indian sisters. When she received her posting to South China, she was so shocked that she first refused it. Not without reason, MacBean and her family considered China to be hostile to missionaries and worried that she would not be under the formal protection of the British Empire.[12] Yet steeped in the literature of mission work, which emphasized selflessness, she eventually agreed to go to South China. We know from the few studies focusing on Canadian women missionaries that they already had a deep connection to the world outside of the North Atlantic region at the end of the nineteenth century.[13] Mostly active in South and East Asia, they were not only missionary wives but were also single career women like MacBean. In Canada, as well as in the United States, there was a strong link between the training of women physicians and the Christian missionary enterprise. For example, when the Ontario Women's Medical College (formerly the Women's Medical College), MacBean's alma mater, was created in 1883, its purpose was twofold. On the one hand, its founder, the suffragist Dr. Emily Stowe, the first woman physician to practice medicine in Canada, wanted to give women the opportunity to study medicine. Indeed, gender roles were defined by relatively strict boundaries at the time, and women studying and practising medicine were generally considered a social abnormality. Most medical faculties in North America were closed to women, as was the case at the University of Toronto until 1906, or imposed formal and informal quotas on female entrants.[14] On the other hand, the school also aimed to prepare women physicians "for work in the Foreign Missionary Field and elsewhere."[15]

This is hardly surprising, because when male missionaries were sent abroad, they soon discovered that they were often barred from preaching, let alone providing health care, to the female populations they were supposed to convert. Therefore, it became essential to organize a female component to the various activities of the missions, what was called "women's work for women," including for medical work.[16] Women missionary physicians gradually began to appear as indispensable to the provision of medical treatment and the training of female medical staff in societies that more carefully observed the convention of sex segregation. Chinese women, especially if they belonged to the elite, were confined to the domestic realm and prevented from contact with male outsiders. As scholars have shown, sex segregation was less strict in South China, particularly in the Pearl River Delta, and it was not unusual for women, not only within the peasant class and smaller trading communities, but also among the richest landowner families, to contribute to the family economy by working outside the home.[17] Nonetheless, like everywhere else in China, female modesty had to be respected to a certain degree, and women preferred being treated by medical practitioners of their own sex, especially for health conditions involving genitalia and reproductive functions.[18] Consequently, in the eyes of the missionaries, there was a great need for female doctors in South China, as well as in the other parts of the country.

The need for women physicians in the missionary field drove the development of women's medical education in North America, generating a noticeable increase of female medical graduates at the end of the nineteenth and the beginning of the twentieth century. Between 1880 and 1900, the proportion of female physicians in the United States doubled from 2.8 to 5.6 percent.[19] In Canada it grew more slowly, but increased from 1.7 percent in 1891 to 2.7 percent twenty years later.[20] Graduating in 1905, MacBean benefited from the medical profession's grudging openness to woman graduates. But as these percentages show, female doctors were still very marginalized and their prospects for career advancement quite limited. Management positions were generally out of reach and recognition from their male peers difficult to obtain. As Jill Campbell-Miller's chapter in this volume also discusses, in these conditions it is not surprising that many female medical graduates chose the foreign medical field, where they were more needed and respected, to pursue their careers. Like MacBean, many women even pursued a medical degree for this specific purpose.[21]

For MacBean, the choice of a medical career was motivated first and foremost by her faith and desire to become a missionary. Her biographer quotes MacBean as saying: "I knew I wanted to be a missionary, though I could not see how I could ever get to College, but I made up my mind that somehow or other I would certainly be a missionary and a medical doctor at that!"[22] Unsurprisingly, her dedication to the missionary endeavour is reflected in the pioneering work she undertook in Jiangmen. When she sailed to South China in 1906, she was one of the first two women, and the only female physician, to be sent there by the Canadian Presbyterian Church. Although male colleagues had been stationed in the area since 1902, there was practically no missionary infrastructure and no medical facility when she arrived.[23] During her first years in Jiangmen, a part of her work was religious. She not only provided medical care, but also proselytized Christianity to the local populations.[24]

Her missionary vocation and her work as a physician were embedded within the "civilizing mission" that justified Western imperialism and colonization. Long before her arrival in Jiangmen, China had been forced to open its door to foreigners by Great Britain, the United States, and other European powers. In the wake of the opium wars of the early 1840s and late 1850s, the British Empire demanded major concessions from a defeated Qing dynasty. In addition to forcing the opium trade on China, Britain and other Western powers, and eventually Japan, sought exclusive trade privileges in several major ports and cities. They also obtained concessions, or leased territories, in strategic locales, evaded Chinese justice by the principle of extraterritoriality, and were allowed to circulate freely throughout the country. Consequently, Christian missionaries were able to establish themselves throughout China and to proselytize to the local populations.[25] Although China was never formally colonized, Western imperial expansionism, which intensified following China's defeat in the Sino-Japanese War of 1894–95, allowed Christian missions to set up schools and medical services throughout the country.

In a very intricate way, missionaries, including MacBean, were tied to Western imperialism. They also originally saw health care as a conversion strategy. Despite the benevolent intentions underlying their medical work, it was intended not only to heal the body, but also to conquer the soul. As historian David Hardiman argues, the era's popular philosophy of social Darwinism and associated racist beliefs in the superiority of white civilization informed this strategy.[26] By providing medical treatments, some quite effective, that were generally unknown to the Chinese, Christian missionaries not only wanted to prove their altruism, but also to demonstrate the "higher nature" of their medicine and, by extension, of their culture and religion. As Carol C. Chin puts it, they were engaged in a form of "beneficent imperialism."[27] They were eager to pass on their "superior" knowledge in order to help, but also to evangelize or "civilize" the local populations. They were generally very comfortable with the implicit backing they enjoyed from the Western powers and rarely expressed concerns about their privileged position in Chinese society.[28] They also remained hesitant to recognize as equal those they managed to convert to their ideas and way of life.

For these reasons, many Chinese argued that the missionaries and their institutions embodied foreign expansionism. Like other symbols of the Western presence in China, they often were targets of anti-Christian and anti-imperialist movements. Like most missionaries in China, MacBean experienced these sometimes violent demonstrations first-hand. In her early days in Jiangmen, it was not unusual for regional officials to send an armed guard, including as many as twelve soldiers, to protect her when she travelled to see patients.[29] In the mid-1920s, following the student protests that occurred in Beijing on May 4, 1919, nationalist fervour was at its peak in China. The weak response of the Chinese government to the Treaty of Versailles, which actually reinforced the foreign presence on Chinese soil despite its claims to be rooted in self-determination, led to political protests nationwide. Anti-imperialist demonstrations, bringing together students and workers, multiplied in Guangzhou in 1925. In June, after an intervention by Franco-British soldiers resulted in the deaths of fifty people, anti-imperialist activists launched a boycott of foreign products and organized a series of strikes in order to paralyze the activity of foreign companies. The atmosphere was so tense in the region that the Canadian Presbyterian Mission evacuated its entire staff from Jiangmen. Along with her colleagues, MacBean took refuge in Hong Kong until conditions became peaceful. In her absence, the women's hospital, as well as the rest of the mission compound, was vandalized and looted.[30]

Immediately after this episode, MacBean moved to Hackett Medical College in Guangzhou and did not engage in direct proselytization anymore. Her focus seemed to have shifted from evangelization to strictly meeting the health care needs of the local populations. However, her changing attitude cannot be ascribed to this single event but must be understood as part of a broader transformation inside the missionary endeavour, and the medical mission in particular. Indeed, by the first decades of the twentieth century, the Protestant missions had engaged more deeply in what the American missionaries called the "social gospel," which emphasized the development of professional institutional and social services.[31] In this context, the medical component of the medical missionary work had started to take precedence over its religious dimension.[32] Like the Canadian nurses in North China studied by Sonya Grypma, and following a larger movement within Christian medical missionary work, MacBean probably believed that her medical work was in itself the expression of her faith and Christian commitment.[33] Nevertheless, she was still a foreign missionary and benefited from her position of social and racial privilege.

When MacBean was hired as chief of obstetrics at Hackett in 1925, the institution already had a well-established reputation among the local populations and authorities. The school of medicine, as well as the adjunct Turner Training School for Nurses, graduated at least a dozen women doctors and nurses each year, and the affiliated hospital, the David Gregg Hospital for Women and Children, which counted one hundred beds, ran at full capacity.[34] Despite Hackett's relative prominence in the region, as with other medical missionary institutions established in China, Hackett faced a constant shortage of women missionary doctors, resulting in part from the declining number of female medical graduates in North America. Consequently, MacBean's services were desperately needed.[35]

At the beginning of the twentieth century, segregated medical education for women was gradually becoming outdated in North America. This process accelerated after the publication of educational reformer Abraham Flexner's influential report on medical education in 1910, sponsored by the Carnegie Foundation, which favoured the laboratory approach to medicine embodied by Johns Hopkins University School of Medicine. Like other marginal medical institutions, women's medical schools could not afford the state-of-the-art equipment demanded by these new standards and consequently closed their doors one after another.[36] Since coeducational training programs adhering to the new Flexnerian standards tended to impose quotas on female applicants and failed to provide a supportive environment to female students, the proportion of women doctors rapidly decreased after 1910. Indeed, the proportion of female medical graduates in the United States was almost as low in 1915 as it had been in 1880. In Canada, the percentage of women doctors decreased substantially as well.[37]

Although Hackett had routinely employed its Chinese female graduates since its foundation, positions of responsibility were reserved for missionary doctors. As the institution's annual reports reveal, Chinese women were usually hired as assistant doctors; most promotions to the level of department head were on an acting or temporary basis. They acted as substitutes until a missionary doctor was available. Those very few Chinese women who could aspire to a high position on an official and permanent basis were lucky enough to work in a field where there was no missionary competitor and had had an opportunity to pursue their medical training in the West. Under these circumstances, MacBean's status as a white missionary certainly weighed heavily in her appointment as chief of obstetrics at Hackett.

The Accomplished Woman Doctor

In the context of South China, MacBean benefited from these professional privileges bestowed on white missionaries, but being a woman also turned out to be an unexpected asset. By the time she arrived at Hackett in 1925, the institution was no longer the preserve of women. Over the years, citing the shortage of female missionary doctors and the transformation of Chinese society, the mission board had become increasingly reliant on male doctors to run the institution. In fact, this change of attitude had a lot to do with the waning of the gendered "separate spheres" approach initially endorsed by the missions, which was increasingly seen as an obstacle to improving missionary professionalism.[38] Gradually, Hackett became dominated by men. When MacBean took office, the position of president had just been given to a man, and almost all the departments had been entrusted to male doctors. The only departments where women were still allowed positions of leadership were gynecology and obstetrics.

Although sex segregation in China by the 1920s was not as strict as it had been during the Qing dynasty, Chinese female patients with gynecological and obstetrical conditions still expected to be treated by female practitioners. Chinese authorities clearly had the same expectations and acted to preserve female modesty. They required Chinese female medical students receiving government scholarships to specialize in gynecology and obstetrics and tended to favour women doctors to run these departments in hospitals under Chinese jurisdiction.[39] In order to conform to this cultural norm and to continue enjoying a high reputation among the local populations, Hackett's management had little choice but to employ women at the head of its departments of gynecology and obstetrics.

In view of this situation, there is no doubt that MacBean's gender allowed her to be hired as chief of obstetrics at Hackett. Nevertheless, she also had to be up to the task. When she took charge of the maternity service in 1925, it enjoyed a reputation as the most advanced and most popular in the region. Between two and three hundred deliveries were performed every year during her posting. In addition, MacBean and her team were not afraid to resort to Caesarean sections when necessary, carrying out a total of nine in 1933 alone.[40] Considering that the other missionary hospital in Guangzhou, the prominent Canton Hospital ran by interdenominational missionaries, practically never performed this surgery during those years, these figures are particularly impressive.[41] As head of her department, MacBean also had to supervise the work of three to seven residents, as well as the medical interns and nurses perfecting their clinical training. Although her workload was already heavy, she was not content. In order to improve the quality of the medical care offered by Hackett to the mothers and children of the area, MacBean also pioneered the development of preventive health services.

In the early 1920s, the horrific casualties of the First World War sparked concerns about depopulation in Western Europe and North America, and infant mortality became a pressing issue. The medical community began to emphasize the special relationship between mother and child and to redefine motherhood through the extension of medical care and monitoring well before and after birth, and through mothers' instruction on pregnancy and newborn hygiene.[42] Like her colleagues in the West, MacBean considered that the health of Chinese children, and by extension the Chinese nation, depended on the health and the competencies of their mother.[43] Admitted to the China Medical Association's research committee when she was still in Jiangmen, she pursued research work to understand the health conditions of prospective mothers in South China and to provide them with more appropriate medical care. In particular, she presented and published studies on pelvic and fetal morphology, and on menstruation and menopause.[44]

Being a recognized researcher and obstetrician in the medical community in China, MacBean developed several important preventive health projects targeting Chinese women and children at Hackett. She notably sponsored the program "Prevention Better Than Cure," which was the organization's first comprehensive mother and child health services in South China. Under her direction, David Gregg Hospital fully organized its well-baby clinic and established its adjunct prenatal and postnatal clinics in 1926.[45] According to missionary sources, these clinics were the first of their kind not only in the province, but also in the whole country.[46]

In 1927, motivated by the high rate of infant mortality, MacBean and her staff were also instrumental in the organization in Guangzhou of the first major public health campaign focusing on maternal and child health.[47] The campaign invited the population of the city to browse nine booths, more than half of which were devoted exclusively to mother and infant care. The first of these stands, deemed crucial to the public's understanding of the value of preventive care for mothers and children, was staffed by MacBean herself and her students.[48] "Slowly, but surely," MacBean reported, "we are making mothers feel that it is most important to have care before their baby comes, as well as after."[49] As this quotation suggests, and as we have shown elsewhere, Hackett's services for mother and child health under MacBean had been resisted, negotiated, and adapted by the local populations.[50] Still, they were considered successful and valuable enough to inspire other hospitals in the region to offer similar services.

Beginning in the early 1930s, and thanks to the specialized medical and nursing personnel trained at Hackett, Canton Hospital, and Lingnan Branch Hospital, a rural hospital affiliated with these institutions opened urban and rural health centres. These centres provided care for the women and children of the city of Guangzhou and the villages of the nearby Haizhu district (the former Henan island). Together with the Hackett's health centre, they formed the Guangdong Health Center Association in 1933.[51] Undoubtedly, MacBean's work as an obstetrician and preventive medicine specialist influenced her colleagues across South China and reached well outside the walls of Hackett.

Indeed, MacBean's impact was even broader. In the decade from 1925 to 1935, she was also professor of obstetrics at Hackett and at its affiliated school of nursing, the Turner Training School for Nurses. In that role, she was the primary source for the transfer of obstetrical knowledge and practice to a younger generation of physicians and nurses in South China. Using the mother and infant health centre as a training facility, MacBean introduced her students to the basics of obstetrics and preventive medicine. In total, she helped train more than eighty female doctors and even more nurses. In doing so, she pursued Hackett's founding goal of empowering Chinese women through medical education. She played a significant part in the early feminization of the Chinese medical profession, which was exceptionally strong and constant in South China thanks to Hackett, and far more important than in North America at the time. Indeed, in the 1930s, the proportion of women medical graduates in South China reached at least 30 percent, a percentage seven to eight times higher than in the United States and Canada during the same period.[52]

Furthermore, Chinese female doctors and nurses trained by MacBean influenced a subsequent generation of female health practitioners.[53] For instance, several of her former medical students, like Dr. Wang Dexin, who worked at Hackett under MacBean's supervision between 1925 and 1927, and Dr. Wang Huaqing, who was an important member of MacBean's team in the early 1930s, joined the staff of the *Baosheng Chanke Xuexiao* (Baosheng Midwifery School), a renowned private western-style midwifery school attached to a hospital for women and children.[54] This nucleus of female doctors, trained and sponsored by MacBean, not only gained a reputation among the Chinese elite in Guangzhou, but also trained dozens of proficient midwives.[55]

MacBean's commitment to the training of qualified health workers also reached beyond Guangzhou. Although they were not recognized as such by the Chinese nationalist authorities, her health clinics at Hackett became the base in South China for the training of nurses specializing in mother and infant health.[56] As an example, in 1930, through the contact MacBean maintained with the staff of the Canadian medical mission in Jiangmen, Hackett's school of nursing welcomed two graduates from the Marion Barclay Hospital nursing program for a one-year internship at its mother and infant health centre. At the end of their training, they returned home to organize similar services and pass on their knowledge to other nursing students.[57]

Furthermore, while very few of her female peers in North America did so, MacBean trained male medical students. From the end of the nineteenth century, attempts to establish a medical training program for men at Canton Hospital and Canton Christian College (later Lingnan University) had repeatedly failed, until they were indefinitely suspended in 1914. In 1932, Hackett Medical College, Canton Hospital, and Lingnan University resuscitated the plan and agreed to create a coeducational medical faculty under Christian auspices in Guangzhou. Since Hackett was already registered and fully recognized by the Chinese nationalist authorities as a "school of medicine of college grade," it became the home base of the scheme. Its staff, including MacBean, joined with Lingnan University to form a new medical faculty, which welcomed its first male students in 1933. MacBean did not welcome the change, believing that "women put more of themselves into the work they undertake."[58] We can also assume that she probably feared that opening Hackett to coeducation would have the same devastating effect on women's medical education that it had in North America. With her high stature in the medical faculty, she felt sufficiently empowered to express her dissatisfaction, urging her colleagues and superiors to be very selective with male applicants.[59] While MacBean went along with the change, her concerns might have been heard, as the medical school registered only six men out of fifty total students.[60]

Conclusion: Contesting Patriarchy

When Dr. MacBean retired due to ill health in 1935, she was an esteemed obstetrician and full professor at the most important school of medicine in South China. Indeed, Hackett, after incorporating Lingnan University and opening its door to male students, was renamed Sun Yat-sen Medical College in 1936. Now the Sun Yat-sen University Zhongshan Medical School, the institution is still considered one of the most prestigious and prominent medical school in China. Undoubtedly, MacBean's work attracted Chinese patients. According to the superintendent of the David Gregg Hospital, Dr. J. Franklin Karcher, "It was largely through her personality and prestige that her department of obstetrics was the most profitable of the hospital."[61] She was also highly respected by her colleagues. In a 1936 report, the president of Hackett, Dr. Wang Haile (Ross Wong), wrote that "she labored hard for the improvement of her department and finally built it up to the present high standards." According to him, "she was justly famous for all of her work" and must be considered as a "Maker of Hackett."[62]

As MacBean's case study reminds us, at the beginning of the twentieth century Canadian women abroad remained imperial creatures, whose experiences were shaped by their standing in the British Empire and their participation in various American imperial projects. Still, as the young and determined missionary fully embraced the medical component of her mandate, MacBean's story also reminds us that Canadian women have a long history of humanitarian engagement. As a woman doctor, obstetrician, and professor, MacBean was committed to improving the health and the lives of the populations of South China. She was not only instrumental to the development of obstetrics and preventive medicine in the region, but she also played a part in the empowerment of Chinese women. At the same time, she carved out a relatively enviable place for herself in the increasingly male medical missionary community. In other words, she worked with the aim that her patients and students could live what she considered more secure, prosperous, and just lives, and that she herself could obtain more professional equity.

Quietly, but surely, MacBean seized the professional opportunities offered by the combination of the missionary setting and the local cultural environment. In a context where women missionary doctors were rare and where Chinese women doctors were practically barred from positions of responsibility, she benefited from her status as a white missionary. As a woman and an obstetrician, she also took advantage of the enduring social norm that prevented most Chinese women from resorting to male doctors during childbirth.

As a product of a segregated medical education later deemed obsolete, it would have been very unlikely for MacBean to reach a level of professional achievement similar to the one she reached at Hackett if she had stayed in Canada. Indeed, in North America during the 1920s and 1930s, women doctors educated in women's medical school were rarely hired as department chairs in medical schools or hospitals attached to universities.[63] Clearly, MacBean not only adapted to the Chinese context, which initially appeared so hostile to her, but also was resourceful enough to use it for contesting the medical patriarchy produced by her own Western culture, and to arise as a widely recognized obstetrician. She was able to prove to male colleagues with prestigious degrees from Johns Hopkins, Oxford, and McGill that she was not just a white woman missionary doctor, but above all a leader in her field.

As MacBean's case study exemplifies, by being attentive to issues associated with women and gender and by addressing power through them, it is possible to uncover different types of leaders from Canada's international past. To come back to our opening words, MacBean's leadership in China obviously reveals itself in a completely different shape from that of Norman Bethune. However, it had no less impact on the lives of the Chinese populations. While the purpose of this chapter is certainly not to make MacBean a national hero, it is definitely intended to nuance, complicate, and enrich our understanding of the Canadian medical and humanitarian leadership in early twentieth century China. Above all, along with the other contributions in this volume, it aspires to produce a more equitable history of Canada's presence in the world.

Notes

1. For a more complete portrait of Bethune's life and career, see, for example, Jean Deslauriers and Denis Goulet, "The Medical Life of Henry Norman Bethune," *Canadian Respiratory Journal* 22, 6 (2015): e32–e42; Larry Hannant, ed., *The Politics of Passion: Norman Bethune's Writing and Arts* (Toronto: University of Toronto Press, 1998); Roderick Stewart and Jesùs Majada, *Bethune in Spain* (Montreal/Kingston: McGill-Queen's University Press, 2014); and Roderick Stewart and Sharon Stewart, *Phoenix: The Life of Norman Bethune* (Montreal/Kingston: McGill-Queen's University Press, 2011).
2. Hackett Medical College was one of three women's medical schools opened in China and certainly the most important in terms of longevity and number of graduates. For more details about the institution and its founder, see Sara W. Tucker, "A Mission for Change in China: The Hackett Women's Medical Center of Canton, China, 1900–1930," in *Women's Work for Women: Missionaries and Social Change in Asia*, ed. Leslie A. Flemming (Boulder, CO: Westview Press, 1989), 137–57; and Guangqiu Xu, *American Doctors in Canton: Modernization in China, 1835–1935* (New Brunswick, NJ: Transaction, 2011) 131–86.
3. Lereine Ballantyne, *Dr. Jessie MacBean and the Work at the Hackett Medical College, Canton, China* (Toronto: Women's Missionary Society of the Presbyterian Church in Canada, 1934). This is the only published biographical source that deals with MacBean's life and career. As its account of MacBean's work in China can be corroborated by a variety of other primary sources, it may be considered reliable. However, readers should keep in mind that it was written to inspire young women to join the mission and, therefore, emphasizes the "higher nature" and achievements of missionary work.
4. For recent examples, see Larissa N. Heinrich, *The Afterlife of Images: Translating the Pathological Body between China and the West* (Durham, NC: Duke University Press, 2008); Michelle Renshaw, *Accommodating the Chinese: The American Hospital in China, 1880–1920* (New York/London: Routledge, 2005); and Connie Anne Shemo, *The Chinese Medical Ministries of Kang Cheng and Shi Meiyu, 1872–1937: On a Cross-Cultural Frontier of Gender, Race, and Nation* (Bethlehem, PA: Lehigh University Press, 2011).
5. The work of Sonya Grypma and Karen Minden explores the role of Canadian medical missionaries in China, but only that of Grypma looks more specifically at the role of women, particularly as nurses. See Sonya Grypma, *Healing Henan: Canadian Nurses at the North China Mission, 1888–1947* (Vancouver/Toronto: UBC Press, 2008); *China Interrupted: Japanese Internment and the Reshaping of a Canadian Missionary Community* (Waterloo, ON: Wilfrid Laurier University Press, 2016); and Karen Minden, *Bamboo Stone: The Evolution of a Chinese Medical Elite* (Toronto: University of Toronto Press, 2014 [1994]).
6. Yuet-Wah Cheung, *Missionary Medicine in China: A Study of Two Canadian Protestant Missions in China before 1937* (Lanham, MD: University Press of America, 1988).
7. Tucker, "A Mission for Change in China," 137–57; Xu, *American Doctors in Canton*, 131–86.
8. Nancy Janovicek and Carmen Nielson, "Introduction: Feminist Conversations," in *Reading Canadian Women's and Gender History*, ed. Nancy Janovicek and Carmen Nielson (Toronto, University of Toronto Press, 2019), 3–22.
9. See, for example, Karen Dubinsky, Sean Mill, and Scott Rutherford, eds. *Canada and the Third World: Overlapping Histories* (Toronto, University of Toronto Press, 2016); and Patricia Roy and Greg Donaghy, eds. *Contradictory Impulses: Canada and Japan in the Twentieth Century* (Vancouver, UBC Press, 2008).
10. See for example, Laura Madokoro, Francine McKenzie, and David Meren, eds., *Dominion of Race: Rethinking Canada's International History* (Vancouver, UBC Press, 2017).
11. David Meren, "Conclusion: Race and the Future of Canadian International History," in Madokoro, McKenzie, and Meren, *Dominion of Race*, 290.

12 Ballantyne, *Dr. Jessie MacBean*, 9–10.
13 See Ruth Compton Brouwer, *New Women for God: Canadian Presbyterian Women and Indian Missions, 1876–1914* (Toronto: University of Toronto Press, 1990), and *Modern Women Modernizing Men: The Changing Missions of Three Professional Women in Asia and Africa* (Vancouver: UBC Press, 2002); and Rosemary R. Gagan, *A Sensitive Independence: Canadian Methodist Women Missionaries in Canada and the Orient, 1881–1925* (Montreal: McGill-Queen's University Press, 1992).
14 Cheryl Krasnick Warsh, *Prescribed Norms: Women and Health in Canada and the United States since 1800* (Toronto: University of Toronto Press, 2012), 175.
15 Edward Shorter, *Partnership for Excellence: Medicine at the University of Toronto and Academic Hospitals* (Toronto: University of Toronto Press, 2013), 20.
16 Jane Hunter, *The Gospel of Gentility: American Women Missionaries in Turn-of-the-Century China* (New Haven, CT: Yale University Press, 1984), 11.
17 Helen F. Siu and Wing-hoi Chan, "Introduction," in *Merchant's Daughters: Women, Commerce, and Regional Culture in South China*, ed. Helen F. Siu (Hong Kong: Hong Kong University Press, 2010), 4–5.
18 Charlotte Furth, "Concepts of Pregnancy, Childbirth, and Infancy in Ch'ing Dynasty China," *Journal of Asian Studies* 46, 1 (1987): 16; Wu Yi-Li, *Reproducing Women: Medicine, Metaphor, and Childbirth in Late Imperial China* (Berkeley: University of California Press, 2010), 15–18.
19 Paul Starr, *The Social Transformation of American Medicine: The Rise of a Sovereign Profession and the Making of a Vast Industry*, 2nd ed. (New York: Basic Books, 2017), 117.
20 Warsh, *Prescribed Norms*, 201.
21 Warsh, *Prescribed Norms*, 175–222.
22 Ballantyne, *Dr. Jessie MacBean*, 5.
23 Cheung, *Missionary Medicine in China*, 27–28.
24 Ballantyne, *Dr. Jessie MacBean*, 11–12.
25 For more details about foreign encroachment in China see Robert Bickers, *The Scramble for China: Foreign Devils in the Qing Empire, 1832–1914* (London: Penguin Books, 2016).
26 David Hardiman, "Introduction," in *Healing Bodies, Saving Souls: Medical Missions in Asia and Africa* (Amsterdam/New York: Rodopi B.V., 2006), 5–58.
27 Carol C. Chin, "Beneficent Imperialists: American Women Missionaries in China at the Turn of the Twentieth Century," *Diplomatic History* 27, 3 (2003): 328.
28 Chin, "Beneficent Imperialists," 327–33.
29 Ballantyne, *Dr. Jessie MacBean*, 16.
30 Cheung, *Missionary Medicine in China*, 30–1.
31 Ruth Compton Brouwer, "From Missionaries to NGOs," in Dubinsky, Mill, and Rutherford, *Canada and the Third World*, 195.
32 Hardiman, "Introduction," 18.
33 Grypma, *Healing Henan*, 15.
34 *Hackett Medical College for Women and Turner Training School for Nurses, Catalogue 1925–1926* (Canton, China: Hackett Medical College, 1926); *Annual Report of the Hackett Medical College for Women and Affiliated Institutions: Hospital Number, 1933* (Canton, China: Hackett Medical College, 1933).
35 Hattie F. Love, "Chinese Women in Medicine," *China Christian Advocate*, April (1917): 9–10; Tucker, "A Mission for Change in China," 145–46.
36 By the mid-1920s, all but one of the American women's medical schools, namely the Woman's Medical College of Pennsylvania, were closed. See Regina Morantz-Sanchez, *Sympathy and Science: Women Physicians in American Medicine* (Chapel Hill: University of North Carolina Press, 2000; New York: Oxford University Press, 1985), 243–48.

37 In Canada, between 1911 and 1921, the proportion of women in the medical profession decreased from 2.6 to 1.8 percent. See Warsh, *Prescribed Norms*, 201.
38 Compton Brouwer, "From Missionaries to NGOs," 195.
39 See Mirela David, "Female Gynecologists and Their Birth Control Clinics: Eugenics in Practice in 1920s–1930s China," *Canadian Bulletin for the History of Medicine* 35, 1 (2018): 37; and Kim Girouard, "Médicaliser au féminin: quand la médecine occidentale rencontre la maternité en Chine du Sud, 1879–1938" (PhD diss., Université de Montréal/École Normale Supérieure de Lyon, 2017), 95–128.
40 *Hackett Medical College for Women, Turner Training School for Nurses, David Gregg Hospital for Women and Children: Bulletin 1924–1925* (Canton, China: Hackett Medical College, 1925); *Hackett Medical College for Women and Turner Training School for Nurses: Catalogue 1925–1926* (Canton, China: Hackett Medical College, 1926); *Hackett Medical College for Women, Turner Training School for Nurses: Catalogue 1928–1929* (Canton, China: Hackett Medical College, 1929); *David Gregg Hospital for Women and Children, Hackett Medical College for Women, Turner Training School for Nurses: Bulletin, April, 1929* (Canton, China: Hackett Medical College, 1929); *Hackett Medical College for Women, Turner Training School for Nurses: Catalogue, June, 1930* (Canton, China: Hackett Medical College, 1929); *Annual Report of the David Gregg Hospital for Women and Children, Hackett Medical College for Women, Turner Training School for Nurses, Yau Tsai School of Pharmacy, 1931* (Canton, China: Hackett Medical College, 1931); *Annual Report of the Hackett Medical College, Hospital Number, 1933*; *Annual Report of the Hackett Medical College for Women and Affiliated Institutions: Hospital Number, January 1, 1933 to June 30, 1934* (Canton, China: Hackett Medical College, 1934).
41 *Report of the Canton Hospital for the Years 1924–1930* (Canton, China: Canton Hospital, 1930); *Report of the Sun Yat Sen Memorial Canton Hospital for the Year 1930–1931* (Canton, China: Canton Hospital, 1931); *Report of the Sun Yat Sen Memorial Canton Hospital for the Year 1931–1932* (Canton, China: Canton Hospital, 1932); *Annual Report for the 98th Year of the Sun Yat Sen Memorial Canton Hospital, Lingnan University, 1932–1933* (Canton, China: Canton Hospital, 1933); *Annual Report for the 99th Year of the Sun Yat Sen Memorial Canton Hospital, Lingnan University, 1933–1934* (Canton, China: Canton Hospital, 1934); *Annual Report for the 100th Year of the Canton Hospital, Lingnan University, 1934–1935* (Canton, China: Canton Hospital, 1935).
42 Richard A. Meckel, *Save the Babies: American Public Health Reform and the Prevention of Infant Mortality, 1850–1929* (Baltimore: Johns Hopkins University Press, 1990).
43 *Annual Report of the David Gregg Hospital, 1931*, 29.
44 "Amended Report of the Research Committee, 1923–1925," *China Medical Journal* 35, 5 (1925): 452; 456.
45 Ballantyne, *Dr. Jessie MacBean*, 35; Margaret Taylor Ross, "A Child Welfare Clinic," *The China Medical Journal*, 41, 3 (1927): 250–52; *Hackett Medical College for Women, Turner Training School for Nurses*, Catalogue 1925–1926, 21.
46 "To Save Life and Spread True Light, Summer Offering 1931," Presbyterian Historical Society, Presbyterian Church in the U.S.A. Board of Foreign Missions Secretaries' Files: China Missions, RG 82 [hereafter cited as Presbyterian Church in the U.S.A. Board of Foreign Missions], box 44, folder 09.
47 Iva M. Miller, "A Health Campaign in South China," *China Medical Journal* 42, 3 (1928): 155.
48 Miller, "A Health Campaign in South China," 158.
49 "Report for 1930 – Department of Obstetrics, by Jessie A. MacBean," Presbyterian Historical Society, Presbyterian Church in the U.S.A. Board of Foreign Missions, RG 82, box 44, folder 09.
50 For more details about this question, see Girouard, *Médicaliser au féminin*, 164–96.

51 "Report, Health Nursing Work in Canton, 1932–1933," General Commission on Archives and History, Foreign Missionary Society, China, Church of the United Brethren in Christ, file 2279-3-7:04.
52 For a more detailed discussion see Girouard, *Médicaliser au féminin*, 115–17.
53 Hackett's annual reports provide statistics only on medical school graduates, not on nursing school graduates, after 1929. We can safely assume that their number, as is the case for medical graduates, remained at least steady from 1929 to 1935.
54 "Annual Report of the David Gregg Hospital, 1931; David Gregg Hospital, Canton, China, Report of the Superintendent, December, 1, 1933," Presbyterian Historical Society, Presbyterian Church in the U.S.A. Board of Foreign Missions, RG 82, box 05, folder 04; "J. Franklin Karcher, M.D., Superintendent, to the President, 1935," Presbyterian Historical Society, Presbyterian Church in the U.S.A. Board of Foreign Missions, Record Group 82, Box 05, Folder 04.
55 "Qingmo chuangye xing guangzhou xiguan xiaojie: Huang Yuying" [Western Guangzhou entrepreneur at the end of the Qing Dynasty: Miss Huang Yuying], *Guangdong shizhi* 1 (1999): 5.
56 *Hackett Medical College, Bulletin 1924–1925*, 33; "Report of Hackett Medical College and Affiliated Institutions, June, 1926," Presbyterian Historical Society, Presbyterian Church in the U.S.A. Board of Foreign Missions, RG 82, box 05, folder 04; Taylor Ross, "A Child Welfare Clinic," 252.
57 "Report for 1930 – Department of Obstetrics, by Jessie A. MacBean," Presbyterian Historical Society, Presbyterian Church in the U.S.A. Board of Foreign Missions, RG 82, box 44, folder 09.
58 Ballantyne, *Dr. Jessie MacBean*, 30.
59 Ballantyne, *Dr. Jessie MacBean*, 30.
60 *Annual Report of the Hackett Medical College, Hospital Number, January 1, 1933 to June 30, 1934*, 12.
61 "J. Franklin Karcher, M.D., Superintendent, to the President, 1935," Presbyterian Historical Society, Presbyterian Church in the U.S.A. Board of Foreign Missions, RG 82, box 05, folder 04.
62 "Report of the Hackett Medical Center, September 1936, by Ross W. Wong M.D.," President, Presbyterian Historical Society, Presbyterian Church in the U.S.A. Board of Foreign Missions, RG 82, box 05, folder 04.
63 Warsh, *Prescribed Norms*, 218–19.

2

A Mission for Modernity
Canadian Women in Medical and Nursing Education in India, 1946–66

Jill Campbell-Miller

"Jai Hindi!" – Victory to India! This was a slogan of the independence movement led by the Indian National Congress in India and the standard greeting of the speeches of India's first prime minister, Jawaharlal Nehru. It was also the greeting that Edith Buchanan, daughter of Canadian Presbyterian missionaries, chose to use in the preface of her textbook for Indian nurses published in 1953, *A Study Guide in the Nursing Arts*.[1] Buchanan's portrait, still hanging in the principal's office of the Rajkumari Amrit Kaur College of Nursing (formerly known as the College of Nursing at the University of Delhi), features a smiling and matronly middle-aged white woman. Tall and with a wide and pleasing face, Buchanan's Scottish features hardly represent a typical image of immediate post-independence India. Yet by locating her work among the vast array of projects that added up to the first long decade of the Nehruvian developmental state (1948–60), it is possible to touch on a wide variety of themes central to that era and place concerning the role of education, health, mission institutions, and international organizations in the modernization project of the early independent state.

This chapter will examine the work of two Canadian women working in the field of medical and nursing education in India during this immediate post-independence period, doctors Edith Buchanan and Florence Nichols. They were two of the two to three dozen Canadian women engaged in health care–related fields in India, primarily under missionary auspices, during the 1950s and early 1960s. Buchanan was the founding vice-principal,

Figure 1 Portrait of Edith Buchanan in the principal's office of the Rajkumari Amrit Kaur College of Nursing. | Courtesy Jill Campbell-Miller

and later principal, of the College of Nursing at the University of Delhi and author of the first textbook specifically written for use in nursing colleges in India. Nichols was a psychiatrist and medical missionary who played a leading role in establishing the Department of Psychiatry at the Christian Medical College in Vellore. Two questions will be asked of the work of these Canadians in the early years of independent India: First, what do their stories reveal about the presence of Canadian women working abroad in the postwar period in the context of the emerging field of international development? And second, how does their presence and work in India help illuminate the Government of India's ambitions for its medical system in the immediate post-independence period and the international infrastructure that contributed to it? Like David Webster's chapter in this volume, it tries to locate women in the history of early international development efforts.

For the latter half of the nineteenth and the first half of the twentieth centuries, both health care and the mission field provided career opportunities to a certain class of white Canadian women, though within a deeply problematic, imperialist project. During the heyday of the British Raj, the imperial administration that ruled India between 1858 and 1948, many Canadian women travelled to India to work as health care providers within Protestant mission institutions.[2] Cultural norms, including the belief that women were naturally caregivers, allowed them to train as nurses and even doctors; the mission field gave them the ability to travel abroad in a socially sanctioned way and offered professional leadership roles unavailable to them at home.[3] By the 1940s and 1950s, the era that this chapters examines, India had undergone dramatic political shifts that led to its independence from British imperial rule in 1947. However, within Canada and India, cultural norms that limited women's career opportunities, and confined them to caregiving roles, were slower to change. Yet as this chapter will show, the context of the Indian government's ambitions for its independent future opened up new professional opportunities for women working in health care–related fields.

The presence of both Buchanan and Nichols as white women of British descent in India was tied to Canada's imperial linkages with the British Raj, and this put them in a privileged position to be able to take advantage of these new opportunities. Their work in health care during the immediate postwar era can be viewed within the context of what historian Dan Gorman has called the transition from "imperialism to internationalism" in Canada. As Gorman writes, a "lingering but largely implicit discourse of whiteness in public affairs" continued after the Second World War in Canada.[4] Buchanan's and Nichols' individual roles as children of the imperial system made their presence in India possible, and their race was part of the implicit dynamics of power that allowed them to fill leadership positions in the former colony. By recognizing their place within the complex international history of empire and mission work, this chapter will follow David Meren's call to engage with an "expansive international history" and "investigate the diverse manifestations and structures of power and to understand how these shaped the history of Canada and the world."[5]

Despite their place as representatives of empire, both women worked during a time of rapid change in India's history, which they helped to implement. After Buchanan and Nichols vacated their roles, they made space for professional Indian women to take over their leadership positions. As much as their presence in India reflected Canada's ties to British imperialism, their efforts just as equally represented the determination of the newly independent state to modernize its health care system by expanding medical and nursing education as component parts of the Nehruvian developmental, socialistic state. Both women played a role in building the educational infrastructure of the Indian state as it related to medicine and nursing.

Medical and Nursing Education in India in the Early Twentieth Century

The spaces within which Buchanan and Nichols worked in the 1940s and 1950s were quite different from those under consideration by most historiography related to missions and missionaries, which primarily focuses on the late nineteenth and early twentieth centuries. The Christian Medical College, for example, was not a British mission but was started as a Christian hospital by an American, Dr. Ida Scudder. Dr. Nichols went to work there as a missionary through the Anglican Church of Canada's relationship with the hospital. The College of Nursing in New Delhi, where Buchanan worked, was a secular, government-led institution built up by the newly independent Indian state. Buchanan found herself working there by virtue of her family ties as the daughter of Canadian Presbyterian missionaries. Therefore, while Buchanan's and Nichols' life trajectories were shaped by the history of the Protestant mission movement, their own institutions and circumstances of work in the 1940s and 1950s must be seen in a different historical and political context compared with that of the British colonial state of earlier decades.

As Kim Girouard shows in this volume, during the late nineteenth century Canadian Protestant churches began to send, in greatly increased numbers, medical missionaries abroad, primarily to China and India. Just as in the case of China, women played a major role in this development, originally because the Hindu and Muslim practice of segregating elite women meant that only other women could gain access to domiciles. By 1916, roughly a third of the worldwide Protestant medical mission physicians were women, and half of those (159) were in India.[6] Despite their focus on health and healing, British mission institutions in the late nineteenth and early twentieth centuries could be complex spaces, manifestations of the Empire and part of its so-called civilizing mission. Early missions were sites of proselytization, medical missions included.[7] Yet without apologizing for these practices, it remains true that by the twentieth century, Protestant medical missions responded to life and death physical needs and often served marginalized communities excluded by traditional social hierarchies.

As historian David Hardiman points out, medical missions persisted into the 1940s and 1950s, until it became clear that indigenous leadership could easily take over the religious and educational aspects of mission work.[8] After independence, the Indian National Congress government sought to, in the parlance of the era, modernize health care and bring about standards of care based on those predominant in many Western countries. In 1946, a year before independence, the Government of India published a report of its Health Survey and Development Committee, known as the Bhore Committee after its chairman, Sir Joseph Bhore. The report found that there were forty-seven thousand doctors practising in the country, approximately five times fewer doctors per capita than in the UK, and forty-three thousand nurses, representing ten times fewer the number per capita in the UK.[9] As a result, the government was not prepared to do what the communist People's Republic of China had done in 1949, and summarily remove all missionaries from the country's medical system. Medical missionaries were an especially important part of medical and nursing education.

The British government's inconsistent and laissez-faire approach to education in colonial India encouraged private actors, including Protestant missionaries, to play a leading role in developing education systems in India.[10] After independence, the central and state governments not only sought to integrate these efforts into a whole, but they also used education, and higher education in particular, as an important tool in the fulfillment of development planning efforts. This coincided with what Ludovic Tournès and Giles Scott-Smith have called the "golden age" of international scholarship programs.[11] Additionally, the United Nations and development assistance programs such as the Commonwealth-devised Colombo Plan began to promote technical assistance programs to support training and professional development in South and Southeast Asia, Latin America, the Caribbean, and Africa.[12] Designed to win local hearts and minds while shoring up social and professional capacities in newly independent countries, educational support through scholarships and fellowships often represented the leading edge of programs in the rapidly expanding field of international development. Medicine, nursing, and education were acceptable fields for Canadian women to work within a professional context overseas, and during the late 1940s and early 1950s, they still largely arrived through mission-sanctioned activity. As such, for those interested in the role of women within the history of Canada and international development, missions, medicine, nursing, and education are important landscapes of investigation.[13]

While both Buchanan and Nichols were in their own ways products of British imperialism in India, the time and place of their work was quite different from that for white women a generation earlier. Both worked during India's transition from colony to nation, within a context that anticipated the end of roles of people like them – white women – from medicine and nursing in India. For example, at the CMC, Dr. Ida Scudder was succeeded by the highly capable Indian surgeon, Dr. Hilda Lazarus, as principal in 1947, the year of India's independence. By placing Buchanan and Nichols within this larger historical context, it is possible to see not only how their own work shaped the institutions where they worked, but also how their shifting environment changed the work that they did.

Edith Buchanan and *A Study Guide in Nursing Arts*

Edith Buchanan was not a missionary herself, at least not by choice. Though born in Canada, her formative years as a child were spent in her parents' Presbyterian mission in Amkhut, in what is today Gujarat. Her father, Dr. John Buchanan, was a domineering man who ruled his mission as a kind of "fiefdom."[14] Buchanan's mother, Dr. Mary MacKay, was groomed to be a missionary by her family and was sent to the University of Toronto from Pictou County, Nova Scotia, to train to be a doctor for that purpose.[15] They married in India and had four children, one of whom died as an infant of dysentery and the other as a soldier in the First World War. After the death of their parents, this left Edith and her sister Ruth. Neither married nor had children. Unfortunately, what is known about Edith Buchanan must be gained from her actions, rather than from any knowledge of her own intentions or thoughts. A relative who knew her in her elder years said that she rarely spoke about herself or her career.[16] As many chapters in this book demonstrate, the problem of a lack of archival or other sources is a commonplace challenge for historians interested in Canadian women living and working abroad, and Buchanan is emblematic of this difficulty. As a middle-class white woman born in the Edwardian era, Buchanan was likely trained from an early age to be modest about her accomplishments. One insight into this ethic is available in the foreword to a pamphlet written about Buchanan's mother. The cousin who wrote the foreword said of Mary that

Figure 2 Edith Buchanan with her parents, John and Mary, 1918. | Courtesy Robert Coleman

"each day brought its work, and each day she did that work, quietly, cheerfully, and without fuss, having no thought to praise or blame."[17] It is likely that Edith adopted a similar attitude in her own professional life.

Edith Buchanan finished her final years of high school at Harbord Collegiate in Toronto, then went on to do an undergraduate degree at Victoria College at the University of Toronto. She then completed two years of training as a nurse at the McGill School for Graduate Nurses, adding a third year by taking a certificate in teaching and supervision.[18] Buchanan was an excellent scholar and an active student. In Toronto she was captain of the women's intercollegiate basketball team, a member of the swimming team, and part of the Victoria Women Undergraduate Association.[19] She relied on a scholarship from the Royal Victoria College to attend McGill, where she received a prize for the highest mark in her class.[20] In 1936 she returned to India.

Despite her parents' profession, Buchanan's principal interest in her chosen line of work seems to have been professional as opposed to spiritual. She spent only a year as a nurse at a mission hospital in Sialkot, in what is now Pakistan, before joining the staff of the Lady Hardinge Medical College in New Delhi for five years. The Government of India hired Buchanan to become a nursing educator in 1943 at the School of Hospital Administration in Delhi, housed at the Lady Reading Health School.[21] In 1946, the Ministry of Health established the College of Nursing at the University of Delhi. An American, Margaretta Craig, became the founding principal, and Buchanan the founding vice-principal. It was renamed the Rajkumari Amrit Kaur College of Nursing in 1974.[22] Buchanan also worked on attaining advanced degrees to support her work in nursing education, obtaining a certificate in Nursing Education (Advanced) from the University of Toronto in 1945 and a doctorate in education from Columbia University in 1953. For her doctorate, Buchanan received a fellowship from the World Health Organization (WHO), the United Nations agency established in 1948 and dedicated to global health.

The choice of Buchanan, a Canadian white woman, for a WHO fellowship for India during this racially charged post-independence period may seem odd. The decision would have been made by a committee in New Delhi largely composed of Indian government officials and WHO representatives.[23] Their decision reflected the history of nursing in India during the colonial period. Nursing was a stigmatized profession among high caste Hindus and was poorly paid.[24] As a result, nursing attracted virtually no Hindu women. Those that did come to it were mostly Christian, either from the Syrian or Protestant denominations and, even then, no graduate programs existed.[25] By the time of independence, few Indian nurses had had the opportunities afforded to Buchanan through her family ties in Canada to gain the higher education necessary to become educational professionals themselves.

The WHO fellowship program reflected the determination of early Western development agencies to create a structure of post-colonial elite leaders.[26] In collaboration with governments, their ambition was to train a generation of leaders that would train the next generation of professionals. Buchanan, who worked for the government-sponsored College of Nursing at the University of Delhi, was a good fit for these ambitions. The government had a major role in the college's development. Minister of Health Rajkumari Amrit Kaur became directly involved with the institution, once writing that it "always had a very special place in my heart."[27] Kaur's personal connection to the college set it apart from other nursing education institutions in the country and closely tied its development with the nationalist political ambitions of the new government. It also made the college a key location for investment from the international community. A historian of nursing in India, Madelaine Healey, described the Delhi College of Nursing "as the flagship of degree education for nurses in India," attracting attention and assistance from international organizations.[28] Buchanan became college principal in 1958 and launched a two-year master of nursing degree "to introduce a culture of research into Indian nursing," fulfilling the government's expectation that she would use her position to create the structural reforms needed to train the next generation of nursing leaders.[29]

The *Study Guide in Nursing Arts*

The main purpose of the WHO fellowship and Buchanan's doctoral dissertation project was to prepare a textbook specifically for nurses in the Indian context.[30] Kaur's close association with the university's College of Nursing was again evident, as she was credited with the foreword to the *Study Guide*. In it, she praised Buchanan as "highly qualified, both in the field of nursing and in the field of education."[31] The preface is the only part of the book where we consciously heard from Buchanan herself. In it, she presented the work as less a book of her own authorship and rather a collaboration, writing that "the stories and illustrations of real life situations are contributed by a great number of students and colleagues in Delhi, coming, as they do, from every part of India." She then wrote that it is "a Study Guide in Nursing that has come out of India, for India. The illustrations, equipment, and experience are our own. Learning in medicine and nursing belongs to no one country or generation. Each drinks from the life-giving stream to build his own body of knowledge anew, suited to his country and its needs. If this effort leads to the production of more and better teaching materials by many nurses all over India, it will be a dream come true."[32] Buchanan clearly identified herself with India, writing that the materials for the book "are our own." She was keenly aware that there were two audiences for her book, and this was expressed in the text. The first, of course, was the Indian nursing students who would use the book in their classes. The second was the Government of India and the Ministry of Health. The textbook was more than a tool of learning for nurses. It was an expression of the government's hopes for the role of nurses in the health care system. The textbook presents nurses as builders of the nation through community health education and a spirit of self-reliance. The book and the doctorate Buchanan earned by writing it were expressions of the government's own hopes for nursing and its collaboration with international organizations such as the WHO.

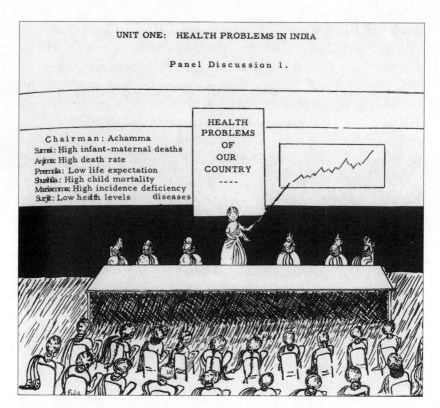

Figure 3 The "panel" of student nurses in *A Study Guide in Nursing Arts*. | Courtesy Robert Coleman

The early sections of *A Study Guide* feature panels illustrated by Buchanan, who drew on real life experiences from her and others' teaching practice to introduce a topic of discussion for the classroom. In these panel discussions, students related a first-hand account of a problem. Buchanan invited students to "tell the story in your own words, give the fact illustrated by the story, summarize possible improvements to the situation, state how to find meanings from charts and graphs," and, finally, "make a chart of this (these) type(s) with statistics supplied."[33] As one contemporary reviewer noted, "The book is a departure from the conventional form of nursing text. It aims to help the Indian nursing student master the principles and practice of nursing through a developmental, self-directive and self-teaching approach."[34] The book is, as the title indicates, a study *guide* – it is meant to prompt students to work independently or in groups.

The *Study Guide* reflected the energy, optimism, and techniques used by the Indian National Congress government. Though the book covered procedures and techniques in caring for the ill, as well as basic nursing principles, tools, and vocabulary, often using vernacular terms, it also made a real effort to place nursing within India's developmental context. It pointed to the types of challenges that the Bhore committee had identified, comparing local indicators of health with similar statistics in Western countries. Despite these challenges, it presented nurses as an integral part of the solution, and a hopeful, positive spirit imbues the writing, with chapter titles such as "Opportunities in Nursing" and "Creative, Positive Nursing for India Today."

Buchanan's text does not spend a great deal of time focusing on specific techniques with, for example, hospital equipment. It is useful to compare this with the second edition of the American nursing textbook *Nursing Arts,* cowritten by a professor at the Teachers College at Columbia, where Buchanan earned her degree, and published in 1953. The American text spends eight chapters exploring subjects specifically related to patients in a hospital setting, two chapters on laboratory and diagnostic tests, and a whole chapter on administering oxygen.[35] By contrast, while Buchanan's *A Study Guide in Nursing Arts* has sections within chapters devoted to caring for patients in a hospital, there are no individual chapters devoted to hospital care and little discussion of medications or equipment. The guide was meant to foster a nurse that is adaptable to many different types of care situations and who can teach herself, as nurses were presumed to be women, to learn the needs of that specific environment. The *Study Guide* was meant as a supplement, not a replacement, for other nursing textbooks.

Buchanan presented the nurse as an instrument of India's advancement, not only in medical care, but also of the entire nation. The Indian government's prevailing focus on self-sufficiency, both at the national and individual level, is obvious throughout the text. In one panel, students identified "Superstition, malpractice, Social custom, Ignorance, Poverty, and Lack of Health Services" as problems for health.[36] In the *Study Guide,* the nurse was cast not only as a weapon against such "ignorance," but also as an educator to promote self-sufficiency in village life. A story told by student nurse "Kamala" illustrates such a case. Her father, a doctor, sometimes took her on his rounds through villages. In one village, a poor man named Kalu would stand on one leg, performing emasculating and socially isolating menial

Figure 4 "Kamala" tells the story of the injured man who, like a crane, stood on one leg "performing some ... child's task." | Courtesy Robert Coleman

tasks while the other men worked their fields. The father told his daughter that Kalu had once been a prosperous farmer too, but that after a snake bite, a tourniquet tied to prevent the poison from leeching into the rest of his body was left on too long, forcing an amputation of the leg. In this case, prevention through education was needed not only for individual care, but also for the economic advancement of the country, since the man's family had fallen into poverty because of his injury.[37]

The government's priorities are seen in other, more self-evident ways as well. One is in the way that the textbook paid attention not only to planning as a concept, but specifically, also to the government's own First Five-Year Plan, which it mentioned several times. In one panel on "Planning Priorities," the chairperson focused on constitutionally defined objectives for the nation as a whole, focusing on equality and redistribution of resources and power, the socialist objectives of many within the Indian National Congress and particularly Nehru himself. The textbook spends a great deal of time on the overall picture of India's economic and social life, urging nurses to "speak with one voice and work with one hand for India."[38]

Though it has been difficult to obtain sources to find out how widely the text was used in India, there is evidence that it has had a sustained life in nursing schools throughout the country. A book on the history of nurses published in 2001 by the Trained Nurses Association of India, the national association of nurses, observes that the textbook is "still found very useful by the teachers and students" nearly fifty years after its publication.[39] Buchanan's obituary in *The Nursing Journal of India,* published in the year of her death, 2003, commented that the book "is still an asset to nurses in India."[40] Yet the book's positive tenor hardly reflected the actual working environment of Indian nurses during the later twentieth century. As Healey wrote, Craig and Buchanan emphasized autonomy and scientific principles and urged nurses to think of themselves as part of a health team. Yet nurses in India, as well as in other parts of the world, faced a challenging and patriarchal context after leaving nursing school.[41]

After leaving the nursing college in 1964, Buchanan went on to work for the WHO on a short-term contract as a consultant in Nepal for a few months.[42] She retired shortly thereafter in 1965 and moved to Musoorie to live with her sister, Ruth.[43] She did obtain a life membership in the Indian Public Health Association in 1975, indicating a continuing professional interest in nursing.[44] Following Ruth's death, Buchanan returned to Canada, passing away in 2003.[45] Her obituary in *The Nursing Journal of India* described Buchanan as Canadian by birth, but "more Indian in her way of thinking and acting."[46] Though Canadian, Buchanan was a product of the historical forces of twentieth-century India – the colonial presence that brought her there in the first place as an infant, the political change that occurred within it, and the international forces than acted on it. She was a living embodiment of the "interactive dimensions," as historian David Hollinger termed it, of both the mission project and the development project that she came to work for on behalf of the Indian government, through the gendered profession of nursing.[47]

Florence Nichols and the Christian Medical College

Florence Nichols, a psychiatrist and medical missionary, left a greater record of her work, including two unpublished memoirs and a paper trail in various archives. One manuscript, an unusual book told from the perspective of her poodle, dealt with her marriage in later life and the death of her husband. The other was about her time living and working in India.[48] She was born in Toronto, in 1913. Like Buchanan, she excelled academically, graduating early from Grade 13 from Humberside Collegiate at only sixteen years of age, receiving high marks across the board. She completed her Bachelor of Arts degree at Victoria College at the University of Toronto, and then her MD a few years later. After a general internship at St. Joseph's Hospital in Toronto, she developed an interest in psychiatry, working in psychiatric hospitals in Brockville and Toronto, and received her diploma of psychiatry from the University of Toronto in 1941. At this time psychiatry was a small specialty of medicine, and Nichols was one of only a handful of female psychiatrists in Canada. The University of Toronto was the first Canadian institution to offer a postgraduate training specialty in psychiatry, and in the first two decades, graduated a total of only ten women and one hundred men.[49] Despite this, Nichols never mentioned sexism as an obstacle to her professional accomplishments.[50]

In 1946 Nichols was able to secure a missionary post at the Christian Medical College (CMC) in Vellore, in what is presently Tamil Nadu, in southern India. In 1902, Scudder, the daughter of American missionaries, began her work by founding a hospital that primarily served women who did not have access to health care. In 1918, she also founded a medical college to train female doctors, though it later became a coed institution.[51] The drive to attract a psychiatrist at the CMC came about as a result of a financial gift from Lord John Paton Maclay, a British shipping magnate, who wanted to build a psychiatric ward at the hospital. It so happened that around the same time, Nichols was training at Toronto's St. Joseph's Hospital in surgery, a specialty she heartily disliked but one she felt was necessary if she were to achieve her lifelong dream of being a missionary. As Nichols tells it, the chief of surgery noticed her unhappiness and questioned her about why she stayed on. When Nichols told him about her quest to become a missionary, he made inquiries with a missionary friend who told the surgeon that a hospital was looking for a psychiatrist in China.[52]

Somehow, word also travelled to Vellore that a Canadian psychiatrist was looking for a mission posting, and the Women's Auxiliary of the Missionary Society of the Church of England in Canada redirected Nichols toward the CMC. Robert Cochrane, the CMC's principal, wrote that though they wanted to have Nichols "at the earliest possible moment" they also wanted her be as "highly trained as possible."[53] All agreed, including Nichols herself, that she required further training outside of Canada.[54] For unknown reasons, this was not arranged, and Nichols ended up sailing to India with her limited Canadian credentials intact.

When Nichols first arrived at the CMC late in 1946, she found an institution neither ready, nor anxious, to embrace psychiatry as a specialty. Instead, the CMC was fully occupied with obtaining the ability to grant its MBBS designation, the equivalent of a bachelor's degree of medicine in North America, from the government.[55] Since a department of psychiatry was not needed to obtain the certification, the CMC did not prioritize her work and was reluctant to allocate space or resources to Nichols.[56] Following an unsuccessful course in the Tamil language and a short stint providing primary health care at a mission site in the small village of Muttathur, Nichols began treating patients in earnest at the CMC in 1948. She found little support for her practice and had no assigned beds for psychiatric purposes. In letters and in her memoir she recorded that her solution to this problem was to care for patients in her own room.[57]

At first, Nichols primarily treated other missionaries rather than Indian patients, partly because of her poor language skills. Due to their lack of progress in building the ward, the CMC lost their gift from Maclay. Though this came as a blow, the loss was perhaps to the long-term benefit of both Nichols and the CMC. Four years in India had given her a course in the cultural life of the region and had exposed the limits of care imposed by scarcity and her own educational shortcomings. With independence, the government stepped up its requirements for medical colleges, and even if the CMC had built a department of psychiatry, she would not have qualified to become a professor in it without further credentials and more training.

In 1949, she left the CMC and returned to Canada on a furlough. However, unusually for a missionary, Nichols took a six-year furlough. While spending time with her family in Toronto, she requested funding to do postgraduate training in psychiatry at the University of Pennsylvania. Her sponsors at the Women's Auxiliary, used to funding short professional development courses, did not understand the benefit of obtaining such a substantial course of education. Not only that, they were suspicious of her motives, believing she was using education as an excuse to spend more time in North America to be closer to her family. They refused to fund her.[58] Undaunted, Nichols secured her own scholarship and supplemented her income by working as an instructor at the University of Pennsylvania.[59] This training and experience in teaching meant that when she returned to the

CMC in 1955, she was qualified to become a professor of psychiatry in a new department.

Nichols encountered a college and hospital much more anxious to develop a psychiatric unit than the one she had left a decade previously. This was partly because she had built some trust with the institution during her previous experience there, but it was also because of the CMC's new-found sense of professional confidence within independent India. Having successfully obtained the MBBS certification, the CMC was rapidly carving out a niche for itself as an institution known for excellence in specialties, making a good case for its value as a developmental tool to the Indian government. In 1949, Jacob Chandy, a neurosurgeon who had trained with Wilder Penfield at the Montreal Neurological Institute, set up a department of neurosurgery, the first of its kind in South Asia; he eventually established India's first neurological training program in 1957.[60] Adding a department of psychiatry made sense in this context, particularly since CMC medical students were forced to travel to Chennai (Madras) for some nominal training in psychiatry.[61] When Nichols returned, she began to organize an outpatient department for psychiatric patients, while the CMC finally began the process of planning and building the department itself.[62] Nichols' new credentials were fundamental to her being accepted as a qualified professor within the department she was establishing.

Nichols also had a direct hand in bringing the department its second fully qualified psychiatrist. Rose Chacko was a medical student who decided to pursue postgraduate training in psychiatry after studying under Nichols. Nichols secured funding for Chacko's studies from Nichols' own parish in Toronto.[63] Chacko went on to train at the University of Pittsburgh specializing in child psychiatry, before returning to the CMC and eventually became chair of the psychiatry department in 1962. Nichols also met and recruited an Indian psychiatric nurse in Philadelphia.[64]

In addition to these efforts, Nichols and CMC director John Carman played a leading role in designing the actual compound that became the Mental Health Centre.[65] She also secured a five thousand dollar contribution for the department from a bishop in the United States, a large sum in the context of a hospital that constantly struggled to find funds for its endeavours.[66] Unlike Buchanan, who worked in an institution directly supported by the government, Nichols was unsuccessful in obtaining funds from international organizations such as the Rockefeller Foundation.[67] Though these organizations may have drawn on the philosophy of mission institutions in supporting the education of leadership, their funding focus was on the secular institutions of government, particularly in this politically charged era of independence.

Nichols, as the head of the Department of Psychiatry, a project she called "her baby," had a major influence on the approach to family-based psychiatry that the Christian Medical College developed and continues to practice to this day.[68] While Nichols was not the first to integrate family members into a psychiatric treatment program in India, the CMC Vellore was one of only two institutions in India during this era to include families directly in a treatment program.[69] While other institutions may incorporate family into their treatment methodologies, the CMC is today one of the few institutions that identifies family-based psychiatry as integral to its treatment practice and care.[70]

Families had been a constant in hospital care in India, partly because of the shortage of nurses. For example, a Canadian mission, the Anglican Maple Leaf Hospital in Kangra, also built accommodations for the relatives of inpatients who "attend to them during their stay in hospital."[71] Nichols took this concept much further, perhaps partly inspired by Dr. Vidya Sagar, a psychiatrist at the Amritsar Mental Hospital in the 1950s, who experimented with having relatives stay with mental hospital patients.[72] Under Nichols, the CMC Mental Health Centre was designed to support care in the context of the family unit both through its programming and the design of its facilities. Rather than simply have families support nursing and cooking tasks in order to relieve pressure on hospital staff, families became part of the treatment process, since it was expected that families would continue to be long-term caregivers upon their discharge from the hospital.

As her writings demonstrate, Nichols integrated family life into the practice of psychiatry as a conscious choice to accommodate both the practical and cultural needs of her patients and the hospital. "In India," she wrote, "the individual is very much a member of a family unit, usually much more so than in the West. Indians prefer to care for their sick members at home rather than be separated from them by sending them to a mental hospital where they cannot remain with the patient. In India, if the patient comes to hospital for any reason, it is customary for some member of his family to accompany him to care for his needs and cook his food. This is not allowed in the existing mental hospitals. The introduction of Western medicine has cut across the tradition of the country in this respect, even in general hospitals, where relatives have been discouraged from attendance on patients

Figure 5 Plaque dedicated to Nichols on the grounds of the Mental Health Centre at the Christian Medical College, Vellore. | Courtesy Jill Campbell-Miller

for hygienic and other reasons."[73] Though Nichols possessed shortcomings as a health care provider and educator, she was deeply dedicated and single-minded in pursuit of her family-centric approach to psychiatric care. Under her direction, patients admitted to the Mental Health Centre's long-term program of about seven weeks lived in a dorm-room-compound environment, with a kitchen and accommodation for family members rather than a standard hospital ward. (Their level of privacy depended on their ability to pay, with private wards subsidizing the costs for poorer families.) Group therapy for family members and patients alike became a core part of the treatment. Occupational therapy also became a major part of the program.[74]

The CMC credits Nichols with pioneering the idea of family participation in mental health care, as a plaque to her on the grounds of the Mental Health Centre attests.[75] In its 2017–18 annual report, the CMC reported having 98 inpatient beds and an average of 300 outpatients per day.[76] They also operate a program of community outreach through a local non-governmental organization.[77] Moreover, the family-centred environment promoted by Nichols provides contemporary researchers with a unique opportunity to study social issues related to mental health.[78] Though her work was less self-consciously tied to post-independence developmental goals than Buchanan's, it aided the same process, with its similar focus on training a new generation of medical leaders in India. By the time Nichols left India in 1959, Indian colleagues were quickly replacing the European missionaries who had formerly held positions of leadership, a process that had been under way for some time. Anna Jacob, an alumna of the CMC, took over from a British predecessor as nursing superintendent even prior to India's independence. Many Indian alumni from Vellore were sent overseas to obtain postgraduate education at the institution's expense, to return and take up leadership positions at the CMC.

Conclusion

There were other Canadian women involved in medical education in India and elsewhere in Asia during this era. Florence Taylor, a Canadian missionary, played an instrumental role in setting up the first bachelor's degree program for nurses at the Christian Medical College in Vellore, in the 1940s.[79] Dorothy Hall, a Canadian nurse, was first a nurse-educator in Thailand before spending ten years in New Delhi as a nurse administrator and regional advisor for the WHO in the 1960s and early 1970s.[80] Lyle Creelman, about whom Susan Armstrong-Reid has written a biography, was the WHO's chief nursing officer from 1954–68.[81] These women's stories largely fall outside of the history of Canadian official development assistance. Neither Buchanan nor Nichols were supported in any way by the Canadian government and are absent from its records.

To excavate women's stories in the histories of Canadian international development assistance, it is necessary to look at the "undiplomatic" past, where women largely worked. Dominique Marshall writes in the conclusion of this volume that the changes made possible by Canadian women's work abroad were not necessarily structural but, rather, cumulative. This is certainly true of the lives and work of Buchanan and Nichols. As Marshall also suggests, looking for women in Canada's international past mirrors the type of work they often did – persistent, quiet, incremental, and sometimes painfully slow investigations that occasionally feel more akin to journalism than to the accustomed archival work of diplomatic historians. This effort often ends up yielding biographies, and thus these histories may seem narrow and contextual. Yet taken together, as this collection demonstrates, they make much larger statements about the role of women as representatives or opponents to the Canadian state.

In the 1950s, health care and education were fields in which Canadian women could travel overseas within a professional context, yet remain within the boundaries of gendered respectability. This was the case whether they worked within older mission postings or took advantage of new opportunities, such as those provided by international organizations and the Indian government. This chapter examined how and where two Canadian women of considerable abilities found fulfilling roles working professionally as health care educators overseas in the postwar era. It contends that their career trajectories and personal ambitions aligned with both established transnational Christian missionary projects and the priorities of emerging international development organizations, and with the modernizing spirit of the Nehruvian developmental state. In their respective unique ways, both Buchanan and Nichols carved out spaces among these complex, overlapping histories where they were able to make substantial contributions to Indian health care. To fully understand the expansive international history in this period of transition from empire to internationalism, it is important to excavate the hidden histories of women like Buchanan and Nichols, who helped to make the global postwar order a reality.

Acknowledgments

I would like to thank AMS Healthcare for funding this research through their postdoctoral fellowship program, as well as Robert Coleman, Margaret and Mary Janack, and the Rajkumari Amrit Kaur College of Nursing.

Notes

1 Edith Buchanan, *A Study Guide in Nursing Arts* (New Delhi: College of Nursing, 1953), v.
2 See Ruth Compton Brouwer, *New Women for God: Canadian Presbyterian Women and India Missions* (Toronto: University of Toronto Press, 1990).
3 Nursing in particular was a field gendered in specific ways in Britain, North America, and India, and concepts of imperial duty, class, and race also played a role within the nursing field in delegating professional designations. See, for example, Rosemary Fitzgerald, "Making and Moulding of the Indian Empire: Recasting Nurses in Colonial India," in *Rhetoric and Reality: Gender and the Colonial Experience in South Asia,* ed. Avril A. Powell and Siobhan Lambert-Hurley (Oxford: Oxford University Press, 2006), 185–222.
4 Dan Gorman, "Race, the Commonwealth, and the United Nations: From Imperialism to Internationalism in Canada, 1940–1960," in *Dominion of Race: Rethinking Canada's International History,* ed. Laura Madokoro, Francine McKenzie, and David Meren (Vancouver: UBC Press, 2017), 141.
5 David Meren, "Getting Over Tragedy: Some Further Thoughts on Canadian International History," *Canadian Historical Review* 96, 4 (December 2015): 593, doi:10.3138/chr.96413.

6 Rosemary Fitzgerald, "Rescue and Redemption: The Rise of Female Medical Missions in Colonial India during the Late Nineteenth and Early Twentieth Centuries," in *Nursing History and the Politics of Welfare*, ed. Anne Marie Rafferty, Jane Robinson, and Ruth Elkan (London: Routledge, 1997), 72.
7 Though the book is about the early nineteenth century and specifically in regard to the United States, Emily Conroy-Krutz offers important insights into conceptual relationship between proselytization, imperialism, and missionary endeavours in the 19th century. Emily Conroy-Krutz, *Christian Imperialism: Converting the World in the Early American Republic* (Ithaca, NY: Cornell University Press, 2015).
8 David Hardiman, *Missionaries and Their Medicine: A Christian Modernity for Tribal India* (Manchester, UK: Manchester University Press, 2008), 192.
9 *Report of the Health Survey and Development Committee, Volume 1: A Survey of the State of the Public Health and of the Existing Health Organisation* (Calcutta: Government of India Press, 1946), 13, https://www.nhp.gov.in/sites/default/files/pdf/Bhore_Committee_Report_VOL-1.pdf.
10 Suresh Chandra Ghosh, *The History of Education in Modern India, 1757–1986* (New Delhi: Orient Longman, 1995), 58; Clive Whitehead, "The Historiography of British Imperial Education Policy, Part I: India," *History of Education* 34, 3 (2005), 320; Hayden J.A. Bellenoit, *Missionary Education and Empire in Late Colonial India, 1860–1920* (London: Pickering and Chatto, 2007), 32.
11 Ludovic Tournès and Giles Scott-Smith, "A World of Exchanges: Conceptualizing the History of International Scholarship Programs (Nineteenth to Twenty-First Centuries)," in *Global Exchanges: Scholarships and Transnational Circulations in the Modern World*, ed. Ludovic Tournès and Giles Scott-Smith (New York: Berghahn, 2018), 15. Shannon writes about American-Iranian relations in Michael K. Shannon, *Losing Hearts and Minds: American-Iranian Relations and International Education during the Cold War* (Ithaca, NY: Cornell University Press, 2017), 3. See also Liping Bu, "Educational Exchange and Cultural Diplomacy in the Cold War," *Journal of American Studies* 33, 3: 393–415, doi.org/10.1017/S0021875899006167.
12 David Webster, "Modern Missionaries: Canadian Postwar Technical Assistance Advisors in Southeast Asia," *Journal of the Canadian Historical Association* 20, 2 (2009): 86–111; Jill Campbell-Miller, "Encounter and Apprenticeship: The Colombo Plan and Canadian Aid in India, 1950–1960," in *A Samaritan State Revisited: Historical Perspectives on Canadian Foreign Aid*, ed. Greg Donaghy and David Webster (Calgary, AB: University of Calgary Press, 2019), 27–52.
13 See especially work by Ruth Compton Brouwer: *Modern Women Modernizing Men: The Changing Missions of Three Professional Women in Asia and Africa, 1902–69* (Vancouver: UBC Press, 2002); *Canada's Global Villagers: CUSO in Development, 1961–68* (Vancouver: UBC Press, 2013); "When Missions Became Development: Ironies of 'NGOization' in Mainstream Canadian Churches in the 1960s," *The Canadian Historical Review* 91, 4 (December 2010): 661–93; "Ironic Interventions: CUSO Volunteers in India's Family Planning Campaign, 1960s–1970s," *Social History* 43, 86 (November 2010): 279–313.
14 Ruth Compton Brouwer, "Canadian Presbyterians and India Missions, 1877–1914: The Policy and Politics of 'Women's Work for Women,'" in *North American Foreign Missions, 1810–1914: Theology, Theory, and Policy*, ed. Wilbert R. Shank (Grand Rapids, MI: Wm. B. Eerdmans, 2004), 210.
15 Ruth Buchanan, *My Mother* (Toronto: Women's Missionary Society of the Presbyterian Church of Canada, 1938).
16 Robert Coleman, in discussion with the author, Toronto, April 26, 2018.

17 Christine Ross Barker, foreword to *My Mother,* by Ruth Buchanan (Toronto: Women's Missionary Society of the Presbyterian Church of Canada, 1938).
18 "Buchanan, Mary Edith McKay," Student Card 28066, McGill University Archives, School for Graduate Studies, 1929–1933.
19 University of Toronto, *Torontonensis 1928* (Toronto: Students' Administrative Council of the University of Toronto, 1928), 48, 231, https://utarms.library.utoronto.ca/archives/online/digitized-publications#yearbooks.
20 "Obituary: Dr. (Ms.) Edith Buchanan," *Nursing Journal of India* 94: 11 (November 2003), 258.
21 World Health Organization (WHO) Records and Archives, correspondence with author, March 11, 2019; Trained Nurses' Association of India, *History and Trends in Nursing in India* (New Delhi: The Trained Nurses' Association of India, 2001), 155.
22 WHO Records and Archives, correspondence with author, March 11, 2019.
23 Oliver Leroux to Ted Giles, September 9, 1954, Library and Archives Canada, RG 29, vol. 1007, file 303-2-1.
24 Madelaine Healey, "'Regarded, Paid, and Housed as Menials': Nursing in Colonial India, 1900–1948," *South Asian History and Culture* 2, 1 (2010): 62.
25 For more on the association between Christianity and nursing historically and to the present day, see Sujani K. Reddy, *Nursing and Empire: Gendered Labor and Migration from India to the United States* (Chapel Hill: The University of North Carolina Press, 2015).
26 Yin-Tang Lin, Thomas David, and Davide Rodogno, "Fellowship Programs for Public Health Development: The Rockefeller Foundation, UNRRA, and the WHO (1920s–1970s)," in Tournès and Scott-Smith, *Global Exchanges,* 142.
27 "College of Nursing: University of Delhi, 10th Anniversary, 22–25 July 1956," Rajkumari Amrit Kaur College of Nursing Library, New Delhi.
28 Madelaine Healey, *Indian Sisters: A History of Nursing and the State, 1907–2007* (London: Routledge, 2013) 130.
29 Healey, *Indian Sisters,* 131. Healey also critiques this approach to training educated nursing elites, writing that it has promoted a classist culture in Indian nursing, where too much attention is paid to graduate education and not enough to the plight of the working nurse; Healey, *Indian Sisters,* 6.
30 Barbara Logan Tunis, *In Caps and Gowns: The Story of the School for Graduate Nurses, McGill University, 1920–1964* (Montreal/Kingston: McGill-Queen's University Press, 1966), 110.
31 Rajkumari Amrit Kaur, foreword to *A Study Guide in the Nursing Arts,* by Edith Buchanan (New Delhi: College of Nursing, 1953), i.
32 Buchanan, *Study Guide,* v.
33 Buchanan, *Study Guide,* 4.
34 Alice Clark, "A Study Guide in Nursing for Indian Nursing Students," *The American Journal of Nursing* 54, 5 (May 1954): 637.
35 Mildred Louise Montag and Margaret Filson, *Nursing Arts,* 2nd ed. (Philadelphia, PA: Saunders, 1953).
36 Buchanan, *Study Guide,* 19.
37 Buchanan, *Study Guide,* 16–17.
38 Buchanan, *Study Guide,* 53.
39 Trained Nurses' Association of India, *History and Trends of Nursing in India,* 155.
40 "Obituary: Dr. (Ms.) Edith Buchanan," 258.
41 Healey, *Indian Sisters,* 136–37.
42 WHO Records and Archives, correspondence with author, March 11, 2019.
43 Ruth Colin Buchanan to Ruth Compton Brouwer, November 11, 1985; Ruth Compton Brouwer, email correspondence with author, March 13, 2019.

44 A copy of the Buchanan's life membership in the Indian Public Health Association in 1975 is held within the private papers of Buchanan's cousin, Robert Coleman.
45 According to her cousin, Buchanan returned to Canada after Ruth's death as she had no remaining family left in India to care for her. Robert Coleman, in discussion with the author, Toronto, April 26, 2018. "Edith Buchanan," August 26, 2003, *Toronto Star*, B6.
46 "Obituary: Dr. (Ms.) Edith Buchanan," 258.
47 David A. Hollinger, *Protestants Abroad: How Missionaries Tried to Change the World but Changed America* (Princeton, NJ: Princeton University Press, 2017), 6.
48 Florence L. Nichols, untitled manuscript. This manuscript has been donated by the family to the General Synod Archives, Anglican Church of Canada, in both hard copy and digital form, as well as in digital form to the Christian Medical College Archives in Vellore.
49 John P.M. Court, "Historical Synopsis: The Department of Psychiatry at the University of Toronto," rev. April 2011, https://www.psychiatry.utoronto.ca/file/1181/download?token=wZLevETF, 10.
50 Margaret Janack, telephone interview by author, August 22, 2018.
51 Reena George, *One Step at a Time: The Birth of the Christian Medical College, Vellore* (New Delhi: Roli Books, 2018), 61, 85, 219.
52 Nichols, untitled manuscript, 6.
53 Robert Cochrane to F.M. Potter and Mrs. Chute, November 2, 1945, Christian Medical College and Hospital, Archives Library, Subject: Psychiatry/Mental Health Centre Correspondence, Aug '45 – June '66, file CMC – P/1/45, box 1 (hereafter cited as Christian Medical College and Hospital Archives).
54 B.C. Oliver to Dr. Robert Cochrane, 1945, Christian Medical College and Hospital Archives.
55 Compton Brouwer, *Modern Women*, 34–65; Meera Abraham, *Religion, Caste, and Gender: Missionaries and Nursing History in South Asia* (Bangalore, India: BI Publications, 1996), 13–14.
56 Florence Nichols to Lord Maclay, October 24, 1949, General Synod Archives, Anglican Church of Canada, Missionary Society of the Church of England in Canada (MSCC) fonds, 103, series 3:3, box 83, file 23, Nichols, Dr. Florence L. 1946–1950.
57 Florence Nichols to St. John's, December 20, 1949, General Synod Archives, Anglican Church of Canada, MSCC fonds.
58 Ruth Soward to Hilda Lazarus, December 3, 1952, Christian Medical College and Hospital Archives.
59 Timothy H. Horning, Public Services Archivist, University of Pennsylvania, correspondence with author, August 27, 2018.
60 Jacob Abraham, K.V. Mathai, Vedantam Rajshekhar, and Raj K. Narayan, "Jacob Chandy: Pioneering Neurosurgeon of India," *Neurosurgery* 67 (2010): 566–76. Wilder Penfield also visited the Christian Medical College during a trip funded by the Canadian Colombo Plan program in 1955. D.W. Bartlett, Memo to Secretary, IGTA, LAC, September 29, 1956, RG 29, vol. 1007, file 303-2-5. Dr. Abraham Verghese, later chair of the department, trained in Chandy's department. Abraham Verghese, "The History of the Mental Health Centre: Some Reminiscences," *The Alumni Journal of the Christian Medical College Vellore: Psychiatry Issue* (2007): 9.
61 P. Kutumbiah to J.C. David, December 29, 1956, Christian Medical College and Hospital Archives.
62 P. Kutumbiah to the Secretary, Indian Council of Medical Research, August 24, 1955, Christian Medical College and Hospital Archives.
63 Mona Purser, "The Homemaker: Missionary Psychiatrist Hopes to End Snake Pit," *Globe and Mail*, September 3, 1953, 13.

64 Nichols, untitled manuscript, 351–52.
65 Nichols, untitled manuscript, 355.
66 Nichols, untitled manuscript, 352. For example, the entire cost of the administration unit of the Mental Health Centre, including doctors' offices, was projected at around eleven thousand dollars.
67 Abraham Verghese, "The History of the Mental Health Centre," 9; Nichols, untitled manuscript.
68 Florence Nichols to Hilda Lazarus, September 2, 1953, Christian Medical College and Hospital Archives. See also Florence L. Nichols, *Life with Father and Mother as Told by Barney Poodle* (unpublished manuscript, 1988), 17. As the title indicates, this unusual manuscript about the marriage of Nichols and the death of her husband was "narrated" by their poodle, Barney.
69 Abraham Verghese, "Family Participation in Mental Health Care – the Vellore Experiment," *Indian Journal of Psychiatry* 30, 2 (April 1988): 117. The other institution that followed this approach in the 1960s was the National Institute of Mental Health and Neurosciences in Bangalore, formerly the All India Institute of Mental Health. Ranbir S. Bhatti, N. Janakiramaiah, and S.M. Channabasavanna, "Family Psychiatric Ward Treatment in India," *Family Process* 19 (June 1980): 193.
70 Dr. Anju Kuruvilla, interview by author, Vellore, November 14, 2018.
71 "Maple Leaf Hospital: Kangra Mission of the M.S.C.C.," General Synod Archives, Anglican Church of Canada, MSCC fonds, 9–14.7, GS75–103, box 137, file 7.
72 Rakesh Kumar Chadda, Bichitra Nanda Patra, and Nitin Gupta, "Recent Developments in Community Mental Health: Relevance and Relationship with the Mental Health Care Bill," *Indian Journal of Social Psychiatry* 31, 2 (2015): 154, doi:10.4103/0971–9962.173296.
73 Nichols, untitled manuscript, 341.
74 Dr. Anju Kuruvilla, interview with author, Vellore, November 14, 2018.
75 Abraham Verghese, "The History of the Mental Health Centre," 7–9.
76 CMC Vellore, "Christian Medical College, Vellore: Facts and Figures, 2017–2018," 4, https://vellorecmc.org/facts-figures-issuu/cmc-facts-figures-2017-2018/.
77 CMC has published a YouTube video about this outreach program: "Our Stories, Our CMC: Mental Health in the Community – Christian Medical College, CMC, Vellore," June 21, 2015, https://www.youtube.com/watch?v=UQtp6zng4IY.
78 See, for example, Helen Charles, S.D. Manoranjitham, and K.S. Jacob, "Stigma and Explanatory Models among People with Schizophrenia and Their Relatives in Vellore, South India," *International Journal of Social Psychiatry* 53, 4 (2007): 325–32, doi:10.1177/0020764006074538; Anadit J. Mathew, Beulah Samuel, and K.S. Jacob, "Perceptions of Illness in Self and in Others among Patients with Bipolar Disorder," *International Journal of Social Psychiatry* 56, 5 (2010): 462–70, doi.org/10.1177/0020764009106621; and Reema Samuel et al., "Development and Validation of the Vellore Occupational Therapy Evaluation Scale to Assess Functioning in People with Mental Illness," *International Journal of Social Psychiatry* 62, 7 (2016): 616–26, doi.org/ 10.1177/0020764016664754.
79 George, *One Step at a Time*, 218.
80 WHO Records and Archives, correspondence with author, March 11, 2019.
81 Susan Armstrong-Reid, *Lyle Creeman: The Frontiers of Global Nursing* (Toronto: University of Toronto Press, 2014).

3

Life Stories, Wife Stories
Women Advisors on Economic Development

David Webster

OVERSEAS DIPLOMACY IS CONDUCTED not only by diplomats working for the Canadian foreign service. It has also been carried out by Canadians working for other international agencies like the United Nations (UN). It has been carried out, unofficially, by missionaries and merchants and development workers. Even more unofficially, but perhaps just as significantly, the work of diplomacy has been aided by wives and secretaries and servants and stenographers.

This chapter traces episodes from the lives of four women who were unconventional diplomats. The research method is prosopography, a form of collective biography of a linked group – in this case, Canadians who went overseas in the 1950s, 1960s, and 1970s as economic development advisors for the UN technical assistance programme. In writing what historians Glenda Sluga and Sunil Amrith call the "life stories" of UN workers,[1] I have been increasingly struck by the importance of what might be called "wife stories" – the experiences of the women married to the UN workers. Historians are increasingly seeing the role of everyday, day-to-day lives in international affairs.[2] Within that move to de-centre the high politics of security and international politics, there is also increasing attention paid to women. After all, as historian Joan Scott wrote: "High politics is itself a gendered concept, for it establishes its crucial importance and public power, the reasons for and the fact of its highest authority, precisely in its exclusion of women from its work."[3] Even the 1948 Universal Declaration of Human Rights declared the family unit as "the natural and fundamental group unit of society," despite the efforts of India's delegate Hansa Mehta to centre the individual.[4] Diplomatic history, as this volume stresses, needs to see women and gender more clearly.[5]

It goes without saying that most women in the twentieth century were wives.[6] (This is so much taken for granted that historians rarely mention it.) As their husbands moved overseas, they inevitably entered the realm of foreign relations, becoming unofficial agents of exchange between their home country and their host country. The politics of marriage needs to be more visible when writing about women and international affairs. Marriage diplomacy played an "indispensable function" in Europe until very recently.[7] "Marriage has in fact been treated as serious business by the makers of foreign policy," political scientist Cynthia Enloe writes.[8] This chapter aims to make marriage, and wives as diplomatic actors, more visible.[9] Men in colonial contexts, from the fur trade to nineteenth-century Vietnam, often portrayed women as sources of pollution or risk.[10] Still, women as wives became diplomatic assets necessary to the success of men's development work in the middle decades of the twentieth century.

These UN development advisors played roles that were inescapably diplomatic. Technical assistance saw the UN interact with and influence governments in Africa, Asia, and Latin America in significant ways, which forced the world organization to develop its own diplomatic service. Canadian technical assistance advisors in many ways functioned as part of this service, carrying out what researchers Mary Young and Susan Henders have called "other diplomacies."[11] Whether based at UN headquarters, attached to government departments in capitals across the world, or in the field, advisors shaped the economic development trajectories and thus the political direction of dozens of countries. UN field and headquarters work in turn required coordination, which would quickly come to be handled by UN Technical Assistance Resident Representatives (TARRs). These TARRs, as they were called, served as the equivalent of ambassadors, with the similar diplomatic accreditation, supervising a similar in-country staff, and attending similar diplomatic meetings and social events.

Some technical advisors, and even a few TARRs, were women. The UN's first TARR was Margaret Anstee, who came to UN work after a spell in the British foreign service that ended when she married, for married women were not permitted in the British foreign service until the 1970s.[12] The same was true in Canada. While the unmarried Elizabeth MacCallum could become Canada's first head of mission as ambassador to Turkey in 1954, women who married were required to resign from the Department of External Affairs. Even unmarried women diplomats were "a little more limited and the careers of a slightly different character than that of the men," one prominent Canadian diplomat wrote in 1964. "They cannot, for example, serve at all posts – for reasons of health and other reasons."[13] The opinion says more about views generally held by male diplomats at the time, and about societal expectations, than it does about women's diplomatic abilities. Single women could be diplomats but admission to the club was always contingent. If she married, the woman was expected to give up her own career in favour of her husband's. In Canada, the barrier persisted until diplomat Margaret Catley-Carlson broke the bar in 1970.[14]

The UN offered a refuge for some women. In the late 1950s, for instance, it named Margaret Anstee as the first woman to be a TARR.[15] She had no Canadian women counterparts, though Canada's Hugh Keenleyside, who headed the UN's Technical Assistance Administration, eventually promoted his influential secretary, Phoebe Ross Kidd, to programme control officer.[16] The first Canadian to serve as a TARR, the poet-professor F.R. Scott, left his wife, Marian Dale Scott, behind in Montreal when he embarked on a world tour prior to taking up his post in Burma. He seems to have taken advantage of being a solo male traveller to engage in extramarital affairs – a widely accepted but little discussed topic.[17]

Few women served directly in prominent development roles, though countries like Burma sought the occasional "lady health visitor."[18] As Jill Campbell-Miller explains in this volume, Canadian nurses led the way. Still, they tended to be women without children or husbands. For instance, Joan Goodall, supervisor of the Department of Therapy at the British Columbia Cancer Institute in Vancouver, "a tall, fine looking woman with a sense of humour ... able to cope with any situation," established a cancer facility in Rangoon, then Burma's capital, in the late 1950s.[19] But Goodall and others like her were the exception. Normally, when asked to locate technical advisors, Canadian officials judged married women as unsuitable, since a placement would require their husband to postpone his own career. Most Canadian women, therefore, went into the technical assistance field as wives.

Drawing on the work of historian Ruth Compton Brouwer on the way modern women "modernized" men,[20] we can see that Canadian women in Africa and Asia championed Western ways of life as more proper, more efficient, more modern. In this they echoed the colonial role of wives as participants in "civilizing" local people, following the footsteps of British women homesteaders in the Canadian prairies, Dutch women policing the lines of European identity in the Netherlands East Indies, or American missionary wives in China.[21] In exploring wife stories, this paper draws on the work of political studies scholar Cynthia Enloe on diplomatic wives and on historian Donica Belilse's work on academic wives.[22] The case studies address Barbara Cadbury in Ceylon and Jamaica; Beatrice Keyfitz in Indonesia and Ceylon; Beatrice Harding in Indonesia and Guyana; and Eleanor Hinder at UN headquarters and in the Soviet Union.

Each of these women was vital to the work carried out, even when authorities in the UN and governments (as well as scholars, later) rendered the women's influence or key aspects of their lives invisible. At the same time, they were ambiguous agents of postcolonial transformation in the Global South, carrying a gospel of progress and modernity that sought to remake Southern countries in Northern images. Where men preached that gospel, women performed it in more private spheres that their husbands could not reach. Like the missionary women described by historian Carol Chin, they can be described as "beneficent imperialists" seeking to transform foreign societies.[23]

In addition to discussing case studies of four women, this chapter is concerned about the ways in which their stories have been downplayed, silenced, erased, and about gaps in the historical record created by archival and historical practices. Archives preserve men's stories more than women's. Historians amplify the silences in the way we tell stories. Institutions and individuals exert power as they downplay women's stories as somehow less important. The stories, told, then reinforce power relations.[24] The archives we use and the stories we tell are also about power. So is this chapter, but it tries to see some of what is less seen and tell some of what is less spoken about, in order to tell a more complete story about Canadian diplomacy and development assistance.

Barbara Cadbury: Family Planning Pioneer

Barbara Pearce Cadbury's stories emerge in the margins of the personal papers left by her husband, George, on file in Saskatchewan and New York. Her own presence is harder to discern in the archival record, but it was significant.

As a young woman, Barbara Pearce formed a branch of the League of Nations Union youth section in Balham and Tooting, in South London, in 1930, delivering a plea for international cooperation against opium smuggling and arguing that the job of the League of Nations was to "organize peace just as England was organized as a country."[25] This came at a time when League of Nations Union meetings could be thrown into chaos when all the scheduled speakers "pleaded their wives as excuse" for not showing up to events.[26] She entered politics at age twenty-four, when she won election as a Labour party councillor to the North London borough of Stoke Newington, both helping Labour take control of the borough and becoming the youngest elected councillor in London. She married fellow socialist George Cadbury, a son of the Quaker chocolate family, who was at the time a councillor in the city of Birmingham. The couple moved their home base to Canada when incoming Co-operative Commonwealth Federation (CCF) premier, Tommy Douglas, of Saskatchewan, offered George a job as chief industrial advisor. George had been to Saskatchewan once before, as a temporary agricultural worker threshing wheat in the province, but won the job more on the strength of a recommendation by CCF luminary David Lewis, who had met the Cadburys while he was a Rhodes scholar at Oxford.[27]

George Cadbury's work in Saskatchewan was significant in the CCF's economic development efforts, a role that is recognized in the literature.[28] His family almost vanishes, though one article notes laconically that his "wife and children follow[ed]" him to Regina.[29] Unseen are what Belisle has described as the "caring labour" and "social labour" carried out by the wife.[30] Referring to the writer Mary Quayle Innis's support of her academic husband, Harold Innis, Belisle pointed out the way Mary's baking, hosting, child care, and household management released him "from the tasks involved in his own everyday bodily welfare, including food and clothing preparation. More than this, it created a nurturing home environment, one from which he could emerge refreshed each day. Most importantly, it gave him the luxury of uninterrupted time."[31]

This vital point can be extended to diplomats and development workers, with the added element of motion: the household must be rebuilt again and again after moves every few years or even months, and the social duties of hosting are significant. No man in diplomacy or development in this period could manage without a wife. Terence MacDermot, who headed missions in Australia, Greece, and South Africa, noted the wife's role as chief of the household servants, responsible for hostessing and "checking the silver" to prevent theft.[32] Multiple examples of wifely duties appear in the official history of the Department of External Affairs.[33] Historian Molly Wood noted that the US diplomatic wives "organized and managed social functions, packed and unpacked households, hired and fired servants, met new people, threw lavish dinner parties, volunteered in the local community, and learned new languages, customs, and rules of protocol all over the world. An efficient and popular wife, one who entertained successfully and maintained an elegant home, would undoubtedly help her husband earn promotion."[34]

In another rarely acknowledged aspect that recalls the colonial idea of women as civilizers and restraints on their husbands, sending a man along with his family reduced the chance of open philandering that might reflect poorly on the UN presence in host countries. In this sense, the UN reflected its own simultaneously liberal-internationalist and bureaucratic self-protection aspects.[35]

Like many prominent activists, Barbara Cadbury subordinated her own career to her husband's. In Regina, she raised two daughters and won election to the board of a local cooperative but was largely sidelined with very little to do, her husband wrote in letters to friends in England.[36] The Saskatchewan CCF, George Cadbury recalled later, was a leader on race issues but lagged on inclusion of women.[37] Things were not much better after George moved to become operations director and then advisor to the UN Technical Assistance Administration in the 1950s.

To see Barbara Cadbury, it is necessary to take the advice of historian Ann Laura Stoler and read both along and against the archival grain.[38] The Saskatchewan archives and the UN archives both preserve George Cadbury's personal correspondence but not Barbara's. George's family appears only occasionally, as when he added a joke from Barbara to one letter or lamented how tough it was to obtain Canadian citizenship while working for the United Nations. His family enters his letters from Regina in such lines as "No one would live in this climate unless their wheat was wanted abroad," implying awareness of winter's effect on family life.[39]

Yet George's extensive correspondence makes no mention that Barbara started work in 1951 as editor of the Planned Parenthood Federation of America's magazine, *Round the World News of Population and Birth Control*.[40] Nor do the archived papers show everything that was happening while the Cadburys were posted in Ceylon and Jamaica. Where George promoted industrial productivity increases in Ceylon and spoke of Colombo one day becoming "another Chicago," Barbara also pushed the government to adopt the attitudes of Western capitalist modernity. George wanted the "creation of a new attitude to industry in Ceylon." Barbara worked in parallel, striving to internationalize the gospel of family planning.[41] Later in life, George was celebrated for his involvement in family planning. Yet his first involvement in that realm came when he joined Barbara in 1954 to cofound the Family Planning Association of Ceylon. It is not clear how much this step reflected his own interest and how much was the necessary involvement of a prominent man in making a new organization acceptable. What is clear is that Barbara was already active in family planning activism.

Drawn by the promise of more influence, George moved to Jamaica as senior economic advisor to prime minister Norman Manley in 1955. Barbara founded another Family Planning Association there. In 1960, the International Planned Parenthood Federation appointed both Cadburys as special representatives, and the couple began family promotion efforts throughout Asia.[42] Yet it was George, the former UN man, who became the author, the advocate, and the Planned Parenthood representative at international meetings in the 1960s and 1970s.

Historian Matthew Connelly's five-hundred-page global history of population control does not mention Barbara Cadbury, whereas George figures prominently in his role as international representative. The reason is probably her relative absence from what has been preserved in the written archival record. After all, as literary scholar Linda Morra wrote, women's presence is often "located beyond the purview of formal institutions, or embedded in archives that did not intend to focus exclusively on their work or accomplishment."[43] To escape scholarly erasure and make Barbara's role as thinker and activist more visible, we have to turn to obituaries and the publications of the Planned Parenthood Association of Toronto, which she cofounded in 1961 "with a group of church leaders and prominent doctors" and the Family Planning Federation of Canada, which she cofounded two years later. While George travelled and made international family planning his realm, Barbara worked at the local and national level to bring together and mobilize people, a role that made her husband's work possible. Meanwhile she kept the family home in Oakville and continued to raise their two daughters. One might even say she was confined to the home front. Yet her role as family planning advocate was as significant as her husband's, and her interest in the issue preceded his own.[44]

Beatrice Keyfitz: No Typical Expat

The story of Beatrice Keyfitz, too, has to be told through her husband's rather patchy archives, the archival traces he left in Ottawa, and an unpublished memoir that concentrates on his professional life. The demographer, statistician, and sociologist Nathan Keyfitz was noted for his ability to come across as a sympathetic student of the societies he was sent to advise and transform. Travel writer Norman Lewis encountered him as an advisor in 1950s Burma, noting that Keyfitz "wore the national costume whenever he could find an excuse, and finally moved out of the hotel and went to live with a Burmese couple he had persuaded to take him as a paying guest."[45] The couple assigned Keyfitz to one of their two rooms and lived together – husband, wife, and four children – in the other.

The young Nathan travelled to Burma alone. In his next assignment, a year in Indonesia, Nathan came along with his wife Beatrice, a fellow Montrealer. This had become standard procedure for UN experts posted for more than a few months, since men in so-called hardship posts were expected to need their wife and children with them. A diary entry by F.R. Scott while he was posted as UN Technical Assistance Resident Representative in Burma serves as one example. Scott "meditated on my incapacity to make a splash for UN in Rangoon. Need wife, house and money for that, plus inclination."[46] He had the inclination and the funds but lacked the wife and household.

Without caring labour, it would have been impossible to meet the social obligations in diplomatic circles and in the home that allowed experts to function with some degree of effectiveness. The point shines through in an examination of Nathan Keyfitz's assignments as population advisor in Indonesia and head of the Commonwealth's Colombo Plan Bureau in Ceylon. Seeing him embedded in a family and a home, not simply as solo expert toiling in an office, paints a fuller picture of his impact.

A year of Beatrice's letters from Indonesia, preserved in her husband's archive, tell the story and document her role in keeping Nathan's social networks active. The "Canadian colony" in Jakarta was small, she wrote. It consisted of "the Embassy people, a few flying instructors hired through the International Civil Aviation Organization, half of a Dutch couple, and the Keyfitz family."[47] Although she was keen on Indonesia and its people, she disliked expatriates. "The other experts' wives are a sad lot," she wrote in one letter. "I suppose they are all right at home, but like the better French wines they don't travel well. They tend to visit one another all morning while their husbands are at work, and after a great deal of unbosoming they naturally come to loathe one another."[48] Beatrice's community, in other words, was not her fellow foreign women.

She first reached this view in the "quite awful" Hotel des Indes, where all foreigners stayed on arrival. It was "full of U.N. flotsam on technical missions of one useless sort or another, tobacco and oil salesmen, and other people whose bills are being paid by the firm, and it's about as second-rate as you would expect. It is also very noisy and full of cats wandering around in a perpetual state of rut and howling their heads off."[49] Things improved greatly with a move to Jakarta's North American–style satellite town of Kemayoran. There, Beatrice wrote, the "40-odd Technical Assistance families milling about at one time or another" were all "trying to create their own little America, Canada, Switzerland, France, Bulgaria or whatnot on Indonesian soil."[50] The Keyfitzes lived between an American and a British family, both working for the International Civil Aviation Organization, and one house away from a Canadian couple who hated Indonesia and counted the days until they could go home to Chilliwack, BC.[51] Although the country ran inefficiently and the clerical help was "the worst in the world," Beatrice adored "the balmy wealth, the palm and banana trees, and, most of all, the seemingly inexhaustible kindness and good humour of the Indonesian people. We like everything about them." And Nathan was "delighted with the young students of economics and sociology who are his assistants at the Planning Bureau."[52] He later coauthored a book with his star pupil, Widjojo Nitisastro, who went on to be the chief architect of Indonesian economic planning under President Suharto. Beatrice introduced Widjojo to such elements of Canadian domesticity as baked beans.[53] As with all development advisors, there were racial stereotypes and echoes of the colonial push to change other societies, of course. Yet compatriots hailed the Keyfitzes for their relative lack of racism.

Finishing his term in Jakarta, Nathan returned to the Dominion Bureau of Statistics in Ottawa but was soon headed back across the Pacific to become director of the Colombo Plan for Technical Cooperation in South and Southeast Asia, "which, whatever else it is, is certainly the longest title he has ever had," as Beatrice wrote in her 1956 Christmas letter, another indication of her role in maintaining her husband's social networks. Ceylon was keen to heed "the gospel of technical assistance," she reported, adding that "the number of foreign experts per head of local population must set a world record."[54]

The couple became the masters of Bank House, a seaside villa once belonging to the Bank of Ceylon. It was large, with several servants, and notably damp: "Razor blades rust over-night, books get covered with green fuzz, and fungus grows on the inside of our watch crystals; at the same time we have a lovely view and cool breezes at night." Nathan was already tired out from his main duty, "showing the flag" from Saigon to Karachi to convey what the diplomatic cables glossed as "sympathetic interest." In other words, he could make no commitments, since donor governments made the decisions.[55]

According to Under-Secretary of State for External Affairs Jules Léger, Nathan quickly gave "new vitality and sense of direction to the Bureau ... Clearly he is going about his job very ably – and very pleasantly."[56] The Canadian high commission in Ceylon similarly reported that "he has increased Canada's reputation and enhanced Canada's prestige."[57] Nathan pushed against the constrictions of his job. Within Ceylon, it was confined to hosting local Colombo Plan experts for periodic social gatherings to boost their morale and reduce their sense of isolation. Again, the job centred on hosting and caring work and required a wife in order to work. The role of diplomatic wife was vital. Beatrice despised the other expat wives and the way their husbands "rode desks" in Jakarta, but she spoke more highly of men in the field working directly on development projects. She accompanied Nathan to the drudgery of cocktail parties and took care of their house and family. Yet the records render her nearly invisible. She authored letters that spoke often of her husband, but his professional reports say no more about her than do the Canadian technical assistance placement and reporting files. She lives more in Nathan's memoirs, which acknowledge her throughout. The absence in official archives and the need to read between the lines in order to see Beatrice suggest that researchers must look harder and read more carefully to tell life stories and see women's important roles, hidden by their husband's archival footprint. Archives, after all, do not just neutrally reflect what happened in the past. Rather, they exert and reflect power through their choices. Societal power has often told women, too, that their records are less worthy of preservation than their husband's records. Thus Beatrice Keyfitz, unlike her husband, left no archive.

Beatrice Harding: Tending the Diplomatic Garden

Another Beatrice is more visible in the Harding family papers preserved at the University of Regina archives, though Beatrice's papers fill fewer boxes than her husband's. Cadbury's work in Saskatchewan was governmental and is thus preserved in the provincial archives, while his UN work is in the UN archives. The Harding papers reflect both Bill and Beatrice and are in a smaller archive less often consulted, less often catalogued, but no less important.

Beatrice (Bea) Harding hailed from rural Manitoba and earned a Bachelor of Science degree in home economics at the University of Manitoba and a Bachelor of Fine Arts at the University of Regina before marrying William Harding of Swift Current, Saskatchewan. She also self-published two memoirs, one on Liberia and one more complete autobiography.

Bill and Beatrice Harding embraced the heady atmosphere of CCF Saskatchewan in the 1940s and 1950s. Bill worked with the Prairie Farm Rehabilitation Administration, then with the Saskatchewan CCF as advisor to the minister of agriculture, and served from 1952 to 1957 as secretary to the Saskatchewan Royal Commission on Agriculture and Rural Life. Saskatchewan at this time was dynamic. It had "entered the exciting era of democratic socialism," Beatrice Harding wrote. "Great challenges lay ahead."[58] The Hardings bought a modest house on Smith Street in central Regina, which remained their home base until Bea's death. Bill was politically active in CCF circles and, with fellow employee Betty Barlow, broadcast advice to farmers for fifteen minutes a day on topics from feed storage to grasshopper control.[59] Their broadcasts were often photographed. In 1960, he was recruited for UN work by Julia Henderson, head of the UN Secretariat's Department of Social Affairs, a woman from Minnesota who had worked on US president Franklin Roosevelt's New Deal as an officer of the Farm Security Administration. Like several other New Dealers, she ended up at the United Nations and was seeking like-minded rural community development experts. The largely unheralded Henderson stood at the centre of UN recruiting networks. Margaret Anstee called her "the real female star" at the UN and credited her for devising its financial system. On her retirement, George Cadbury recruited her to take over as director-general of the International Planned Parenthood Federation upon the death of fellow UN veteran David Owen. International networks remained in play.[60]

Bill Harding accepted the idea of a UN field posting. When the call in 1961 came with an opening, it was for work in the interior of Liberia. "My mind went in somersaults," he recalled in an unpublished memoir. "[W]here in hell was Liberia?" He "phoned home and told Bea to look up Liberia in the atlas." "I know where Siberia is," she replied, then called back

Figure 6 Bill Harding and Betty Barlow broadcast for Your Ag Report, Saskatchewan, 1940s. | Saskatchewan Film Board photo, S73.2547. Courtesy Harding family papers, University of Regina Archives. Used with permission of Saskatchewan Provincial Archives

to report that Liberia was "a small country in West Africa."[61] Bea Harding embraced the adventure promised by a year in Liberia, where the United Nations ended up with two workers in exchange for the eleven thousand dollar salary it paid Bill. She came, Bill wrote, "not as an appendage, but as her own person."[62] She did so at the cost of delays to her career as a visual artist and adult education teacher but seems to have embraced the job fully.

The project near the village of Kpain aimed to resettle Indigenous peoples on new plots of jungle land, twenty-five acres each, that they were to clear and farm.[63] Harding's Saskatchewan community development experience seemed to offer models for Liberia, and UN authorities hailed his mission as relatively successful – though the resettlement ultimately contributed to troubles during Liberia's more recent wars, rather than being an example of UN success. Bill's work earned him subsequent postings as a respected UN Technical Assistance Resident Representative in Guyana, Somalia, and, finally, the Philippines.

The Kpain project was a challenge from the start. Its ambitious mandate from the Liberian government was "to develop a number of community settlements ... on the basis of private, as distinct from communal, ownership of land with a view to demonstrating the superior advantages of intensive and diversified agriculture."[64] After initial misgivings, Bill soon saw potential in Kpain, reporting that both he and Beatrice were "stimulated and excited" by being in the field.[65]

Since Bill eventually concluded that the project would probably fail, he and Beatrice instead devoted themselves to community-building among its people. Bea formed close links with a teenager nicknamed "Smallboy." The importance of good relations with local society mattered in the settlement areas as much as it did on the diplomatic circuit, and the presence of a wife skilled in personal relationships was crucial to Bill's success. The settlers, he wrote, "were a little surly with me but they fairly beamed and come running from all directions when Bea goes around with me."[66] While he busied himself with planning and organization and construction, Bea undertook caring labour as an amateur nurse and seamstress. After this, Bill wrote, "I really felt that I belonged and that they accepted me completely. It was heartwarming – exhilarating."[67] The project was not a success, but the Hardings took pleasure from what they had managed to do in social relations.

After a time back in Regina, the couple took up another job, this time in British Guiana, in 1964. Bill's job as community development advisor shifted into one of Technical Assistance Resident Representative when Guyana became independent in May 1966. The wives of UN representatives, Bea learned, were not allowed to work for any UN agency, and there were few other employment options in Georgetown.[68] Bea therefore worked as a volunteer with the Red Cross and with injured children. This caring labour enhanced Bill's position as resident representative and the UN's reputation and image as a selfless aid provider. "Not only did Bill's responsibilities increase," Bea recalled, "but my social responsibilities for entertaining accelerated also. We had to entertain more often and reciprocate for invitations from embassies and ambassadors. There were cocktails and dinner parties and luncheons at noon to attend. Suddenly we were plummeted

CLOCKWISE FROM TOP LEFT:

Figure 7 Beatrice Harding with "Smallboy" and settlers, Kpain, Liberia, 1960. | Courtesy Harding family papers, University of Regina Archives

Figure 8 Bill Harding places sign at entrance to Kpain project, Liberia, 1960. | Courtesy Harding family papers, University of Regina Archives

Figure 9 Beatrice Harding dresses a wound, Kpain, Liberia, 1960. | Courtesy Harding family papers, University of Regina Archives

LIFE STORIES, WIFE STORIES 77

into a new state of society subjected to protocol and other rules. Fortunately I had my training as a home economist to fall back on."[69] Indeed, when David Owen, chief of the UN Development Programme (UNDP), visited in 1965, the Hardings scrambled to spruce up their home and bring their gardens up to UNDP diplomatic standards. Since the UNDP did not offer official residences or fund their upkeep, gardening became a necessary piece of the preparations to receive Owen, and it was up to Bea Harding to see to this diplomatic necessity. So, while the UNDP report noted that the Owen visit was "tightly and effectively organized by Mr. William H. Harding, Resident Representative," the visit's success also required the unrecorded work of his unnamed wife. Gardening was also diplomacy.[70]

"Bill Harding had become what some describe as one of the 'conscience men' of the UN ... completely devoted to the objectives of this world forum in spreading peace around the world and providing a better life for all mankind," one local journalist wrote.[71] Yet this was hardly a success by a heroic solo UN employee, but rather the product of a partnership. Similar stories could be told about Bill's subsequent posts as UNDP representative in Mogadishu and Manila. In these field postings, Bea developed a new career as a writer, selling stories to Asian and Canadian English-language publications and studying with a famous Filipino printmaker. This experience launched her on a visual arts career back in Regina after Bill's retirement from UN work in 1975. In the later years of his career, she finally won a UN consulting appointment in her own name, based on the knowledge at UN headquarters that she and Bill had been acting as a team for years.

Eleanor Hinder: Technical Assistance Ambassador

A final, contrasting case study begins with a photograph. In 1955, a team of government officials from India toured the Soviet Union, examining everything from coal mining to civil aviation. Distinctive in their group photograph was Australian Eleanor Hinder, the only woman and the only non-Indian on the mission. She is identified with a line drawn in pencil on a photograph of the group posed in front of the Kakhovka Dam construction site, part of the great Donbass industrial complex taking shape in what was then the Ukrainian Soviet Socialist Republic. The photo came from the official trip report submitted by the UN Technical Assistance Administration, sponsor of the study tour. The pencil was wielded by Viola Smith, Hinder's partner in life and love, on the copy of the report housed in Hinder's

Figure 10 Indian delegation to the USSR. Photo printed in the United Nation's 1955 report, "Observations on Technical Development and Training Opportunities in the USSR: Report of a Study Tour of Indian Government Officials." | UN document TAA/IND.15, 1955; courtesy Eleanor M. Hinder papers, MLMSS 770, State Library of New South Wales

personal papers, which Smith donated to the University of New South Wales. The image indicates the occasional visibility of key actors like Hinder, whose names are seldom recalled when stories of international politics are penned. Unlike other women discussed here, Hinder reached a high level in her own right. Yet like the others in this chapter, she also contended with the politics of marriage and diplomacy.

Eleanor Hinder started work as superintendent of welfare at a department store in her native Sydney, then in 1925 moved to Shanghai to run social welfare operations in the International Settlement. Alongside her social welfare work in Shanghai factories, Hinder was named by the League of Nations

LIFE STORIES, WIFE STORIES   79

as Protector of *mui tsai*, "girl slaves" working in the city. There she met A. Viola Smith, who, in 1920, became the first woman to join the American diplomatic service, as clerk to the US trade commissioner in China. Smith won promotion as US trade commissioner in Shanghai in 1928, and later added the job of US consul in the city. The *Australian Dictionary of Biography* describes their partnership in this way: "Continuing to live and work in that city until 1941, they became devoted to each other, shared a house, and created a garden."[72] Their lifestyle was typical for Europeans in Shanghai: "The couple owned the latest cars, a houseboat, took numerous vacations, and employed Chinese servants," according to one sketch of Smith's career.[73]

Hinder went on from Shanghai to various posts with the British Foreign Office and the UN Relief and Rehabilitation Administration, and as an advisor on welfare and labour to Burma, Malaya, and Hong Kong, ending up with an OBE awarded by the British government. Smith spent the Second World War as a China specialist in Washington but left US government service to work as the first director of the trade promotion division of the secretariat for the United Nations Economic Commission for Asia and the Far East in Bangkok.

In some ways, Hinder was the trailing spouse, more junior in status, but the two wanted to live together after the war's end and were eventually able to find ways to do so that centred Hinder's career.

With no claim to US residency, Hinder moved to Toronto, finding a temporary home close to her partner and a brief Canadian connection that ties her, however tenuously, to the other women in this chapter.[74] From there, she sought work at the United Nations, succeeding in 1951 with the Technical Assistance Administration (TAA). Hinder rose to important roles at the TAA partly because she had expertise in international development. Yet her presence in New York was the result of her "life-long friend," as she phrased it, being an American.[75] Talk of lifelong companionship was open language for the time but did not help Hinder gain US residency. While she worked at the UN, this was not an issue, but it would require the couple to relocate on Hinder's retirement back to her Australian birthplace. During her UN years, it worked well, as Smith found work as UN representative for the International Federation of Women Lawyers.

Hinder became an influential figure as chief of the TAA's Office of Asia and the Far East. Numerous files in the UN archives bear Hinder's stamp, showing her in constant and friendly contact with Technical Assistance

Resident Representatives and with many individual advisors, and in constant motion through numerous field trips. Advisors at times addressed her as an almost mother-like figure, an indication of the caring labour she exerted in assisting them with their culture shock. The TAA pushed governments, especially in Asia, to develop indicative national economic development plans. Hinder was one of those doing the pushing, though she did so with more diplomatic touch than some colleagues. She also took a key role, along with George Cadbury, in trying to diversify the source countries of expert advisors, especially through plans to direct Japanese reparations money for Southeast Asian countries into UN channels to fund Japanese technical assistance advisors.[76] This worked well in Asia, where governments tended to cooperate with UN schemes, but less well when Hinder was transferred to the TAA's Latin America office. She retired in 1956, soon after the transfer, but when she still did not win a US residency lottery, she took on a series of consultant positions with the United Nations until her death in a plane crash, in 1963. These positions allowed her to maintain her US residency and were driven more by her relationship with Viola Smith than by her commitment to UN work, strong though that was.

When the TAA agreed to accept Soviet aid, the first step was to put flesh on the bones of the deal by exploring what sort of help the USSR could offer. India was the first country to express interest in accepting Soviet aid under the UN programme, and thus the first country to send a delegation to see what the Soviets had to offer. Although she had just retired, the TAA tapped Eleanor Hinder for the "very important" job of accompanying this group, giving her the title of Ambassador without Portfolio. If the mission succeeded, it could lead to Soviet integration into the UN's technical assistance system and better relations between the USSR and the world body.[77] If not, there were dangers: the Moscow papers published a Soviet letter to the UN secretary-general complaining that none of the Soviet technical assistance pledge had yet been spent.[78] The five-week mission included separate tours of as many as ten cities for senior Indian civil servants.

The Indian delegation appeared pleased with their reception. Their final report described a warm welcome and assured readers that they had "perfect freedom" to travel and inquire as they wished.[79] The trip was not easy. The group flew over the mountains to Kabul, then descended to Tashkent, and finally arrived in Moscow three days after leaving New Delhi. Six subgroups criss-crossed the country to study water and power, mining and mineral development, coal mining, agriculture and forestry, civil aviation, heavy chemicals, and surveys. They were greeted with great interest, heightened by the parallel arrival of Indian prime minister Jawaharlal Nehru in Moscow for a state visit. Hinder had engineered a diplomatic triumph for the United Nations during the height of the Cold War.

Hinder's travelogues, mostly written while in flight with a special ink pen designed to work at high altitudes, captured the personal side of this story. They reflect her admiration for and fascination with the Soviet Union, flushed with the success of its postwar reconstruction and the sense of opportunity that flourished after the death of Stalin. Women held positions of authority everywhere, far different from in the West, she wrote. Four thousand women had started building a mighty dam on Ukraine's Don River during the Second World War and finished soon after the war's end, launching a heroic tale in which the region now generated 10 million kilowatt-hours of power – and the Soviet Union added 4 million kilowatts more each year. Development in the USSR, Hinder reported, was pushed forward by popular dedication and hard work and a vast range of specialist institutes. She was especially impressed by the great canal in the Uzbek Soviet Socialist Republic. The contrast with hardscrabble Afghanistan, its women all clad in burkhas, struck her most of all. "On the Uzbek side – fine strapping women, all of them working it seems, striding along freely."[80]

In Moscow, Hinder "felt indeed that I was participating in a historic moment, that the sharing of technical knowledge between these two peoples through the United Nations had significance beyond even the great benefits involved in the sharing."[81] The "wider significance" included the value, for many other countries, of impressions that India's team would bring back. There was the possible relevance of models for development offered by the constituent republics such as Georgia and Uzbekistan. The chances for Soviet technical assistance, with the UN as channel, were much more favourable in the new Soviet Union of the mid-1950s. "If we have the wisdom to grasp it," Hinder urged, "an opportunity is at hand."[82]

The Soviets were happy with the avenues now opening to non-communist Asian countries. Indian officials were happy at a chance to draw on a major new source of aid. And UN aid officials were happy that they had opened a new channel for technical assistance and were integrating the Soviet Union into the multilateral technical assistance world. Hinder, previously TAA bureau chief for Asia, was not given the ambassador title idly. She was crucial in negotiations and throughout this story acted as both capable aid administrator and canny diplomat.

The 1955 Indian study tour of the USSR allowed Hinder to retain residency in the United States as a UN ambassador even after her formal retirement. When final retirement came, Smith joined Hinder in Australia. Borders constrained the couple. Both made career choices that sacrificed opportunities in order to be together, even as both could point to impressive careers. The personal and the political intertwined. Hinder was an early proponent of Margaret Joan Anstee's dictate for women at the UN: "Never learn to type."[83] In common with many visitors to the USSR, Hinder saw Soviet industrial muscle – but she also saw that women workers were as much a part of that as men, a far less common observation. Neither Hinder nor Smith needed to act as a diplomatic wife. Instead, both acted as single women in the diplomatic realm. Yet the story of their partnership has to be seen in order to understand the trajectories of their diplomatic lives.

Conclusion

The four cases of Barbara Cadbury, Beatrice Keyfitz, Beatrice Harding, and even Eleanor Hinder illustrate the vital importance to diplomacy of caring labour and social duties, whether in national capitals or in field settings. They also reveal women's agency and the importance of personal ties in diplomacy. The personal is international, to cite Cynthia Enloe once again, and personal relationships shape networks and actions in far-flung locations.[84]

"No archive is neutral," to borrow a chapter title from one book on archival studies.[85] What is preserved and archived is a political decision, one that reinforces existing ideas about whose stories and experiences are important. The first two case studies here left no papers to official archives. To find their stories, historians need to read against the archival grain and seek out the "unarrested," uncatalogued archival traces.[86] The other two case studies have papers in archives, but these are far-flung and university-based, not more formal government archives. This chapter has used their own archives alongside government records in Ottawa and UN records in New York to try to shed light on less visible aspects of women's diplomacy. Historians of Canadian foreign relations will need to continue to extend their research methods to see the more complete story about Canadian diplomacy.

Among this chapter's own absences are the many daily racisms inherent in technical assistance work and their intersections with the way ideas of women's roles evolved in the mid-twentieth century. We still "need to perceive white femininity as a historically constructed concept," as feminist scholar Vron Ware wrote at the century's end.[87] None of the cases examined here should be hailed as triumphs and none of the women as heroic figures. Quite the contrary. Development efforts were as often as not modernization that tried to transform the Global South in the image of former colonial powers. Population interventions by the Cadburys aimed to control population and impose Western models on Sri Lanka and Jamaica, then took the effort global. Similar interventions by the Keyfitzes in Indonesia had negative effects by promoting "transmigration" of Javanese settlers to "outer Indonesia" in ways that consciously echoed the settler colonialism of the North American frontier, with all the assimilationist approaches to Indigenous peoples that entailed. The Hardings themselves ended their UN careers with a negative assessment of the UN's impact on less developed countries. Eleanor Hinder promoted often-harmful UN interventions that aimed to integrate Asian countries as producers of primary products in a global trading system in which they lacked power, and she went on to endorse the environmentally devastating effect of Soviet colonialism in Uzbekistan. This far from positive balance sheet is the topic of future research.

Still, the women discussed in this chapter all pushed against the roles assigned to white women overseas, each in their own way. Structural factors left them highly constrained in their actions, as other chapters in this collection show, but they expanded the boundaries of women's roles, shaping diplomatic outcomes through their actions. Hinder was a diplomat in her own right, though she chose the less glamorous work of the UN for personal reasons. The role of diplomatic wife was not available to her, even as she spent her life with a diplomat. The other women profiled acted as diplomatic wives, but still proved influential.

No UN development worker or diplomat could succeed without the unacknowledged work of their wife. In his classic work on the Canadian diplomat, Marcel Cadieux wrote that the diplomat lacked local ties and so had to "ensure that the charm of his society, the attractiveness of his home, replace the customary background of relationships." A diplomat had to be "an active and popular member of the local society," and "he must be undisturbed by an unsettled life."[88] This was equally true for development diplomats working as UN advisors around the world, whose wives (and partners) created the domestic spaces, parties, and networks necessary for success. Historians need to see those partners' roles more clearly in order to understand the diplomatic past. This requires a rethinking of the way we research and remember diplomatic successes and diplomatic trajectories.

Acknowledgments

I am enormously grateful to the late Greg Donaghy for encouraging me to write this essay and pushing me to be a better historian. I also appreciate edits from Greg, Jill Campbell-Miller, and Stacey Barker and comments (formal or informal) on earlier versions from Donica Belisle, Karen Dubinsky, Linda Morra, and participants at a Queen's University Arthur Lower Workshop in Canadian history in 2019 and at the virtual annual conference of the Academic Conference on the United Nations System in 2020.

Notes

1. Sunil Amrith and Glenda Sluga, "New Histories of the United Nations," *Journal of World History* 19, 3 (2008): 251–74.
2. Laura Ishiguro, *Nothing to Write Home About: British Family Correspondence and the Settler Colonial Everyday in British Columbia* (Vancouver: UBC Press, 2019).
3. Joan Wallach Scott, *Gender and the Politics of History* (New York: Columbia University Press, 1988).
4. Glenda Sluga, "Women, Feminisms and Twentieth-Century Internationalisms," in *Internationalisms: A Twentieth-Century History*, ed. Glenda Sluga and Patricia Clavin (Cambridge: Cambridge University Press, 2017), 80; Universal Declaration of Human Rights, United Nations General Assembly resolution A/217 A, December 10, 1948, https://www.un.org/en/ga/search/view_doc.asp?symbol=A/RES/217(III).
5. In addition to the essays in this book, the point is discussed historiographically in Kristen Hoganson, "What's Gender Got to Do with It? Gender History as Foreign Relations History," in *Explaining the History of American Foreign Relations*, 2nd ed., ed. Michael J. Hogan and Thomas G. Paterson (Cambridge: Cambridge University Press, 2004), 304–22. See also Whitney Wood, "Spreading the Gospel of Natural Birth: Canadian Contributions to an International Medical Movement, 1945–60" and Amanda Ricci, "Making Global Citizens? Canadian Women at the World Conference of the International Women's Year, Mexico City 1975," both in *Undiplomatic History: The New Study of Canada and the World*, ed. Asa McKercher and Philip Van Huizen (Montreal: McGill-Queen's University Press, 2019), 137–60, 206–29.
6. In 1961, 91.6% of census families were headed by married couples. "Distribution (in percentage) of census families by family structure, Canada, 1961 to 2011," Statistics Canada, censuses of population, 1961 to 2011, https://www12.statcan.gc.ca/census-recensement/2011/as-sa/98-312-x/2011003/fig/fig3_1-1-eng.cfm.
7. Silvia Z. Mitchell, "Marriage Plots: Royal Women, Marriage Diplomacy and International Politics at the Spanish, French and Imperial Courts, 1665–1679," in *Women, Diplomacy and International Politics since 1500*, ed. Glenda Sluga and Carolyn James (London: Routledge, 2016), 87.

8   Cynthia Enloe, *Bananas, Beaches, and Bases: Making Feminist Sense of International Politics*, 2nd ed. (Berkeley: University of California Press, 2014), 93.
9   At the original conference from which this volume is drawn, retired diplomat Margaret Catley-Carlson pointed out that there may also be "husband stories" that could be told.
10 See, for instance, Sylvia Van Kirk, "The Role of Native Women in the Fur Trade Society of Western Canada, 1670–1830," *Frontiers: A Journal of Women Studies* 7, 3 (1984): 9–13, https://www.jstor.org/stable/3346234; and Ann Laura Stoler, "Sexual Affronts and Racial Frontiers: European Identities and the Cultural Politics of Exclusion in Colonial Southeast Asia," in *Tensions of Empire: Colonial Cultures in a Bourgeois World*, eds. Frederick Cooper and Ann Laura Stoler (Berkeley: University of California Press, 1997): 198–237.
11 Mary M. Young and Susan J. Henders, "'Other Diplomacies' and World Order: Historical Insights from Canadian-Asian Relations," *Hague Journal of Diplomacy* 11 (2016): 351–82.
12 On diplomatic "marriage bars" see Jennifer A. Cassidy, ed., *Gender and Diplomacy* (London: Routledge, 2017).
13 Terence MacDermot, unpublished manuscript on the Canadian foreign service, Bishop's University Archives, T.W.L. MacDermot fonds, MG-023.
14 John Hilliker, Mary Halloran, and Greg Donaghy, *Canada's Department of External Affairs*, vol. 3, *Innovation and Adaptation, 1968–1984* (Toronto: University of Toronto Press/Institute of Public Administration of Canada, 2017), 72.
15 Margaret Joan Anstee, *Never Learn to Type: A Woman at the United Nations* (London: Wiley, 2004); interview with Margaret Joan Anstee, United Nations Intellectual History Project, December 14, 2000.
16 P.R. Kidd, report on Technical Assistance Committee debates, July 27, 1953, United Nations Archives and Records Management Section (UNARMS), Technical Assistance Records, file 330/4.
17 F.R. Scott diary, Library and Archives Canada (LAC), Francis Reginald Scott fonds, MG30 D211, vol. 92, http://www.bac-lac.gc.ca/eng/CollectionSearch/Pages/record.aspx?app=fonand col&IdNumber=103891&new=-8586236177400020532.
18 E.M. Mills, "The Essential Qualifications of a Lady Health Visitor," *Perspectives in Public Health* 24, 3 (1903): 306–18.
19 Canadian High Commission in Kuala Lumpur to DEA, January 14, 1959, LAC, RG25/7375/11038-A-4-40[5.1].
20 Ruth Compton Brouwer, *Modern Women Modernizing Men: The Changing Missions of Three Professional Women in Asia and Africa, 1902–69* (Vancouver: UBC Press, 2002).
21 Sarah Carter, *Imperial Plots: Women, Land, and the Spadework of British Colonialism on the Canadian Prairies* (Winnipeg: University of Manitoba Press, 2016); Ann Laura Stoler, *Carnal Knowledge and Imperial Power: Race and the Intimate in Colonial Rule* (Berkeley: University of California Press, 2010); Jane Hunter, *The Gospel of Gentility: American Women Missionaries in Turn-of-the-Century China* (New Haven, CT: Yale University Press, 1984).
22 Enloe, *Bananas, Beaches, and Bases;* Donica Belisle, with Kiera Mitchell, "Mary Quayle Innis: Faculty Wives' Contributions and the Making of Academic Celebrity," *Canadian Historical Review* 99, 3 (September 2018): 456–86.
23 Carol G. Chin, "Beneficent Imperialists: American Women Missionaries in China at the Turn of the Twentieth Century," *Diplomatic History* 27, 3 (2003): 327–52.
24 Linda M. Morra, *Unarrested Archives: Case Studies in Twentieth-Century Canadian Women's Authorship* (Toronto: University of Toronto Press, 2014).
25 "Opium Traffic. League of Nations Busy. Foiling Smugglers." *Norwood News*, October 10, 1930, 7, British Newspaper Archive, britishnewspaperarchive.co.uk.
26 "War Must End. Tooting Rector's Plea for League of Nations," *Norwood News*, June 21, 1929, 12, British Newspaper Archive.

27 George W. Cadbury, "Planning in Saskatchewan," in *Essays on the Left*, ed. Laurier LaPierre et al. (Toronto: McClelland and Stewart, 1971), 51–2; George W. Cadbury, "Saskatchewan: Democratic Social Ownership," *Public Affairs* (December 1948); Jean Larmour, "The Douglas Government's Changing Emphasis on Public, Private and Co-operative Development in Saskatchewan, 1955–1961," in *Building the Co-operative Commonwealth: Essays on the Democratic Socialist Tradition in Canada*, ed. J. William Brennan (Regina, SK: Canadian Plains Research Centre, 1984), 161–80; John Richards and Larry Pratt, *Prairie Capitalism: Power and Influence in the New West* (Toronto: McClelland and Stewart, 1979); "Government, Co-operatives and Private Enterprise in Industry," September 24, 1946, Saskatchewan Archives Board, R-757, file 4 [3].

28 Meyer Brownstone, "The Douglas-Lloyd Governments: Innovation and Bureaucratic Adaptation," in *Essays on the Left*, ed. Laurier LaPierre et al. (Toronto: McClelland and Stewart, 1971); Larmour, "The Douglas Government's Changing Emphasis on Public, Private and Co-operative Development in Saskatchewan, 1955–1961"; Richards and Pratt, *Prairie Capitalism*; and David Quiring, *CCF Colonialism in Northern Saskatchewan* (Vancouver: UBC Press, 2005).

29 Robert I. Maclaren, "George Woodall Cadbury: The Fabian Catalyst in Saskatchewan's 'Good Public Administration,'" *Canadian Public Administration* 38, 3, 472.

30 Belisle and Mitchell, "Mary Quayle Innis."

31 Belisle and Mitchell, "Mary Quayle Innis," 471.

32 MacDermot, unpublished manuscript on the Canadian Foreign Service, Bishop's University Archives.

33 John Hilliker, Mary Halloran, and Greg Donaghy, *Canada's Department of External Affairs*, vol. 3, *Innovation and Adaptation, 1968–1984*.

34 Molly M. Wood, "Wives, Clerks, and 'Lady Diplomats': The Gendered Politics of Diplomacy and Representation in the U.S. Foreign Service, 1900–1940," *European Journal of American Studies* 10, 1 (2015): 2, doi.org/10.4000/ejas.10562.

35 Ellen Ravndal and Edward Newman, "The International Civil Service," in *Oxford Handbook of Global Policy and Transnational Administration*, ed. Diane Stone and Kim Moloney (Oxford: Oxford University Press, 2019), 165–81.

36 Letters appear in Provincial Archives of Saskatchewan, George W. Cadbury fonds, file R-757, Cadbury, George W., correspondence files.

37 Jean Larmour interview with George Cadbury, January 1982, Provincial Archives of Saskatchewan, file R-757, Cadbury George W.

38 Ann Laura Stoler, *Along the Archival Grain: Epistemic Anxieties and Colonial Common Sense* (Princeton, NJ: Princeton University Press, 2008).

39 George Cadbury to Tommy Douglas, March 21, 1955, Provincial Archives of Saskatchewan, file R-757, correspondence files; Cadbury letters in UNARMS, Keenleyside files.

40 "Passionate Campaigner for Choice: Barbara Cadbury," Section15.ca, July 9, 2002.

41 Cadbury to Arthur Goldschmidt, August 11, 1954, United Nations Archives, S-0441 –1431–04.

42 "Passionate Campaigner for Choice"; Matthew Connelly, *Fatal Misconception: The Struggle to Control World Population* (Cambridge: Harvard University Press, 2009).

43 Morra, *Unarrested Archives*.

44 "Passionate Campaigner for Choice"; "George Cadbury, 88, Canadian Economist," *New York Times*, March 8, 1995; "Barbara Cadbury Was a Pioneer in Family Planning in Canada," *Oakville Beaver*, May 13, 2001; Connelly, *Fatal Misconception*.

45 Norman Lewis, *Golden Earth: Travels in Burma* (London: Eland Books, 1952), 72. Details can also be found in Nathan Keyfitz, *Notes of a Wayfarer*, unpublished memoir.

46 F.R. Scott, diary entry, May 16, 1952, LAC, Franklin Reginald Scott fonds.

47 Beatrice Keyfitz (BK) to Lois, November 27, 1953, Harvard University Archives, Nathan Keyfitz Papers, correspondence 1953–4, box 2 (hereafter cited as Keyfitz Papers).
48 BK to Grace, December 1, 1953, Keyfitz Papers.
49 BK to "Dear Oswald," February 14, 1954, Keyfitz Papers.
50 BK to Grace, December 1, 1953, Keyfitz Papers.
51 BK to Mama and Papa, January 8, 1954, Keyfitz Papers.
52 Keyfitz Christmas letter, October 1, 1953, Keyfitz Papers, box 6.
53 The reference to Canadian domesticity echoes Kristen Hoganson, *Consumers' Imperium: The Global Production of American Domesticity, 1865–1920* (Chapel Hill: University of North Carolina Press, 2006); Emily S. Rosenberg, "Consuming Women: Images of Americanization in the 'American Century,'" *Diplomatic History* 23, 3 (July 1999): 479–97; and Donica Belisle, *Purchasing Power: Women and the Rise of Canadian Consumer Culture* (Toronto: University of Toronto Press, 2020).
54 Keyfitz Christmas letter from Colombo, November 1, 1956, LAC, RG74, vol. 266, file 36–8C-K1[1].
55 *Notes of a Wayfarer;* Keyfitz Christmas letter from Colombo.
56 Léger to Herbert Marshall, Dominion Statistician, August 24, 1956, LAC, RG74, vol. 266, file 36–8C-K1[1].
57 James J. Hurley, Canadian High Commissioner to Ceylon, August 16, 1957, LAC, RG74, vol. 266, file 36–8C-K1[1].
58 Beatrice Harding, *Around the World in 80 Years* (Regina, SK: self-pub., 2004), 103.
59 William M. Harding personal history, University of Regina Archives, Bill Harding fonds, CCF broadcast series script, February 1952, WMH 91–29, box 4, file 3.
60 Interview with Margaret Joan Anstee, United Nations Intellectual History Project, December 14, 2000; "Obituary: Julia Henderson," International Planned Parenthood Federation, September 17, 2013, https://www.ippf.org/blogs/obituary-julia-henderson.
61 William M. Harding (WMH), unpublished Liberia memoir, 1–3, Bill Harding papers, 91–29 box 13 file WMH/LIB/1; *Around the World in 80 Years*, 124.
62 WMH, unpublished memoir, iii.
63 Harding, Report No. 1, June 17, 1961, Bill Harding fonds, WMH 91–29, box 13, file WMH/LIB/4.
64 Liberian Information Service, *Liberia: Story of Progress* (Monrovia: Liberian Information Service, n.d.), 54, cited in Bill Harding, unpublished memoir, Chapter 5, page 1.
65 Harding, circular letter, August 30, 1961, Bill Harding fonds, WMH/LIB/5.
66 WMH, letter to ladies, August 14, 1961, WMH/LIB/5 letters.
67 WMH, letter to friends and family, August 17, 1961, WMH/LIB/5 letters.
68 Harding, *Around the World in 80 Years*, 145.
69 Harding, *Around the World in 80 Years*, 166.
70 WMH, UN Day speech 1967, Bill Harding fonds, WMH 91–29 box 11, file 5; Report on Visits to UNDP Projects in Guyana, by Thomas F. Power Jr., January 18, 1967, WMH 91–29, box 10, file 6; Harding, *Around the World in 80 Years*.
71 Rickey Singh, "Goodbye to a Friend of Guyana," *Sunday Graphic*, November 19, 1967, Bill Harding fonds, WMH 91–29, box 11, file 6.
72 Heather Barker, "Smith, Addie Viola (1893–1975)," in *Australian Dictionary of Biography*, National Centre of Biography, Australian National University, http://adb.anu.edu.au/biography/smith-addie-viola-11717/text20945.
73 Alexandra Epstein, "International Feminism and Empire-Building between the Wars: The Case of Viola Smith," *Women's History Review*, 17, 5 (2008): 711.
74 Eleanor Hinder (EH), letter to R.D. Ledward, UK delegation to UN, June 4, 1951, State Library of New South Wales, Eleanor M. Hinder Papers (EMHP), vol. 770, file 7.

75 EH, letter applying for US visa, EMHP 770/7.
76 See, for instance, UNARMS, E.M. Hinder and G.W.C. Cadbury travel files.
77 Arthur "Tex" Goldschmidt, TAA, to Hinder, February 15, 1955, EMHP, 770/8/1.
78 EH to Syed Ahmed, TAA, from Moscow, June 5, 1955, EMHP 770/8/1.
79 "Observations on Technical Development and Training Opportunities in the USSR: Report of a Study Tour of Indian Government Officials, 31 May – 6 July 1955," UN document TAA/IND/15, EMHP 770/8/1; Canadian embassy New Delhi to USSEA, July 11, 1955, LAC, 5475-DU-1-40[14].
80 EH, Travelogue No. 7, Uzbek-Afghan border, July 5, 1955, EMHP, 770/8/1.
81 EH to Ahmed, July 3, 1955; EH to Hugh Keenleyside, TAA director-general, and Goldschmidt, June 4, 1955, EMHP, 770/8/1.
82 EH, report to Keenleyside, July 16, 1955, EMHP 770/8/1.
83 Anstee, *Never Learn to Type*.
84 Enloe, *Bananas, Beaches and Bases*. On this point, see also Leila J. Rupp, *Worlds of Women: The Making of an International Women's Movement* (Princeton NJ: Princeton University Press, 1997).
85 Linda M. Morra and Jessica Schagerl, "Introduction: No Archive Is Neutral," in *Basements, Attics, Closets and Cyberspace: Explorations in Canadian Women's Archives* (Waterloo, ON: Wilfrid Laurier University Press, 2012).
86 Stoler, *Along the Archival Grain*; Morra, *Unarrested Archives*.
87 Vron Ware, *Beyond the Pale: White Women, Racism and History* (London: Verso, 1992), xiii.
88 Marcel Cadieux, *Canadian Diplomat: An Essay in Definition* (Toronto: University of Toronto Press, 1963), 35, 94, 98. See also Harold Nicolson, *Diplomacy* (New York: Harcourt Brace, 1939).

PART 2

Women in International Resistance

4

Historically Invisible
The Women's International League for Peace and Freedom, 1914–29

Sharon Anne Cook and Lorna McLean

When historian Harriet Alonso set out to retrieve the biographies of Jane Addams and Emily Greene Balch from the ashcan of history, Alonso asserted that even though both women had been Nobel Peace Prize laureates, each was and still is virtually unknown in the land of her birth.[1] And while they are well documented within the peace movement, that has guaranteed them little visibility within the broader historical record.[2] It has often been observed that as a topic, peace is itself under-recognized in the public's consciousness. When women peacemakers like Jane Addams or Emily Greene Balch are remembered, it is often for other achievements than their peace initiatives. Why have we so conveniently forgotten women working on behalf of peace, including the practical ideas they promoted to regain and maintain international peace?[3]

Founded in 1915, during the cataclysm of the First World War, the Women's International League for Peace and Freedom (WILPF) was one of the most ambitious of the experiments initiated by women to bring about global peace. Led by women with elevated public profiles from the United States, Canada, the United Kingdom, Germany, the Netherlands, Belgium, and beyond, the WILPF gained access to important public authorities during the First World War, through discussions of the peace treaty, during preparations for establishing the League of Nations, and on into the 1920s. In the process, it championed a novel and practical approach to peacemaking called Continuous Mediation, developed by Canadian academic Julia Grace Wales. Wales suggested that the United States, then a

Figure 11 Julia Grace Wales, 1916. | Photograph by DeLonge Studio of Madison, Wisconsin. Courtesy Library and Archives Canada, PA-182511

neutral power, mediate a continuous conference to consider peace proposals as the war continued. This was a notion that Woodrow Wilson seems to have incorporated into his famed Fourteen Points, a list of guiding principles on which peace between the warring nations was to be based. Nevertheless, despite developing useful proposals like this one, Wales and her female international peace associates in this era have fallen into obscurity.

This chapter begins by surveying the range of women's peace-based organizations before and during the First World War that resulted in the founding of the WILPF, in 1915. It considers the ideas promoted to re-establish and maintain international peace and justice by the WILPF. We offer profiles of six prominent women from the United States, Canada, and the United Kingdom who were recognized as leaders in peace ideology and who were closely associated with the WILPF. None, except for social reformer Jane Addams, whose work to alleviate urban poverty through the settlement house movement made her well known prior to her peace activism, have retained any significant recognition in public memory. Finally, we speculate on the reasons and effects of this collective amnesia as it relates to women as international peace-seekers.

Precursors of the Women's International League for Peace and Freedom

Many national and international women's organizations deplored war and attempted to promote peace through resolutions at conferences, letter-writing campaigns, and interviews with policy-makers. As early as 1883, for instance, the World's Woman's Christian Temperance Union had established a Department of Peace and International Arbitration, with a similar Department of Work established at the Canadian national level of the Woman's Christian Temperance Union after 1900.[4] Their stated objective was to subvert nations' tendencies to declare war by creating a third-party arbitration process, and several models were proposed. But no organization took up this aim with more commitment, knowledge, and energy than the WILPF.

The direct line of succession to the WILPF came through at least three separate, but closely connected, women's organizations.[5] One source was the Woman's Peace Party in the United States, headed by Jane Addams.[6] Founded in 1914, it was an important constituent of the anti-war 1915 International Women's Congress which met in The Hague, Netherlands.[7] The Woman's Peace Party was a supporter of female suffrage, as were all of these associated women's groups. One of its key demands was for a continuous process of mediation. In reviewing the resolutions of The Hague conference, Woodrow Wilson observed that these ideas were "by far the best formulations which ... has been put out by anybody."[8]

A second organization that fed members and procedure into the WILPF was the British non-militant National Union of Women's Suffrage Societies. Historian Jo Vellacott defined the members as "tough, logical and consistent" feminists who were not only committed to peaceful principles, but who had developed procedures for productive parliamentary debate to settle disputes.[9] This they achieved as a result of being caught between the British militant suffragists of the Women's Social and Political Union and forces resisting women's suffrage on any terms. And as with all of these constituent groups, the members were accused of disloyalty during the war.

A third constituency that constituted the WILPF originated in the International Congress of Women, organized in 1915 by German, Belgian, British, and Dutch pacifists. This group comprised representatives from twelve neutral and belligerent nations, and they too supported continuous mediation of international tensions. The International Congress of Women was feminist and in favour of female suffrage. It adopted much of the Woman's Peace Party platform, forming the International Committee of Women for Permanent Peace, with Addams as president. Along with other associations outlined in this volume, all three of these organizations and the WILPF demonstrated women's personal agency as they sought a variety of routes to influence international norms of peacemaking from outside the corridors of power.

These groups formed the WILPF, eventually setting their headquarters in Geneva, Switzerland, in order to be near the League of Nations. They denounced the Treaty of Versailles that ended the First World War as a vengeful act, injurious to all world citizens, but particularly so to women and children. As a feminist and pacifist organization, the members decried economic imperialism in any form, including its guise in the peace treaty. The women of the WILPF represented transnational ideals that transcended national interest. In the process, by not linking their cause to national interests, the key leaders of the WILPF might have sentenced themselves to obscurity.

Policies of the WILPF

The policy position of the WILPF between its formal founding in 1915 and the date of its clear decline in 1930 (when the rise of fascism made organizations based on pacifism untenable) are outlined by Vellacott in her masterful study of the WILPF. The WILPF demanded, among other things:

- International support for the League of Nations, which it saw as the key bulwark between lawless militarism and innocent people;
- The reinstatement of the principles of the 14 Points to the Covenant;
- Open membership to all nations;
- Reduction of armaments, and eventually, disarmament;

- Acceptance of the principle of self-determination in matters of nationality and territory;
- All nations' free access to raw materials;
- Easier amendment of the League of Nations' Covenant;
- Machinery for arbitration and conciliation;
- Abolition of secret treaties;
- Provision for the revision of treaties;
- Promotion of freedom of transit;
- Efforts to combat disease and improve health;
- Establishment of full equal suffrage, and the full equality of women with men politically, socially and economically.[10]

Prominent Members of the Women's International League for Peace and Freedom

Emily Greene Balch
A recipient of the Nobel Peace Prize in 1946 for her work with the WILPF, Emily Balch is, as noted, virtually unknown in the United States, or almost anywhere else, today.[11] She joined the WILPF in 1919 and remained committed to peace activism until her death in 1961. Throughout her career and her long life (b. 1867), Balch declared herself a socialist, pacifist, and anti-capitalist, eliciting criticism and even hatred for her policy positions. She challenged the norms for women with apparent relish throughout her life. Descended from an anti-slavery lawyer father and a domestically ensconced mother, Balch was a graduate of Bryn Mawr College in Pennsylvania, and the Sorbonne in Paris. At Bryn Mawr, she adopted views on female equality and the Quaker ideal to be "useful."[12] She taught economics and was chair of the Department of Economics and Sociology at Wellesley College. Though Balch's sophisticated approaches to the study of sociology – encompassing race, gender, and ethnicity – are completely lost to the historical record, historian Andrew Johnston argues that her critical work on immigration deserves greater respect.[13] She championed the study of international organizations and reconciliation long before they became topics of public interest. Johnston credits her academic methodology as a type of "ontological transnationalism," which placed her far in advance of her academic peers in the 1920s, in a field that squeezed her out.[14]

In 1915, Balch joined forces with Addams and other feminists, including Emmeline Pethick-Lawrence of Britain, and Rosika Schwimmer of

Figure 12 Emily Greene Balch. | Photograph by Harris and Ewing. Courtesy Library of Congress, LC-DIG-HEC-18336

Austria-Hungary, to found the Woman's Peace Party, which eventually became the American branch of the WILPF. That year, Balch, along with forty-five other American women and over one thousand Europeans, met at the International Congress of Women. She rapidly rose to a leadership position there, being named to a delegation (with Schwimmer, Chrystal Macmillan, of England, and Cor Ramond-Hirsch, of the Netherlands) that had the aim of convincing political leaders of the wisdom of using mediation to end the war. When the WILPF was established in 1915, Balch became the first secretary-treasurer, afterwards called the international secretary. She accepted this position after being fired by Wellesley for her radical views.

During the Red Scare following the First World War, when the Russian Revolution gave rise to panicky fears of leftist subversion in the United

States, Balch was smeared by a Senate subcommittee as being "dangerous, destructive and anarchistic." The Daughters of the American Revolution, a conservative women's organization, denounced the WILPF as part of a "world revolutionary movement" out to "destroy civilization and Christianity ... and the government of the United States."[15]

As the chief administrator of the WILPF throughout the 1920s, Balch wrote a number of influential reports encouraging disarmament, surveying the inhumanity arising from militarism, and calling for mediation of the Spanish Civil War (1936–39). In this period, she concentrated on the needs of refugees and called for an end to anti-Semitism. She succeeded in her campaign to have the WILPF declared a non-governmental organization associated with the United Nations in 1948.

On being named a Nobel laureate that year, she characteristically gave ten thousand dollars of the prize to the WILPF. And doubtless, she could have used that money to good effect for her own needs. Never possessed of much money, she only survived financially in Geneva because her good friend, Helen Cheever, also a member of the WILPF, supported her financially and personally.[16]

In retrospect, Balch's invisibility is especially perplexing. Her place on the world stage through the first half of the twentieth century and her recognition as a Nobel Peace laureate would seem to have guaranteed her fame. But this was not to be the case. Was the lack of regard after 1950 due to her radical political and economic views, which had alienated so many in America? Was it rooted in her close association with the WILPF, which rapidly lost traction after 1930? Johnston hypothesized that Balch's move toward settlement houses and social work (through her close association with Addams) removed her from the theoretically infused field of sociology then in vogue, effectively erasing her significant contribution to sociological research, both as an academic and in her work with WILPF. The discipline became dominated by male researchers, and liminal figures like Balch "lost their professional platform."[17] Did Addams's stronger personality mean that she could be the only star?

Catherine E. Marshall
Harkening from the non-violent wing of the British suffrage movement to the Women's International League – the British counterpart to the international WILPF – Catherine Marshall played an important role in the

suffrage movement in England through the National Union of Women's Suffrage Societies, for which she served as honorary parliamentary secretary. From 1914, she helped to coordinate women's peace efforts, both in Britain and internationally. Although she seems not to have had a formal role with the WILPF, she remained in its service throughout the interwar period. Suffragist, pacifist, humanitarian, and socialist, she "looked to socialism which she hoped could change political, economic, and social structures by peaceful means."[18]

Marshall was a woman of exceptional ability, both in articulating the nature of women's peace work and in working productively (and peacefully) during rancorous debates at WILPF forums. These skills drew heavily on her experience in working to obtain women's suffrage in Britain. In 1917, she set out her view of the dimensions of the problem of war:

> I am convinced that the great constructive task for us of the WIL faith is not simply to oppose war in a negative way ... but to help to find an *alternative* to war that shall be as creative of free and fruitful of life as war is destructive of them, that shall make as urgent a call on men's and women's courage and devotion and self-sacrifice, and that abolish not only armaments, offensive and defensive, but the spirit of *domination* on the one hand, and of *defensiveness* on the other. And to achieve this fruition of the pacifist faith we have got to have a *revolution* of our whole social, industrial and political systems ... a revolution that will bring about change without resort to the methods or spirit of war.[19]

Marshall brought her capacity for productive parliamentary debate with her to Geneva, to the WILPF headquarters at Maison Internationale. She ensured that the few women officially named by governments or organizations to the League of Nations were made welcome at WILPF headquarters, and she lobbied any group that might be prepared to support the WILPF. She effectively chaired meetings of these lobby groups and managed to insist on conduct of mutual respect among women who had suffered much at the hands of "enemies" sitting next to them at conferences. At one particularly fiery meeting in 1927, when Marshall allowed open debate on conflicting resolutions by the delegates, "the composed confident chairman [Marshall] arose and assured the audience ... that each speaker was at liberty to speak her views from the floor, but that no resolution would be presented that was not in harmony with the purpose for which the meeting was called [peace]."[20]

As the meeting progressed, it remained quiet and measured, despite the rancour just below the surface of women from belligerent powers.

Marshall also directed her energies in support of the League of Nations itself. Before the first session of the League opened, she suggested modifications to some of its procedures, and these were accepted.[21] Marshall unofficially acted on behalf of the WILPF from 1920, and in that capacity travelled extensively throughout Europe. When the WILPF was first organized, some money was available to the executive, but not much. As a consequence, Marshall travelled almost exclusively by using her own slender resources: first, those of her father who financed her work until his death and, thereafter, by cobbling funds together from friends and relatives.

In addition to her role as a negotiator and activist, Marshall was called on to act with Balch as hostess for many receptions and dinners at Maison Internationale. Like the profile of Jean Casselman Wadds in this collection, Marshall, Balch, and indeed most of the leaders of the WILPF recognized the importance of entertaining as a component of diplomacy. But despite this being an essential part of the organization's strategy to bring national representatives on board, it was expensive, and this too she had to underwrite, as Vellacott noted.

> Her contribution to the international work in the early years was probably the largest of any single member other than Emily Balch (who was employed full-time), her skills outstanding and the range of areas in which she became expert phenomenal, and indeed the amount she did was remarkable, yet she would surely have done even more if a little more money had been available, and unquestionably she would have been spared some stress.[22]

Yet despite her many achievements and her deserved respect and even fame within the organization, her name too has been lost to history. How can we account for this absence? The fact that Marshall did not have a formal role with the WILPF might have been a factor, although her name is inexorably linked with the organization in all historical accounts. Did her financial limitations impose limits on her fame? Undoubtedly. Possibly the very range of the issues with which she became associated meant that her public recognition was diluted, while a single cause might have preserved her historical position. While her name was intimately associated with the cause of obtaining suffrage for women in Britain, this did not protect her from invisibility.

Mary Sheepshanks

Possessed of a Cambridge degree and a tough and committed mind, Mary Sheepshanks was the daughter of a British clergyman. In her youth, she had known straightened finances and since her university days had to provide for herself. Her heightened recognition of the importance and justice of a living wage stood against her when she was being considered for the important role of WILPF international secretary. She was repeatedly passed over because of her insistence on being adequately paid and being provided with modern equipment with which to work in the office at Maison Internationale. She was finally named to the post in 1927. In that capacity, she was called on to serve on committees and often produce their final reports, work with delegations to the League, host all delegations journeying to Geneva, lobby both behind the scenes and publicly, organize conferences, write letters, and give public speeches. Like Marshall, she found the hosting most onerous. She was eventually forced to move out of the headquarters and into small quarters close by in order to find quiet and time for her many administrative tasks.[23]

Long before Sheepshanks was given the formal role to lead the WILPF, however, she played a significant part in that organization and before that, in the British women's suffrage movement. She had worked with Marshall to achieve suffrage, meeting with all parliamentary parties to develop their support. By 1919, she attended the Zurich conference, where she emphasized the importance of including women from all belligerent nations, rather than just the victors.

> Women from the warring as well as the neutral nations joined hands in grief and horror at the misery and devastation, the loss of millions of lives, the mutilation and ruined health of millions more, and the wretched plight of the hundreds of thousands of refugees now scattered over the face of the earth, homeless and deprived of everything that makes life worth living.[24]

Sheepshanks also had to travel a good deal. The WILPF periodically sent missions to troubled locales to engage in mediation with disputing parties or to fact-find. Sheepshanks visited the Ukraine in 1930 with one delegation, requiring her superb research as well as negotiating skills. She also had to find the money to finance the trip. Always with too much to do, Sheepshanks held up under the stress and financial limitations.

But even as one of Britain's most prominent prewar suffragists,[25] and then the administrative head of the WILPF in regular touch with the newsworthy international actors of her era, Sheepshanks too has been almost completely forgotten. Like Marshall before her, her public recognition might well have been hampered by addressing too many issues, including the burdensome task of hosting delegations on little money. Spread thinly as she was, Sheepshanks suffered from too little administrative support, a product of the WILPF's chronic underfunding. Accounts of her prodigious energy also spoke of her exhaustion and frustration, which might have caused her to be sharper and demanding with people around her. Of all of the women in this survey, she presents as the most difficult and even demanding personality, long on principle and short on tolerance for the working conditions she endured. And like the other women in this survey, her removal from her home nation to an international organization, and one which attempted to influence a far more weighty one like the League of Nations, meant that even in the interwar period, she laboured in relative obscurity.

Chrystal Macmillan

Chrystal Macmillan's career spanned forty years of championing women's rights as a suffragist, college student, peace activist, and lawyer. Born in Edinburgh, in 1872, she grew up in an upper-middle-class family, the only girl with seven brothers. She began her schooling in an all-girls private school and later studied at the University of Edinburgh. She was the first woman to graduate in science from the university, where she also received the highest honours in mathematics. Continuing her studies, in 1926 she was one of the first group of women to become barristers in London.[26]

At the beginning of the First World War, Macmillan launched her career in peace activism. As secretary of the International Woman Suffrage Alliance, she supported the work of the International Women's Relief Committee and joined Sheepshanks and other members of the relief committee to provide food and clothing to refugees in Europe. Her involvement in the war effort led her to join the British women's delegation to the International Congress of Women. As the English Channel had been declared a war zone, Macmillan was one of only three British women who managed to make their way to the congress.[27]

Along with Balch and others, the women travelled back and forth between countries in Europe and the United States, meeting with twenty-four

Figure 13 Chrystal Macmillan. | Courtesy LSE Library

influential leaders, including prime ministers, foreign ministers, presidents, the King of Norway, and Pope Benedict XV.[28] The women urged these leaders to take up the plan for continuous mediation, developed by Julia Grace Wales, to end the war.

At the end of the war, Macmillan served as a delegate to the Second International Congress of Women, which established the Women's International League for Peace and Freedom. Her goal was to pursue her longtime interests in women's rights for both married and single women, permitting them to hold full citizenship in their professional careers.[29] Despite her leadership in the suffrage and peace movements and, later, as a legal scholar, few historical sources document Macmillan's ongoing efforts for social justice. A former student of the University of Edinburgh, a refurbished building, the School of Social and Political Science, was named after Chrystal Macmillan.[30]

Along with the naming of the building, the University of Edinburgh also created a doctoral scholarship for a student studying in a field relevant to Macmillan's achievements.[31] These are significant tributes at the University of Edinburgh, but still we are left wondering why Macmillan's status as a peace activist was not recognized until almost a century after the war ended. An exhibition about her life at the University of Edinburgh includes her many "firsts" as a student and a legal scholar. One panel out of nine acknowledges her role in organizing "Women's Voices for International Peace and Conflict Resolution," while a second poster identifies her as a "Prominent voice for social justice."[32]

Jane Addams

The culmination of Jane Addams's lifelong career as a peace activist and social reformer occurred in 1931. Just four years before her lengthy illness and untimely death in 1935, she was awarded the Nobel Peace Prize. Yet, popular knowledge about Addams has centred on her work as the leader of the settlement movement and as the founder of Hull-House – a facility that offered programs geared toward the needs of recent immigrants and impoverished mothers and children residing in the United States. But her career was far more diverse than this. It was devoted as well to the peace movement, both nationally and internationally.

Much like Wales, Macmillan, and Balch, Addams was born, in 1860, into an upper-middle-class family in Illinois where her father was a prosperous miller and banker. Her mother died when she was very young, leaving her to be raised by her stepmother, Anna Haldeman Addams, who worked at home to raise the family. Addams was well schooled in a private girls' academy and enrolled briefly in medical school, departing before graduation because of ill health. Upon travelling to Europe and visiting the London settlement house, Toynbee Hall, in 1887, she returned to the United States the following year and established Hull-House in the slums of Chicago. This mission house operated as a retreat for women, offering a day nursery, gymnasium, dispensary, playground, and a cooperative boarding house for single working women, known as the Jane Club.[33]

As historian Alonso rightly declares, "Hull House made Jane Addams famous."[34] As the founder of Hull-House, Addams went on to be elected in 1909 as the first woman president of the National Conference on Charities and Correction and the first head of the National Conference of Settlements, a position she held until her death. As a well-known and respected

Figure 14 Jane Addams. | Photograph by Harris and Ewing. Courtesy Library of Congress, LC-DIG-HEC-03453

public figure, she attracted political attention early in her career. In 1912, she was invited to second Teddy Roosevelt's nomination for president on the Progressive Party ticket. She was a keen supporter of women's suffrage and held a series of leadership positions in career and volunteer organizations, resulting in her election as the first vice-president of the National American Woman Suffrage Association, followed by her involvement in the International Woman Suffrage Association.[35]

Upon the declaration of war in August 1914, Addams and Balch, along with other social-work professionals, organized the American Union Against Militarism. As indicated previously, at the urging of two European suffragists, Emmeline Pethick-Lawrence and Rosika Schwimmer, and on behalf of several American suffragists including Balch, Addams convened a meeting of women from various organizations on January 1915, in Washington, DC. This meeting resulted in the formation of the Woman's Peace Party, which later became the American section of the WILPF.[36] Described by Alonso as a "uniquely feminist group," it proclaimed that women had a "peculiar moral passion of revolt against both the cruelty and waste of war."[37] The success of the organization under Addams's leadership is evident in the membership of twenty-five thousand women, peaking in February 1917, the same year that the United States entered the war.[38]

Returning to the United States as president of the newly formed International Committee of Women for Permanent Peace, Addams spoke about the dangers of war. For several years, the United States' government and opponents of communism during the Red Scare protested her motives as unpatriotic and subversive. Addams's reputation as a social reformer served to counter these slurs and denunciations of her status as a patriotic American.[39]

From the end of the war to her death in 1935, Addams laboured on at Hull-House and the WILPF and, despite her failing health, continued to travel internationally. She adopted this strategy of speaking at conferences abroad in part to avoid the ongoing harassment that she faced in the United States. Her supporters continued to mount active campaigns on her behalf between 1916 and 1931 for the Nobel Peace Prize. Finally, in 1931, at a time when peace activism was seen in a more positive light, Addams received the Nobel Peace Prize along with Nicholas Murray Butler of Columbia University. Although no longer active because of ill health, Addams persevered as honorary president of the WILPF. To mark this international honour and in recognition of her activism, hundreds of letters and telegrams arrived along with a box of flowers from the White House, where a former food relief colleague, Herbert Hoover, now president, resided.[40]

Among the peace activists in this chapter, Addams achieved national and international fame predominantly because of her role in founding Hull-House as part of the American settlement movement. As a noted social reformer, she gained the support of national political leaders to whose support she reciprocated, thereby lending an air of authenticity to their political aspirations. Acknowledging Addams's role as a reformer is not intended to overshadow her significant leadership in the peace movement. However, without her role as a social reformer, it is doubtful that anyone would remember her actions as an international peace activist, despite their significance.

As noted by Wales in writing to her family, Wales celebrated Addams's unique contribution to the international peace movement where "she will be the most needed, because there the hard intellectual struggle will begin."[41]

Julia Grace Wales

As the Canadian architect of the Continuous Mediation without Armistice Peace Plan, passed by the Wisconsin Peace Society and state legislature, acclaimed by the American National Peace Conference, presented to President Woodrow Wilson, and later embraced by the WILPF, one might expect Wales to be recognized as a hero. Rarely mentioned in history – including among some of the references cited in this chapter – Wales's accomplishments deserve attention and recognition. As one author has written elsewhere, the ambiguity about Wales's national identity as a Canadian peace activist and hidden authorship of what became known as the "Wisconsin Plan" explain, in part, her historical absence.[42] Nonetheless, her role as a champion in the international peace movement and later as a public intellectual resulted in her invisibility in both Canada and the United States.[43]

Wales's career as a peace activist originated in December 1914. After witnessing the devastating effect of the war on her friends, family, and students, she spent the December holidays at her family home in Quebec, conceiving her plan to bring an end to war. Born in Bury, Quebec, in 1881, Wales grew up in a privileged, socially conscious family in which her father practised as a physician. Given her mother's ill health, she was often responsible for running the family household and did not attend the local girls' academy until age eleven. Without doubt, Wales was an exceptional scholar. She continued her studies at McGill, graduating with first-class honours in English literature, delivering the Prophecy Speech (valedictorian), and winning the Shakespeare Gold Medal Award.[44]

She moved to the United States in 1903 to accept a scholarship at Radcliffe College, Harvard University, to complete her master's degree. From 1904 to 1908, she was employed as a teacher of mathematics and science at a girls' school in Montreal. The following year, she accepted a position as an instructor in the English department at the University of Wisconsin at Madison.[45]

We can gain insight into Wales's lack of public recognition for writing her peace plan by examining the early days of its promotion. Although Wales was invited to attend the National Peace Conference in 1915, in the United States, to promote her plan, she declined because of her citizenship as a Canadian and belligerent in the war. She sought to stay in the background.

Equally telling, she thought her ideas would be taken more seriously if a man put them forward. And indeed, in February 1915, District Attorney John Aylward of Madison, Wisconsin, successfully presented the "Wisconsin Plan." As a modest, religious woman, Wales may have preferred anonymity, despite pursuing peace initiatives throughout her life.[46]

Wales's plan received great acclaim in North America and Europe. In April 1915, after receiving a personal invitation from Addams, Wales travelled with a contingent of American women to The Hague to attend the International Congress of Women.[47] In writing about the ambitions of the women who acted on their peace convictions by travelling to The Hague, Wales recounted how,

> After the conference began, our brains were kept so busy that we had no time to realize our feelings. The "collective mind" was at work under complex conditions. Despite difficulties of language and point of view, the work went forward almost without misunderstanding. During the first day or two we were all timorous, more fearful of wounding each other, however, than of being wounded. But as we proceeded, we gained confidence, for we found that every woman, because she knew her own national sensitiveness, was prepared to take infinite pains in her consideration for the sensitiveness of others.[48]

Wales remained in Europe, travelling with members of the International Congress of Women and promoting her plan. She returned home in the summer of 1915, and by the fall she was back teaching at the University of Wisconsin. Her return to university life was curtailed in December 1915, when she was invited by American businessman and industrialist Henry Ford to travel with Addams and other peace activists to Europe to, once again, pursue the peace plan.[49]

Upon returning from Europe a second time, Wales once again resumed her career as an instructor at the University of Wisconsin. It is difficult to trace her further involvement in the WILPF once she returned to Canada and the United States. In 1920 she was awarded a scholarship (the first ever to a female academic from North America) to study in London while completing her PhD on Shakespeare. Following graduation in 1926, Wales began her lengthy career of twenty-one years as a professor at the University of Wisconsin. Throughout those decades, Wales waged a campaign for international peace, wrote poetry, music, magazine and academic articles, and letters to government, religious leaders, and university presidents, and penned a textbook championing the role of civics to maintain human rights.[50] Although Wales's ideas and her proposal for a " a world thinking organ" or "peace league" eventually came to fruition in the form of Woodrow Wilson's Fourteen Points, the League of Nations and the United Nations, the extent of the contribution attributed to Wales is not clear.[51]

Despite her authorship of the Wisconsin Plan, her professional career supporting peace initiatives, and an extensive archival collection in the Library and Archives Canada, the only book-length manuscript written about Wales's peace activism is aptly titled, *Julia Grace Wales: Canada's Hidden Heroine and the Quest for Peace, 1914 to 1918*.[52] Why was Wales hidden as a heroine in Canada and the United States? Although she returned to academia after the war, she continued to promote her ideas as a public intellectual and as the author of a resolution for the United Nations. Was Wales correct in assuming that only if a man put forth an idea it would be taken seriously and recorded in history? Did she learn from Emily Balch's experience in academia, where radical ideas about peace and economics earned her dismissal? Because Wales herself did not reflect on her lack of visibility, we will never know.

What we do know is that she felt a deep responsibility to promote global peace and social justice – a characteristic she shared with others in the peace movement. In a brief article written in 1949, two years after she had retired from the University of Wisconsin, she wrote an essay titled "The Condensed Statement of My Experience with the Ford Conference." In recounting her motivation to engage in the Ford Peace Mission, she recalled how at the time she "set out from Madison in Dec. 1915, with a feeling of dread, which proved to be not unjustified. Nevertheless, I am more profoundly thankful that I went on the Ford Expedition and if I could have known what was before me, though I should have dreaded it more, I would have felt doubly the necessity of going."[53]

The Invisibility of Women Active in the International Peace Movement, 1914–29: A Summary of Causes

As was the case with other women identified in this volume who also contributed to international diplomacy, much of the work of the women we have profiled was invisible. Why were these smart, driven, and accomplished professional women forgotten? First, as women of academic and idealistic orientations, they had little popular following among powerful organizations or politicians. Andrew Johnston noted that Balch, in direct contrast to Addams, was reserved and remained out of the spotlight if possible. Even when Balch was fired from Wellesley, she asked her supporters not to intervene on her behalf.[54] This was even truer of Wales. In many cases, even the most senior League of Nations' leaders failed to recognize what the women of the WILPF achieved or proposed.

Second, by allying themselves exclusively with the international peace movement (unlike Addams, who made her name as a social activist in a variety of movements) the remaining women activists fell victim to ambivalent assessments about peace activism, popular definitions of national heroism that favoured military men, and the apparent lack of patriotism to their own nations. As Canadian historian Dianne Dodd has observed, women's accomplishments, especially if the women were involved in unpopular causes, were often overlooked or forgotten. She underscored this point in an article on Canadian heroines and historic sites. According to Dodd, women such as Agnes Macphail, the first female Member of Parliament elected to the House of Commons in 1921, did not have the same appeal for commemoration at the federal level as other prominent women such as Nellie McClung, the notable social activist and suffragette. Dodd speculated that Macphail's neglect stemmed, in part, from the fact that she was not a "colourful 'character' in her community," nor did she promote popular reform causes.[55] Hence, the usual "cheerleaders" who promoted individuals were absent in their cases. Although our chapter is not about commemorating Canadian women, the same principles that apply in the Canadian context, apply internationally to women peace activists.

Third, as pacifist feminists, several of these women regularly broke norms associated with respectable womanhood in the western world. Unlike the women analyzed in this volume by Jill Campbell-Miller, the leaders of the WILPF did not always hold to accepted standards of gendered respectability. The prevailing norms associated with women's "goodness" ascribed this to "maternal feminism," an early feminist belief that women's role in society and public affairs was due to their special status as mothers and nurturers. Women who argued their case from an academic standpoint, rather than from a position of moral superiority grounded in the maternalist dogma of the household, as all of these women did, were outside the realm of honour. As Wales remarked about the women in the peace mission, "as we proceeded, we gained confidence." Who would promote their achievements but other "abnormal" women? The six single women whom we profile in this chapter experienced lives in sharp contrast to the four stories profiled in David Webster's chapter in this volume. In his study, he illustrates the vital importance to diplomacy of "caring labour" and social duties, whether in national capitals or in field settings that these wives performed. As single women, the members of the WILPF pursued their peace work without the diplomacy of caring labour provided by life partners.

Fourth, the League of Nations that WILPF sought to support and amend was in decline by the end of the 1920s, blighting everyone associated with it, including the women of the WILPF.

Finally, we can explain these women's invisibility by referencing their own decisions. Wales's unwillingness to have her name associated with her influential strategy to reach and maintain peace is mirrored in the self-effacing approach of many of these women. Using their own money, limited as it was, to promote international peace meant that their "fame" was also limited, their profiles blurring into those of the organization of which they were a proud element. We remember the Women's International League for Peace and Freedom; we forget the women who created and propped it up.

Conclusion

By the end of the 1920s, the WILPF was rapidly losing popular support. Much of this decline was due to the deteriorating international political climate where fascism made positions favouring pacifism increasingly difficult to maintain. The unity of purpose that had characterized the WILPF during the First World War and into the 1920s fractured as the organization sought to address the depth of international problems.[56]

Throughout the rest of the century, the WILPF continued on with fluctuating levels of membership, an expansion in their topics of interest, and new international activities. Celebrating its centennial in 2015, the members returned to The Hague for their annual meeting, focusing on resolutions that centred on The Human Right to Healthy and Safe Food.[57] Actions listed on their website in 2021 identify categories to promote socio-economic justice, leverage feminist perspectives on peace, redefine security and build the movement.[58]

Although the women we have profiled made different professional and personal choices in their approach and engagement with international peace and activism, their interests reflected common concerns with peace, poverty, and human rights, embracing a transnational perspective. The independent nature of their beliefs and actions, as demonstrated by the many "firsts" in their careers, may further explain their isolation historically. Perhaps these lone women, who moved through male environments of academia, religious institutions, and government, understood the limited options that led them to develop a reliance on their own singular abilities and willingness to persevere.

What significance did these women have for Canada and the cause of peace? As Jill Campbell-Miller and Greg Donaghy argue in the introduction, women from Canada, the United States, Britain, and beyond helped to shape international policy and agencies through their paid and unpaid work. The activists in the WILPF did not "represent" their national origins; rather, they developed effective transnational organizations that applied pressure in support of peacemaking and peace-sustaining on international organizations like the United Nations. In so doing, they created a powerful extra-organizational structure, in this case composed of women pacifists from all countries, not just western democracies. In turn, countries like Canada developed a tradition of supporting organizations like the United Nations and also the many specialized agencies and lobby groups that make that organization effective. The WILPF was instrumental in developing this "informal" layer of organizational resolve to support international peace.

Notes

1. Harriet Hyman Alonso, "Nobel Peace Laureates: Jane Addams and Emily Greene Balch; Two Women of the Women's International League for Peace and Freedom," *Journal of Women's History* 7, 2 (Summer 1995): 6.
2. See, for example, Ruth Roach Pierson, *Women and Peace: Theoretical, Historical and Practical Perspectives* (London, UK: Croom Helm, 1987); Betty A. Reardon, *Women and Peace: Feminist Visions of Global Security* (New York: State University of New York Press, 1993); Janice Williamson and Deborah Gorham, eds., *Up and Doing: Canadian Women and Peace* (Toronto: The Women's Press, 1989).
3. Within Canada, much of the focus on women's peace activism looks at later movements, particularly the Voice of Women, including the work of Susan Colbourn in this volume. For example, see chapters by Ian McKay, Marie Hammond-Callaghan, Braden Hutchinson, and Tarah Brookfield, in *Worth Fighting For: Canada's Tradition of War Resistance from 1812 to the War on Terror*, ed. Lara Campbell, Michael Dawson, and Catherine Gidney (Toronto: Between the Lines, 2015).
4. Sharon Anne Cook, "'Through Sunshine and Shadow': The Woman's Christian Temperance Union, Evangelicalism, and Reform in Ontario, 1874–1930 (Montreal/Kingston: McGill-Queen's University Press, 1995), 109.
5. Beverley Boutilier, "Educating for Peace and Cooperation: The Women's International League for Peace and Freedom in Canada, 1919–1929" (master's thesis, Carleton University, 1988).

6 Marie Louise Degen, *The History of the Woman's Peace Party* (New York: Garland, 1972).
7 L. Costin, "Feminism, Pacifism, Internationalism and the 1915 International Congress of Women," *Women's Studies International Forum* 5, 3–4 (1982), 301–15.
8 Jo Vellacott, "A Place for Pacifism and Transnationalism in Feminist Theory: The Early Work of the Women's International League for Peace and Freedom," *Women's History Review* 1 (1993): 15.
9 Vellacott, "A Place for Pacifism," 27.
10 Vellacott, "A Place for Pacifism," 34–35.
11 Alonso, "Nobel Peace Laureates," 6.
12 Andrew M. Johnston, "The Disappearance of Emily G. Balch, Social Scientist," *The Journal of the Gilded Age and Progressive Era* 13, 2 (April 2014): 174.
13 Johnston, "The Disappearance of Emily G. Balch," 166 – 199.
14 Johnston, "The Disappearance of Emily G. Balch," 170.
15 Alonso, "Nobel Peace Laureates," 14.
16 Leila J. Rupp, "Sexuality and Politics in the Early Twentieth Century: The Case of the International Women's Movement," *Feminist Studies* 23, 3 (1997): 29.
17 Johnston, "The Disappearance of Emily G. Balch," 196.
18 Jo Vellacott, *From Liberal to Labour with Women's Suffrage: The Story of Catherine Marshall*, 2nd ed. (Montreal/Kingston: McGill-Queen's University Press, 2016), 368.
19 Catherine E. Marshall, quoted in Jo Vellacott, "Feminism as if All People Mattered: Working to Remove the Causes of War, 1919–1929," *Contemporary European History* 10, 3 (2001): 381.
20 Vellacott, "A Place for Pacifism,"46.
21 Vellacott, "Feminism as if All People Mattered," 388.
22 Vellacott, "A Place for Pacificism," 49.
23 Vellacott, "A Place for Pacifism," 50.
24 Vellacott, "Feminism as if All People Mattered," 391.
25 Suffragists were people who advocated to extend suffrage (voting) for women. Suffragettes supported direct political action.
26 Katrina Gass and Helen Kay, "Chrystal Macmillan, 1872–1937," in *These Dangerous Women* (London, UK; Women's International League for Peace and Freedom/The Clapham Film Unit), http://www.wilpf.org.uk/wp-content/uploads/2015/05/Macmillan-Chrystal.pdf.
27 Gass and Kay, "Chrystal Macmillan, 1872–1937."
28 Alonso, "Nobel Peace Laureates," 11.
29 Gass and Kay, "Chrystal Macmillan, 1872–1937."
30 "Chrystal Macmillan exhibition," School of Social and Political Science, University of Edinburgh. 2021, https://www.sps.ed.ac.uk/sites/default/files/assets/pdf/CM_Banners.pdf.
31 "The Chrystal Macmillan PhD Studentship," School of Social and Political Science, University of Edinburgh, 2021, https://www.ed.ac.uk/student-funding/postgraduate/uk-eu/humanities/social-political-science/chrystal-macmillan.
32 "In Honour of Chrystal Macmillan," School of Social and Political Science, University of Edinburgh, 2021, https://www.sps.ed.ac.uk/sites/default/files/assets/pdf/CM_Banners.pdf.
33 Alonso, "Nobel Peace Laureates," 7–8.
34 Alonso, "Nobel Peace Laureates," 8.
35 Alonso, "Nobel Peace Laureates," 7–8.
36 Alonso, "Nobel Peace Laureates," 10.
37 Alonso, "Nobel Peace Laureates," 10.
38 Alonso, "Nobel Peace Laureates," 11.
39 Alonso, "Nobel Peace Laureates," 13–20.
40 Alonso, "Nobel Peace Laureates," 15–16.

41 Julia Grace Wales fonds, "Letters to Family," Library and Archives Canada, MG 30, C-238, vol. 1, no. 58.
42 Lorna McLean, "'The Necessity of Going': Julia Grace Wales's Transnational Life as a Peace Activist and Scholar," in *Feminist History in Canada: New Essays on Women, Gender, Work, and Nation*, ed. Catherine Carstairs and Nancy Janovicek (Vancouver: UBC Press, 2013), 77–95.
43 Lorna McLean and Jamilee Baroud, "Democracy Needs Education: Performance, Peace and Pedagogy, Julia Grace Wales," *Paedagogica Historica: International Journal of the History of Education*, 56, 4 (2019): 503–509, doi:10.1080/00309230.2019.1616783.
44 McLean, "'The Necessity of Going.'"
45 Mary Jean Woodward Bean, *Julia Grace Wales: Canada's Hidden Heroine and the Quest for Peace, 1914–1918* (Ottawa: Borealis Press, 2005): 35–37.
46 Woodward Bean, *Julia Grace Wales*, 54–58.
47 "Jane Addams to Julia Grace Wales, March 25, 1915," Jane Addams Papers Project, https://digital.janeaddams.ramapo.edu/items/show/10395; Woodward Bean, *Julia Grace Wales*, 63.
48 Julia Grace Wales fonds, "Correspondence" Library and Archives Canada, MG 30 C 238, Vol. 1, no. 22, cited in Woodward Bean, *Julia Grace Wales*, 9.
49 Julia Grace Wales fonds, "Correspondence." Library and Archives Canada, MG 30, series C-238, vol. 4, no. 31.
50 McLean and Baroud, "Democracy Needs Education."
51 Woodward Bean, *Julia Grace Wales*, x.
52 Woodward Bean, *Julia Grace Wales*. See also Wendy Sharer, *Vote and Voice: Women's Organizations and Political Literacy, 1915–1930* (Carbondale: Southern Illinois University Press, 2004).
53 Julia Grace Wales fonds, "The Condensed Statement of My Experience with the Ford Conference," Library and Archives Canada, MG 30, series C-238, vol. 4, no. 28.
54 Johnston, "The Disappearance of Emily G. Balch," 167.
55 Dianne Dodd, "Canadian Historic Sites and Plaques: Heroines, Trailblazers, the Famous Five," *Canadian Historic Sites and Plaques* 6, 2 (2009): 50.
56 Vellacott, "Feminism as if All People Mattered," 392.
57 "WILPF Resolutions, 31st Congress, The Hague, The Netherlands, 2015," accessed July 5, 2019, https://wilpf.org/wp-content/uploads/2015/10/WILPF_triennial_congress_2015.pdf.
58 Women's International League for Peace and Freedom, "Our Vision," 2021, https://www.wilpf.org/vision/#actions.

5

Collecting Teeth for Peace
The Voice of Women, the Baby Tooth Survey, and the Search for Security in the Atomic Age

Susan Colbourn

AFTER ITS FOUNDING IN 1960, the Voice of Women/la Voix des Femmes quickly became one of Canada's most prominent peace organizations.[1] Successive generations of members worked for peace in diverse ways: they protested the Vietnam War, campaigned against the proliferation of children's toys that promoted militarism, picketed NATO headquarters to oppose allied plans for a multilateral nuclear force, and spoke out against nuclear policies from the acquisition of the Bomarc missile to the testing of air-launched cruise missiles over Canadian territory.

No shortage of histories delve into these peace campaigns and the countless others championed by the Voice of Women over the years.[2] This chapter revisits one of the organization's earliest: the group's opposition to nuclear testing in the early 1960s. Alarmed by the dangers of radioactive fallout, members of the newly formed Voice of Women pressed the federal government for greater monitoring and spearheaded the collection of baby teeth from cities and towns across Canada to study the impact of repeated US, Soviet, and British nuclear tests. Reconsidering this episode, this chapter situates the Voice of Women within a much larger surge of opposition to nuclear testing, one that swept Canada along with much of the globe.

Such activism can be understood, as the historian Tarah Brookfield shows, in the context of Cold War maternalism or as part of a broader internationalism that motivated concerned citizens to challenge the binary divisions between East and West.[3] Others have tied opposition to nuclear testing, including the campaigns spearheaded by the Voice of Women, to a burgeoning sense of environmentalism.[4]

Focusing on the circulation of ideas, like the opposition to nuclear testing, also sheds new light on how women participated in broader national and global conversations about security.[5] Members of the Voice of Women warned of the dangers of nuclear testing programs and, in doing so, blended personal, national, and global understandings of security. As they made the case for a nuclear test ban, these activists' arguments incorporated maternal appeals, angst about the Cold War confrontation, and concerns about the environmental damage caused by weapons testing. These arguments illustrated diverse and entangled concepts of security, ones that grappled with the globalizing power of atomic weapons and their radioactive by-products.

With campaigns like the baby tooth survey, the Voice of Women helped to shape a national – and international – discourse about nuclear testing and the associated risks. These conversations transcended traditional boundaries of participation in the making of foreign policy. Far from being confined to the corridors of power in Ottawa, where women remained scarce in the early 1960s, debates over nuclear testing played out in the Department of External Affairs and between grassroots activists, many of them women, working out of their kitchens and basements. Each viewed the issue of nuclear testing as one central to questions of war and peace and of preserving Canadian security and that of the planet in the atomic age.

A Swell of Opposition

In March 1954, the United States conducted its first test of a hydrogen bomb. Conducted at the Bikini Atoll in the Pacific, the test (dubbed "Castle Bravo") sent radioactive fallout far beyond the perimeter demarcated by the Atomic Energy Commission of the United States.[6] A Japanese fishing vessel, *Daigo Fukuryu Maru* (*Lucky Dragon 5*), out trawling during the Castle Bravo test, ended up caught in the fallout. On the morning of March 1, within hours of the Castle Bravo test, the *Lucky Dragon*'s crew exhibited painful signs of acute radiation poisoning.

News of the *Lucky Dragon* spawned anti-nuclear campaigns focused on the dangers of testing nuclear weapons. After the Castle Bravo test, groups like the Federation of American Scientists and the National Committee for a Sane Nuclear Policy launched campaigns to put an end to these tests. Over the remainder of the decade, there was a groundswell of grassroots anti-nuclear activism. In 1957, for instance, the American Friends Service Committee and the Women's International League for Peace and Freedom, both active for decades, delivered a petition with ten thousand signatures to US president Dwight D. Eisenhower, supporting an end to testing.[7] The sheer number of nuclear tests alone was enough to galvanize opposition: between 1951 and 1958, the United States conducted upwards of 180 tests. The Soviet Union, for its part, conducted 83 between its first in 1949 and 1958.[8]

Canadians, too, worried about the dangers of nuclear testing and began to mobilize to stop the existing nuclear powers from conducting further tests. The United Church of Canada spoke out against the damage arising from nuclear testing. New organizations formed to raise awareness about the problems of radiation, including the BC Women's Committee Against Radiation Hazards and the Canadian Committee for the Control of Radiation Hazards. Students at McGill University, Sir George Williams University, and the Université de Montréal came together to form the Combined Universities Campaign for Nuclear Disarmament and, on Christmas Day of 1959, eighty members of the fledgling group took to the streets of Ottawa. It was the first student demonstration of any real size since the end of the Second World War.[9] Like so many across the globe, countless Canadians wrote to their government to express their concern about the dangers of nuclear weapons. Starting in the spring of 1958, John Diefenbaker's Conservative government saw a sizable swell in anti-nuclear letters and telegrams.[10]

The Voice of Women formed in response to many of these same anxieties, made worse by events in the spring of 1960. On May 1, Soviet Air Defence Forces shot down a US reconnaissance overflight not far from Sverdlovsk. After the Soviet Union captured parts of the Lockheed U-2 and its pilot, Francis Gary Powers, Dwight Eisenhower reversed his earlier line that it had been a weather research aircraft, admitting that it was, in fact, an espionage overflight. Soviet general secretary Nikita Khrushchev responded, furious that the United States had conducted overflights in the weeks leading up to a four-power summit. "It was an unintelligent move, sheer stupidity," he later recalled.[11] When the much-touted summit between the United States, the United Kingdom, France, and the Soviet Union opened in Paris a few weeks later on May 16, Khrushchev immediately threatened to walk out. Unsatisfied with Eisenhower's response and determined to scuttle the summit, Khrushchev made good on his threat. The Paris Summit collapsed.[12]

Concerned about the increasing tensions between the two Cold War superpowers, Lotta Dempsey, a columnist at the *Toronto Daily Star*, appealed to women to take up collective action against the threat of nuclear war. "In some way," she wrote in a May 21 column, just days after the breakdown in Paris, "women the world over must refuse to allow this thing to happen."[13] Responding to Dempsey's call, a group of women began to lay the groundwork for a women's peace organization. At the Toronto Committee for Disarmament's gathering at Massey Hall in July of 1960, the Voice of Women was formally established. Within five months, the nascent peace group boasted a membership of two thousand and a mailing list of some ten thousand.[14]

Even before the Massey Hall meeting, some of the group's founders headed to Ottawa to meet with political leaders. Josephine Davis and Dorothy Henderson met with Secretary of State for External Affairs Howard Green and with Lester Pearson, the leader of the Liberals in opposition. Green, according to Dempsey, who accompanied Davis and Henderson, reassured the women that he shared their concerns. "If they were being naive," Green told Davis and Henderson, "then he, too, was naive."[15]

Members of the Voice of Women walked a fine line when it came to how, when, and on what terms women should engage in public debates about foreign policy and security in the atomic age. Often the group's messages appealed directly to their societal role as women and as mothers. "It is a fact of nature that the female of the species is the giver of life and instinctively is endowed with concern for the preservation of life, at least of the young and the helpless," the Voice of Women's first president, Helen Tucker, began one column in the group's regular newsletter.[16] This instinct to protect one's young needed to be extended, projected out on a global scale to protect the planet and all of its inhabitants. "V.O.W. believes that women united in common concern for their families' survival," one open letter put it, "can exercise a positive influence upon the course of world affairs."[17] Letters to the editor underscored these same themes with their concerns framed "as the mother of young children" or "as a wife and a mother."[18]

At the Massey Hall meeting where the Voice of Women was officially formed, one attendee cautioned those considering membership "to seek their husbands' approval before joining."[19] Josephine Davis, one of the group's early members, described the Voice of Women as "a useful auxiliary effort" to the work already being done by men on these same issues.[20] The group's newsletters underscored this orientation: members of the central committee, for instance, were listed as "Mrs. W.D. Tucker" and "Mrs. Fred Davis." Early membership forms solicited information with these conventions in mind, asking prospective members to provide their name, as well as their husband's initial.[21] In the popular press, too, the group's leaders tended to be described as "'prominent' or as 'wife of the well-known...'" phrases that framed their activism with their status as the wives of elite men.[22] These familial and societal ties, then, conferred a degree of respectability on the Voice of Women's activities. Maryon Pearson's affiliation with the group underscored such connections; after all, even the wife of the Leader of the Opposition was an honorary sponsor of the Voice of Women.[23] Members later argued that this maternal image contributed to the group's legitimacy, particularly when compared to other peace groups and campaigns to ban the bomb.[24] But members of the Voice of Women still faced problems familiar to peace activists throughout the Cold War, as they were accused of naïveté or communist sympathies.

From the outset, the Voice of Women's activities focused on a wide array of issues, not just the dangers of nuclear weapons tests. Members worried about the Diefenbaker government's plans to acquire the Bomarc, an anti-aircraft missile to be equipped with nuclear warheads if, in the words of the prime minister, the "full potential of these defensive weapons" were to be reached.[25] Early activities extended far beyond the nuclear realm. The Voice of Women, for instance, endorsed the Women's International League for Peace and Freedom's "Share a Loaf" program to combat hunger, expressed concern about the superpowers' involvement in Cuba, advocated for the United Nations to recognize the People's Republic of China, pushed for official federal legislation on bilingualism and biculturalism, and lobbied for the creation of a Canadian Peace Research Institute.[26] Despite the diversity of these early campaigns, the group remained primarily concerned with nuclear questions.

Motherhood, Mutations, and Morality

From its founding in the summer of 1960, the Voice of Women drew attention to the dangers of nuclear testing. The group's newsletters reprinted and circulated other appeals that highlighted the issue, such as the famed French humanitarian and Nobel Peace Prize recipient Dr. Albert Schweitzer's "Peace or Atomic War?" which addressed the threat posed by the testing of hydrogen bombs.[27] Along with efforts to raise awareness among its members, the Voice of Women lobbied Prime Minister John Diefenbaker's government to oppose nuclear tests. As part of the group's eight-point program, adopted in June 1961, the Voice of Women appealed to the Diefenbaker government to do everything in its power to bring about an end to nuclear testing.[28]

In March 1962, approximately three hundred members and friends of the group travelled from Montreal to Ottawa aboard the Voice of Women's so-called Peace Train to deliver a brief to Prime Minister Diefenbaker.[29] Focused on the recent US decision to resume nuclear tests, the brief homed in on the seeming futility of conducting more tests with a quotation from Dr. Hans Bethe, a German American physicist who had helped to build the hydrogen bomb. "It was true before and it is true now," the brief quoted Bethe, "that the Russians would be able to destroy us and that we would be able to destroy them if we chose. We already know so much about atomic weapons that there is not much more to learn."[30] When *Saturday Night* covered the Peace Train, the coverage expressed doubt that any other "ban the bomb" group would have received the same reception in Ottawa. "Motherhood, mutations and morality are a mighty powerful and explosive mixture," the article concluded.[31]

Within the Diefenbaker government, some were sympathetic to the concerns raised by peace campaigners like those active in the Voice of Women. Secretary of State for External Affairs Howard Green expressed strong public opposition to nuclear tests on numerous occasions.[32] The Voice of Women pointed to Green's public remarks against testing, like a February 1962 speech in Vancouver, in subsequent appeals to the prime minister.[33] Green gained a reputation for optimism and idealism with nuclear disarmament as the flagship issue in his portfolio. "Green's major obsession in office," Peter C. Newman wrote in one *Maclean's* portrait of the foreign minister, "has been to cajole the major powers into realistic disarmament talks."[34] To that end, the Diefenbaker government dispatched letters to the United Kingdom and the United States underscoring the critical importance of an agreement on nuclear testing. It was crucial for London and Washington to redouble their efforts to conclude an agreement with the Soviet Union.[35]

Green put the department to work drafting resolutions to put the brakes on nuclear testing and to call for monitoring of atmospheric radiation for consideration at the United Nations General Assembly and the Ten-Nation Disarmament Committee, a short-lived disarmament forum bringing together delegations from the two blocs, established in 1959.[36] Canadian representatives stressed the significance of an agreement on the cessation of nuclear tests. A treaty could serve as a logical starting point, an opening to pursue broader disarmament agreements.[37] Canadian diplomats also lobbied other governments to sponsor these resolutions. Green, in particular, was relentless in these efforts. George Ignatieff, working as a prime ministerial advisor on nuclear weapons policy, later recalled watching the foreign minister work potential cosponsors, even going so far as to follow them into the washroom.[38]

As he championed nuclear disarmament proposals, Green flatly rejected the idea of unilateral disarmament. "I think if we suddenly decided to give up our arms we'd lose our influence with our friends," he told the press after meeting with members of the Voice of Women.[39] After Green's remarks appeared in the *Globe and Mail* as part of a story on the chapter's visit to Ottawa, representatives from the Voice of Women wrote to the newspaper to correct the record. The Voice of Women, like Green, did not endorse unilateral disarmament.[40]

Members of the Voice of Women did not confine their appeals to their own elected representatives. In February of 1962, the national group dispatched messages to Eisenhower's successor, President John F. Kennedy, and to British prime minister Harold Macmillan, registering their opposition to the resumption of nuclear tests. The Voice of Women's board also dispatched three of its members to Europe: Thérèse Casgrain, a prominent women's rights activist from Quebec who took over as Voice of Women's president later that year, Ghislaine Laurendeau, a charter member of the group's Quebec chapter, and Ghislaine Roy.[41] Message in hand, Casgrain, Laurendeau, and Roy appealed to the delegations meeting at the Disarmament Conference in Geneva.[42]

The Voice of Women's efforts coincided with those of other activist groups, also present in Geneva. Over the course of a few short days, this group of women developed an International Statement presented to the Disarmament Conference's delegations. Signed by women from Austria, Canada, France, the Federal Republic of Germany, Norway, the Soviet Union, Sweden, the United Kingdom, and the United States, the statement implored delegates to oppose all nuclear testing, to put a stop to the "dispersion" of nuclear weapons, and to remain relentless in the pursuit of complete, general disarmament.[43] When, in the summer of 1962, Nikita Khrushchev announced that the Soviet Union would undertake a new round of nuclear tests, the Voice of Women implored the Soviet premier to rethink his decision.[44]

The Voice of Women kept up their efforts to draw attention to the issue of nuclear testing. On November 1, 1962, in the immediate aftermath of the Cuban Missile Crisis, three hundred women traversed downtown Ottawa in silence, weaving their way toward Parliament Hill. With them, they carried letters, notes, and telegrams from twelve hundred fellow concerned Canadians. Green assured them that the government's position had not changed: Ottawa still supported a test ban and hoped to see one in place in the first months of 1963.[45]

It remained difficult, however, to disentangle the test ban issue from other contentious nuclear questions like the acquisition of the Bomarc missile.[46] The Voice of Women pushed for Canada to resist the Bomarc missiles, and their appeals incorporated concerns about the dangers of atomic testing. "We Canadians cannot say, 'We don't want to get into politics.'" The realities of nuclear weapons, the group's board argued, were such that they could not be ignored. Ongoing nuclear tests scattered radioactive pollutants, unconfined by national borders or considerations about sovereignty. As far as the Voice of Women's membership was concerned, these tests posed a clear threat: nuclear tests and the associated radioactive fallout impacted Canadians' immediate surroundings, the food they ate, and the air they could breathe. "The life and death of our children is now political. Governments made decisions for war or peace, but it is WE who elect the governments."[47]

Diefenbaker's minority government fell in February of 1963, brought down by the nuclear question. Lester Pearson's Liberals had indicated that, if in power, they would accept the warheads; the Liberals' positions set the stage for an electoral standoff. Suggested questions for candidates in 1963's "nuclear election" kept testing front of mind, even as the dominant issue remained the Bomarc. Circulated in the group's newsletter, these queries implored readers to ask their local candidates whether their party knew that Canada possessed a higher recorded degree of radiation than both the United States and the United Kingdom. Despite these radiation figures, the Canadian government possessed "a totally inadequate system of monitoring and information," at least in the estimation of those involved in the Voice of Women.[48] Even after Lester Pearson's Liberals won the election, the Voice of Women kept up their appeals to refuse new nuclear weapons in the hopes of creating the most favourable international climate for a treaty banning nuclear testing.[49]

"Teeth Collecting for Peace"

The Voice of Women's efforts to highlight the dangers of nuclear tests continued apace, gaining considerable momentum in 1963. That March, the Voice of Women launched a nationwide campaign to collect baby teeth for scientific study with the initial campaigns focused on Edmonton, Halifax, London, Montreal, Toronto, Vancouver, and Winnipeg.[50] In Toronto, members even set up a collection booth at the Canadian National Exhibition. By the summer of 1964, the Voice of Women had collected some twelve thousand baby teeth for study at the University of Toronto's Faculty of Dentistry.[51]

The Voice of Women were not the first to conduct a study of baby teeth for the purposes of tracing levels of radioactivity or of strontium-90. A similar study was already under way in the United States, begun in 1958. Dr. Herman Kalckar, the vice-president of the St. Louis–based Committee for Nuclear Information, recommended the collection and study of baby teeth as a mechanism for evaluating the impact of nuclear tests.[52] By August 1963, when the Soviet Union, the United Kingdom, and the United States signed the Limited Test Ban Treaty prohibiting nuclear tests underwater, in the atmosphere, and in outer space, the Committee for Nuclear Information had collected data on 132,000 teeth.[53] Studies were also under way in Canada. Ethel Kesler, a former social worker and mother in Montreal, started up a similar collection drive in 1960. Kesler worked to solicit teeth to be sent to Dr. A.M. Hunt at the University of Toronto's Faculty of Dentistry, where Hunt was already studying levels of strontium-90 in children's teeth with a grant from the National Research Council of Canada. Over approximately two years, Kesler and a small handful of her fellow Montreal mothers collected between 6,000 and 7,000 baby teeth for Hunt's study.[54]

Kesler's efforts received some support from the Voice of Women. A May 1961 issue of the group's newsletter, for instance, carried a member's suggestion that readers could collect their children's teeth and send them to Dr. Hunt.[55] Another plea in October asked for those who had "a tooth-losing youngster" to send their teeth on for study.[56] In February of 1963, as Kesler geared up for another round of collections, she reached out to Dr. Ursula Franklin, chair of the VOW's research committee, for assistance. Kesler appealed to Franklin for support from the Voice of Women to collect teeth for Hunt's study in communities across Canada.[57] The Voice of Women kicked off their collections the next month.

When the program rolled out nationally, the Voice of Women received support from surprising places. Businesses across the country donated funds to cover the costs of printing the forms used to gather information about the teeth. Numerous national insurance companies, a drug company, and even a brewery all pitched in to cover the printing costs. Other cash donations came from food corporations, soap producers, a dairy, and a steel company, along with grassroots fundraising efforts like bake sales and "Toothsome Teas."[58]

Studies of baby teeth focused on ascertaining the amount of strontium-90 in children's bones. "Strontium-90," as one of the group's pamphlets soliciting submissions of baby teeth for study explained, "is a radioactive material in fallout from atomic and hydrogen bomb explosions. It has been increasing in our food and is retained in the developing bones and teeth of our children. If ever accumulated in large enough amounts, it may cause harmful effects by its radiation."[59] The Voice of Women spearheaded a collection of teeth, along with information about the children and their upbringing relevant to the research study. The child's birthdate, mother's place of residence while pregnant, child's place of residence during their first year of life, as well as current residence, and information about their feeding (e.g., breastfeeding or infant formula) were all solicited as part of the collection.[60]

The Voice of Women viewed the baby tooth study as a prime mechanism to obtain more measurements of radioactive fallout across Canada, in addition to raising public awareness of the issues. Already, some like Ursula Franklin worried about the lack of existing infrastructure to deal with fallout in Canada.[61] Such fears were almost certainly exacerbated by reports that levels of strontium-90 had increased dramatically over the course of 1962, quadrupling within the year.[62] Franklin, a trained physicist affiliated with the Ontario Research Foundation, expressed concerns about the lack of public education regarding radiation and fallout.[63]

The Voice of Women's research committee also undertook studies into the impact of radioactive fallout on food supplies in Canada. Begun in the autumn of 1962, the committee's research reflected many of the same concerns as the baby tooth study. Dr. Franklin, who spearheaded the research, wished to provide the group's members and the Canadian public writ large with more complete information about the degree of radioactive contamination and hoped that this information could be used to press the government into action, perhaps even to institute public health "countermeasures" if necessary.[64]

Franklin provided some of this information to Barbara Moon, a writer on staff at *Maclean's*. Moon's article, drawing on Franklin's work, appeared in the magazine's May 4, 1963, issue. Entitled "What We Can Do about Fallout," the piece drew attention to the dangers of radioactive fallout and the impact on Canadians. "The world is going into the hottest year for fallout since testing began," the article claimed. "Canada is the hottest country in the world."[65] Unsurprisingly, given Franklin's involvement, the article foreshadowed many of the arguments made in the Voice of Women's brief on fallout monitoring put out later that year. The Voice of Women, however, went uncredited in the final article; Franklin was mentioned by name, but with reference to her affiliation with the University of Toronto. Nevertheless, the group's members still felt that it had been time well spent in order to raise public consciousness about radiation fallout.[66]

On July 22, 1963, the Voice of Women presented the results of Franklin's research in Ottawa. The final product, a brief entitled "Fallout Monitoring in Canada," underscored the group's "concern over the discrepancies between the rapidly increasing levels of radioactive contamination of our food and environment and the apparent inactivity of our government in the field of radiation protection."[67] Already, there had been a marked increase in contaminants produced by fallout over the course of 1962. And these were sure to continue increasing, thanks to the vast number of tests conducted.

"Fallout Monitoring in Canada" compared the country's existing efforts to monitor fallout to similar programs in the United States, the United Kingdom, and the Federal Republic of Germany. Based on these comparisons, the brief found Canadian systems to be inadequate. It pointed to a whole host of shortcomings in the existing monitoring programs, including limited studies of food sources, the failure to track differences across the country, and the lack of an independent advisory board to study problems of fallout and associated hazards from radiation. Canadian monitoring, for instance, conducted minimal studies of food sources. Whereas others tracked animal feed and diets, existing Canadian programs only studied fallout in milk. But that tracking showed that Canadian milk was among the most contaminated.[68] Why, then, would the government not study other foodstuffs?

Given these inadequacies, the Voice of Women appealed to the new Liberal government to introduce a series of changes to create a more robust monitoring infrastructure. The brief envisioned the creation of an advisory board, greater provincial participation in monitoring programs, and the regular publication of fallout data along with "sufficient interpretation to be meaningful to the concerned citizen." It also called for more diverse forms of data collection: the monitoring of a greater array of foodstuffs, such as water, processed food, infant formula, and representative overall diets, as well as gathering data from across the country with a focus on areas deemed to be at risk of high fallout like the Canadian West and the Maritimes.[69]

Making the case for a more robust program of monitoring, the brief's language invoked children and the future of the nation. "Canada is a country of young people; one-third of its population is under 15," the brief's preamble reminded readers. "It is for these young people and for their future that we are urging our Government to concern itself with the problems of radiation contamination of the Canadian environment (just as we will continue to urge the governments of major powers to cease nuclear testing)."[70]

When the brief was completed in the summer of 1963, the Voice of Women sent three copies to the minister of National Health and Welfare, Judy LaMarsh, with a request for a meeting. On July 22, Ursula Franklin travelled to Ottawa, along with fellow members Kay Macpherson, Diana Wright, Diane Campbell, and Meg Sears for a full day of meetings. The women met representatives from the major political parties: the ruling Liberals, the Conservatives in opposition, Social Credit, and the New Democratic Party, as well as appointments with the parliamentary secretaries to Judy LaMarsh and Harry Hays, the agriculture minister. They topped the day off with a press conference and a television interview with the CBC.[71] Franklin felt the meetings went well, particularly the one with LaMarsh's parliamentary secretary, Dr. Stanley Haidasz, which seemed to indicate that the Secretary's office was taking some of her concerns seriously.[72]

But there were some disappointments. Some MPs refused to meet with representatives from the Voice of Women, while others insisted that fallout was a non-issue given the imminent Limited Test Ban Treaty. Events also distracted the press and those in Ottawa. That same week, the Pearson government announced the creation of the commission on biculturalism. As a result, none of the French-language press turned up to the Voice of

Women's press conference, a disappointment given the lengths the women had gone to in order to ensure a bilingual briefing.[73] Despite these setbacks, the group's members felt pleased with the outcome. Franklin performed exceptionally, at least in the eyes of her colleagues: she was "unflagging" with a "rare combination of expert knowledge and articulateness." Summing up the visit to Ottawa, Meg Sears wrote that "it is probably no exaggeration to conclude that, of those MPs susceptible to logic, not one failed to be impressed by the brief."[74]

On the heels of the trip to Ottawa, Franklin hammered home the brief's central message. The federal government's existing information about radioactive fallout was insufficient and, at times, inaccurate. Official statements about the current strontium-90 levels confused and misled the Canadian public, she argued. And the government's studies did little to assess the full extent of the problem. Air monitoring programs, for example, were housed at airports across the country. These sites made it difficult, if not impossible, to study how factors like wind currents impacted levels of strontium-90. As evidence of the government's inadequate data, Franklin drew attention to one 1961 study of national strontium-90 levels. In it, the average levels for two age groups had been calculated based on a sample size of one.[75]

Franklin's conclusions came under fire, at least in some corners. C.K. Johns, the head of the dairy section at the Department of Agriculture, felt Franklin had "failed to gain a proper perspective concerning the hazards of fallout." Johns took issue, in particular, with the brief's framing as the language seemed to overlook a basic fact: the scientists and public health officials responsible for monitoring and studying radioactive fallout were themselves parents and grandparents. "They are just as concerned over any health hazard to their kin," Johns wrote to the Voice of Women's corresponding secretary, "as are the most emotional advocates of immediate action to remove fallout from milk."[76] Skeptics also dismissed the value of the group's ongoing efforts to collect baby teeth for Dr. Hunt. Judy LaMarsh, for instance, famously quipped that "a box full of teeth, with no idea where they came from, isn't much help."[77]

Much of the intense interest in radioactive fallout began to subside in late 1963. With the signing of the Limited Test Ban Treaty, the issue simply did not seem so urgent. But the Voice of Women continued to highlight the ongoing damage of fallout from the earlier tests.[78] "Even if no more nuclear testing occurred at any time in the future," one passage in the fallout brief argued, "the present levels of atmospheric pollution will continue to affect the food chain to a considerable extent."[79] The Metro Toronto chapter's August 1963 newsletter, published just after the signing of the Limited Test Ban Treaty, urged members to write to the prime minister, their Member of Parliament, member of provincial parliament, and their dairy and bread suppliers with quotations and figures from the fallout brief as part of a continued push for better monitoring.[80] Franklin herself continued to receive inquiries based on her research. In the summer of 1966, for instance, she received a letter from a concerned woman in New Zealand, Kathleen Dawson, worried about upcoming French nuclear tests and the radioactive fallout it would produce in the South Pacific.[81]

As for the baby teeth, they received a burst of renewed interest when Dr. Hunt released his findings in 1965. After conducting studies on over thirty thousand baby teeth from cities and towns across Canada, Hunt and his team concluded that there were "no harmful effects from the low levels of strontium-90."[82] Press coverage dismissed earlier concerns as nothing more than a panic. Results from the University of Toronto study maintained that it would take some fifty times as many megatons tested to reach a level of real danger, and the levels of strontium-90 were now dropping.[83]

Conclusion

As they underscored the potential threat of nuclear testing, the Voice of Women participated in a global conversation about the dangers of nuclear weapons and their impact on security, broadly conceived. Anti-nuclear campaigns like the baby tooth survey, designed to bring about a halt to nuclear testing, put forward broad concepts of security.

Arguments put forward by the Voice of Women invoked familial connections, environmental concerns, and Cold War anxieties to make the case against continued nuclear testing. Often, members appealed to their societal role as wives and mothers, even using it as justification for their political participation. Some of the group's efforts, like the fallout brief, highlighted the long-term damage to the planet, to agricultural production, and to food and water supplies. Other lines of argumentation probed the complex relationship between nuclear weapons and the Cold War struggle between East and West. At once, the Voice of Women's arguments against nuclear testing responded to the deterioration of relations between the superpowers and illustrated how nuclear questions mattered beyond the binary strictures of East-West competition. Taken together, these arguments all belied a complex and multifaceted understanding of security and how it might be conceptualized in the atomic age.

The basic point here is a simple one, returning to this collection's emphasis on women and the search for global order. No shortage of individuals weighed in on questions of international affairs and security. Members of the Voice of Women did not shy away from participating in these debates, though their status as women did shape the terms of their engagement and inform the arguments they put forward. Centring the circulation of ideas, such as the surge of opposition to nuclear testing in the late 1950s and early 1960s, illustrates how conversations about international security criss-crossed the public and private sectors, as grassroots activists, concerned citizens, and policy-makers debated the same issues.

Acknowledgments

I would like to thank Stacey Barker, Jill Campbell-Miller, Greg Donaghy, and Simon Miles for their comments on earlier drafts, as well as the anonymous reviewers for their suggestions and recommendations.

Notes

1 As of 2021, the Voice of Women remains an active peace organization.
2 Tarah Brookfield, *Cold War Comforts: Canadian Women, Child Safety, and Global Insecurity* (Waterloo, ON: Wilfrid Laurier Press, 2012); Frances Early, "'A Grandly Subversive Time': The Halifax Branch of the Voice of Women in the 1960s," in *Mothers of the Municipality: Women, Work, and Social Policy in Post–1945 Halifax*, ed. Judith Fingard and Janet Guildford (Toronto: University of Toronto Press, 2005), 253–80; Frances Early, "Re-imaging War: The Voice of Women, the Canadian Aid for Vietnam Civilians, and the Knitting Project for Vietnamese Children, 1966–1976," *Peace and Change* 34, 2 (April 2009): 148–63; Frances Early, "Canadian Women and the International Arena in the 1960s: The Voice of Women/ La voix des femmes and the Opposition to the Vietnam War," in *The Sixties: Passion, Politics, and Style*, ed. Dimitry Anastakis (Montreal/Kingston: McGill-Queen's University Press, 2014), 25–41; Marie Hammond-Callaghan, "Bridging and Breaching Cold War Divides: Transnational Peace Building, State Surveillance, and the Voice of Women," in *Worth Fighting For: Canada's Tradition of War Resistance from 1812 to the War on Terror*, ed. Lara Campbell, Michael Dawson, and Catherine Gidney (Toronto: Between the Lines, 2015), 135–45; Braden Hutchinson, "Fighting the War at Home: Voice of Women and War Toy Activism in Postwar Canada," in *Worth Fighting For*, 147–58; Nicole Marion, "Canada's Disarmers: The Complicated Struggle against Nuclear Weapons, 1959–1963" (PhD diss., Carleton University, 2017). Beyond this literature on particular campaigns, much of the scholarship on the early work of the Voice of Women focuses on the organization's place in women's movements, both traditional forms of peace activism and various waves of feminism: Christine Ball, "The History of the Voice of Women/La Voix des Femmes: The Early Years, 1960–1963" (PhD diss., University of Toronto, 1994); Candace Loewen, "Making Ourselves Heard: 'Voice of Women' and the Peace Movement in the Early Sixties," in *Framing Our Past: Canadian*

Women's History in the Twentieth Century, ed. Sharon Anne Cook, Lorna R. McLean, and Kate O'Rourke (Montreal: McGill-Queen's University Press, 2001), 248–51.
3 Brookfield, *Cold War Comforts*, 5–8.
4 Catherine Carstairs, "Food, Fear, and the Environment in the Long Sixties," in *Debating Dissent: Canada and the Sixties*, ed. Lara Campbell, Dominique Clément, and Gregory S. Kealey (Toronto: University of Toronto Press, 2012), 29–46; Michael Egan, *Barry Commoner and the Science of Survival: The Remaking of American Environmentalism* (Cambridge, MA: MIT Press, 2007); Petra Goedde, *The Politics of Peace: A Global Cold War History* (Oxford: Oxford University Press, 2019).
5 This understanding of peace activism as part of a larger debate about security draws on a rich existing scholarship about peace activism during the Cold War. See, for some examples, Holger Nehring, *Politics of Security: British and West German Protest Movements and the Early Cold War, 1945–1970* (Oxford: Oxford University Press, 2013); Holger Nehring, "The Last Battle of the Cold War: Peace Movements and German Politics in the 1980s," in *The Euromissile Crisis and the End of the Cold War*, ed. Leopoldo Nuti, Frédéric Bozo, Marie-Pierre Rey, and Bernd Rother (Washington, DC: Woodrow Wilson Center Press; Stanford, CA: Stanford University Press, 2015), 309–12.
6 The Atomic Energy Commission was the US government agency responsible for the peacetime development of atomic technology, established as part of the McMahon Act (1946) which transferred control of the nation's atomic weapons program from the military to civilian institutions.
7 See the Cook and McLean chapter in this volume for one episode from the Women's International League for Peace and Freedom's earlier activism.
8 Goedde, *Politics of Peace*, 77–81.
9 Bryan Palmer, *Canada's 1960s: The Ironies of Identity in a Rebellious Era* (Toronto: University of Toronto Press, 2009), 256–57.
10 Patricia I. McMahon, *Essence of Indecision: Diefenbaker's Nuclear Policy, 1957–1963* (Montreal/Kingston: McGill-Queen's University Press, 2014), 32–33.
11 Nikita Sergeevich Khrushchev, *Memoirs of Nikita Khrushchev*, ed. Sergei Khrushchev, trans. George Shriver and Stephen Shenfield, vol. 3, *Statesman (1953–1964)* (University Park: Pennsylvania State University Press, 2007), 236.
12 On the U-2 affair and the breakdown of the Paris Summit, see William I. Hitchcock, *The Age of Eisenhower: America and the World in the 1950s* (New York: Simon and Schuster, 2018), 456–74.
13 Lotta Dempsey, "Private Line," *Toronto Daily Star*, May 21, 1960, 62.
14 Josephine Davis, "Letter from the Editor," *Voice of Women*, February 1, 1961, 2.
15 Lotta Dempsey, "The Leaders Listened!," *Toronto Daily Star*, June 16, 1960, 62.
16 Helen Tucker, "Letter from the President of V.O.W. Why 'Voice of Women'?," *Voice of Women*, 1960, 1.
17 "An Open Letter from Voice of Women (Canada)," *Voice of Women*, March 25, 1962, 13.
18 Christine Ball, "Towards a Feminine Perspective on Peace," *Peace Research* 23, 4 (November 1991): 60. Candace Loewen has identified a similar trend in letters to Lester Pearson regarding nuclear issues. For examples, see Candace Loewen, "Mike Hears Voices: Voice of Women and Lester Pearson, 1960–1963," *Atlantis* 12, 2 (1987): 25–26.
19 "Voice of Women: Group Formed to Reinforce Fighters against Nuclear Weapons," *Globe and Mail*, July 29, 1960, 5.
20 Josephine Davis, letter to the editor, "Voice of Women," *Globe and Mail*, March 27, 1962, 6.
21 "Metro Toronto Newsletter – August 1963," University of Toronto and Records Management Services (UTARMS), B1996–0004/041(08).

22 Kay Macpherson and Meg Sears, "The Voice of Women: A History," in *Women in the Canadian Mosaic*, ed. Gwen Matheson (Toronto: Peter Martin Associates, 1976), 72. See, for some examples of this coverage, "Voice of Women: Group Formed to Reinforce Fighters against Nuclear Weapons," *Globe and Mail*, July 29, 1960, 5; Walter Gray, "Blame Sickness ... Political Position Four Senators Withdraw Sponsorship from the Voice of Women Organization," *Globe and Mail*, September 26, 1961, 1.

23 On Maryon Pearson's relationship with the Voice of Women in the early 1960s, see Loewen, "Mike Hears Voices," 25, 28–29.

24 Macpherson and Sears, "The Voice of Women," 72.

25 *House of Commons Debates*, Twenty-Fourth Parliament, Second Session, Vol. II, February 20, 1959, 1223.

26 "Resolutions," *Voice of Women*, November 15, 1962, 20; "French-English Relations," *Voice of Women*, July 1963, 11.

27 Albert Schweitzer, "Peace or Atomic War?," *Voice of Women*, 1960, 5–6. Schweitzer's work was influential in building an international opposition to nuclear testing. His "Declaration of Conscience," broadcast in 1957, called for an end to nuclear testing.

28 Mrs. F.C. Davis, letter, "Voice of Women," *Globe and Mail*, October 20, 1961, 6.

29 "V.O.W. Action," *Voice of Women*, March 25, 1962, 9–11.

30 "Brief to the Prime Minister," *Voice of Women*, March 25, 1962, 10.

31 *Saturday Night* coverage reprinted in *Voice of Women*, March 25, 1962, 9. For a discussion of how motherhood shaped the activism pursued by the Voice of Women and how it was received, see Marion, "Canada's Disarmers," 58–69.

32 On Howard Green's attitudes toward nuclear weapons, see Eric Bergbusch and Michael D. Stevenson, "Howard Green, Public Opinion and the Politics of Disarmament," in *Architects and Innovators: Building the Department of Foreign Affairs and International Trade, 1909–2009*, ed. Greg Donaghy and Kim Richard Nossal (Montreal/Kingston: McGill-Queen's University Press, 2009), 191–206; Daniel Heidt, "'I Think That Would Be the End of Canada': Howard Green, the Nuclear Test Ban, and Interest-Based Foreign Policy, 1946–1963," *American Review of Canadian Studies* 42, 3 (September 2012): 343–69; Michael D. Stevenson, "Howard Green, Disarmament, and Canadian-American Defence Relations, 1959–1963," in *The Nuclear North: Histories of Canada in the Atomic Age*, ed. Susan Colbourn and Timothy Andrews Sayle (Vancouver: UBC Press, 2020), 67–87.

33 "Brief to the Prime Minister," *Voice of Women*.

34 Peter C. Newman, "Howard Green: A Friendly Peacemaker Toughens Up," *Maclean's*, October 7, 1961, 108.

35 "Memorandum from Prime Minister to Prime Minister of United Kingdom," April 24, 1962, Documents on Canadian External Relations, vol. 29, doc. 32.

36 The ten members were divided in half, five from the Atlantic Alliance and the other five from the Warsaw Pact. The Western member states were Canada, France, Italy, the United Kingdom, and the United States; Bulgaria, Czechoslovakia, Poland, Romania, and the Soviet Union represented the Warsaw Pact.

37 General E.L.M. Burns, remarks, "Toward the Cessation of Nuclear Tests," October 30, 1961, in *Canadian Foreign Policy 1955–1965: Selected Speeches and Documents*, ed. Arthur E. Blanchette (Toronto: McClelland and Stewart, 1977), 61–62.

38 George Ignatieff, *The Making of a Peacemonger: The Memoirs of George Ignatieff* (Toronto: University of Toronto Press, 1985), 190.

39 Walter Gray, "Women's Group Fails to Sway PM," *Globe and Mail*, March 8, 1962, 21.

40 Jean E. Mailing, letter to editor, "Voice of Women," *Globe and Mail*, March 12, 1962, 6.

41 Thérèse Casgrain became president of Voice of Women national in September 1962, and the national headquarters moved to Montreal during her tenure. Ghislaine Laurendeau was

married to André Laurendeau, the publisher of *Le Devoir* and cochair of the Royal Commission on Bilingualism and Biculturalism: Kay Macpherson, "Thérèse Casgrain: A Voice for Women," *Broadside* 3, 3 (December 1981/January 1982): 6, reprinted in *Inside Broadside: A Decade of Feminist Journalism*, ed. Philinda Masters (Toronto: Second Story Press, 2019).

42 "V.O.W. Action," *Voice of Women*, March 25, 1962, 12.
43 "V.O.W. at Geneva and in Vienna," *Voice of Women*, July 1, 1962, 2.
44 "Renew Nuclear Protest," *Globe and Mail*, July 26, 1962, 12.
45 "Eye-witness Report by Fran Hill, Our Ottawa Publicity Chairman," *Voice of Women*, December 15, 1962.
46 On the controversy over the Bomarc missiles, see McMahon, *Essence of Indecision*; Asa McKercher, *Camelot and Canada: Canadian-American Relations in the Kennedy Era* (Oxford: Oxford University Press, 2016), esp. Chapter 3; Michael Stevenson, "'Tossing a Match into Dry Hay': Nuclear Weapons and the Crisis in U.S.-Canadian Relations," *Journal of Cold War Studies* 16 (2014): 5–34; Isabel Campbell, "Pearson's Promises and the NATO Nuclear Dilemma," in *Mike's World: Lester B. Pearson and Canadian External Affairs*, ed. Asa McKercher and Galen Roger Perras (Vancouver: UBC Press, 2017), 275–96.
47 "Some Thinking – By a Committee of the VOW Board," *Voice of Women*, March 1963, 8 (emphasis in original).
48 "Some Questions for Candidates," *Voice of Women*, March 1963, 9.
49 "Report from VOW President, July 1, 1963," University of Toronto and Records Management Services (UTARMS), B1996–0004/041(08); "Message Sent to Mr. Pearson by Voice of Women, July 9th, 1963," *Voice of Women*, July 1963, 5; "Brief Presented to the Prime Minister – May 23, 1963," *Voice of Women*, July 1963, 9–11.
50 Franklin to Kessler [*sic*], UTARMS, March 19, 1963, B1996–0004/042(05); "New Program Launched: Teeth Collecting for Peace," *Globe and Mail*, March 15, 1963, 9.
51 "VOW Report: 12,000 Teeth Tested," *Globe and Mail*, June 1, 1964, 13.
52 Yvonne Logan, "The Story of the Baby Tooth Survey," *Scientist and Citizen* 6, 9–10 (September–October 1964): 38, copy of issue in UTARMS, B1996–0004/041(07).
53 Egan, *Barry Commoner*, 66–72; Goedde, *Politics of Peace*, 83–85.
54 Ethel Kesler to Ursula Franklin, February 11, 1963, UTARMS, B1996–0004/042(05).
55 "Action on the Home Front," *Voice of Women*, May 15, 1961, 72.
56 "From the Provinces," *Voice of Women*, October 15, 1961, 138.
57 Kesler to Franklin, February 11, 1963, UTARMS, B1996–0004/042(05).
58 "Tooth Collecting in Canada," n.d. [1965], UTARMS, B2015–0005/060(16).
59 "Will You Help the Tooth Survey?," pamphlet, n.d., UTARMS, B1996–0004/041(02).
60 "Will You Help the Tooth Survey?"
61 Handwritten notes, n.d., UTARMS, B1996–0004/041(01).
62 Laird to Turnbull, February 12, 1963, UTARMS, B1996–0004/042(05).
63 Handwritten notes, n.d., UTARMS.
64 Wright memorandum, "Memo to VoW Provincial Executive Members and Regina VoW Executive, Meeting in Regina Wednesday, December 19, 1962," UTARMS, B1996–0004/042(05).
65 Barbara Moon, "What We Can Do about Fallout," *Maclean's*, May 4, 1963, 11.
66 "Standing Committee Reports," *Voice of Women*, July 1963, 16.
67 "Fallout Monitoring in Canada: Brief to the Minister of National Health and Welfare, Ottawa," 1963, UTARMS, B1996–0004/041(08).
68 For a public presentation of this data, see chart printed in Moon, "What Can We Do about Fallout," 13.
69 "Fallout Monitoring in Canada: Brief to the Minister of National Health and Welfare, Ottawa," 1963, UTARMS, B1996–0004/041(08).

70 Macpherson and Franklin to LaMarsh, enclosure, June 24, 1963, UTARMS, B1996–0004/042(02).
71 Meg Sears, "VOW Presents Fallout Brief," *Voice of Women*, November 1963, 4.
72 "Letter to All Council Members and Regional Chairmen," July 29, 1963, UTARMS, B1996–0004/041(08).
73 "Letter to All Council Members and Regional Chairmen," July 29, 1963.
74 Sears, "VOW Presents Fallout Brief."
75 William MacEachern, "Deliberate Concealment of Fallout Facts Charged," *Toronto Daily Star*, July 23, 1963, 19; William MacEachern, "Strontium in Our Milk Hits Record," *Toronto Daily Star*, August 12, 1963, 1.
76 C.K. Johns to Ursula Bell, November 19, 1963, UTARMS, B1996–0004/042(06).
77 "Teeth Check for Fallout Questioned," *Globe and Mail*, December 4, 1963, 9; "VOW Defends Project Assailed by LaMarsh," *Globe and Mail*, December 5, 1963, 14.
78 Sears, "VOW Presents Fallout Brief," 5.
79 "Fallout Monitoring in Canada: Brief to the Minister of National Health and Welfare, Ottawa."
80 "Metro Toronto Newsletter – August 1963."
81 Ursula Franklin to Kathleen Dawson, June 22, 1966, UTARMS, B1996–0004/041(08).
82 "Strontium-90 Fallout: No Harm to Teeth," *Telegram*, September 1, 1965, clipping, UTARMS, B1996–0004/041(03). See also C.K. Hunt to Ursula Franklin, enclosure, April 9, 1965, UTARMS, B1996–0004/041(10).
83 "Professor Discounts Strontium 90 Scare," clipping, UTARMS, B1996–0004/041(03).

6

Marie Smallface-Marule
An Indigenous Internationalist

Jonathan Crossen

THERE ARE SEVERAL HISTORICAL examples of Indigenous peoples travelling overseas to assert their rights to their land, resources, and ways of living in the face of internal colonialism by the Canadian government. Some of the earliest examples involved Indigenous petitioners seeking audiences with British royalty.[1] A shift in audience occurred nearly as soon as an opportunity appeared; in the early 1920s, Haudenosaunee hereditary leader Deskaheh Levi General travelled to Europe, hoping to convince the newly established League of Nations to support his people's right to sovereignty.[2]

The active participation of Indigenous peoples – independent of the Canadian government at the international level – exploded after the 1982 establishment of the Working Group on Indigenous Populations by the United Nation's Economic and Social Council. Asbjørn Eide, the chair of the Working Group, took the innovative step of allowing any Indigenous representatives to attend the meetings. With help from a Voluntary Fund for Indigenous Populations (established by the UN General Assembly in 1985), sessions of the working group grew to include as many as a thousand participants.[3] That Indigenous peoples were thus able to participate in the drafting of the UN Declaration on the Rights of Indigenous Peoples gave the document increased validity in their eyes. Perhaps more importantly, it served as a demonstration that they had the right to shape their own future and define their own space.

The large-scale participation of Indigenous actors in the creation of a major UN instrument has led to significant (if still insufficient) scholarly attention to recent contributions of Indigenous peoples in international forums, as well as to Indigenous-run international organizations.[4] What has received less attention, however, is the reverse relationship: the impact of that international activity on individual Indigenous people. This chapter will investigate the effect that internationalism had on one early Indigenous internationalist, Marie Smallface-Marule. Her varied personal and professional experiences highlight how she gained a global perspective, informed particularly by pan-African liberation movements, and used it as an effective strategy to advance Indigenous sovereignty and cultural resurgence within Canada's borders and elsewhere. Whether working within local or international contexts, she viewed decolonization as a means to forge links between Indigenous and oppressed peoples all over the world. She also understood that this bond, used effectively, could create substantial political power.

Charting Smallface-Marule's life and activities emphasizes the importance of biography in understanding the effects of internationalism. Observing the ways her activism was a response to both ongoing colonialism and decolonization subverts the state-centred, geographically bounded paradigm of Canadian history and raises the story of Smallface-Marule's life specifically – and Indigenous activism more generally – to a more complex global level of analysis, befitting the platform on which they operated.

"They Treated Me like a Foreign Student"

Marie Smallface was born to Emil and Olive Smallface in the spring of 1944. She was raised as a member of the Káínai (Kainai Nation or Blood Tribe) and given the name Isstoikamo'saakii, meaning "Winter Thief Woman."[5] She spent her childhood on the Káínai reserve, located between the towns of Cardston and Lethbridge, Alberta. Despite the proximity to these communities, the Káínai reserve is the largest section of Indigenous reserve land allotted by the Canadian government, and one of the most populous.

It is possible that Marie Smallface's internationalism began at birth. The Niitsitapi, sometimes called the Blackfoot Confederacy, is a collective name for a number of allied nations, including the Káínai (into which Smallface was born), Siksiká, and the Piikáni. While not commonly described as such, the Niitsitapi might therefore be considered an international or multinational community. Moreover, the imposition of the United States/Canada border formally divided Niitsitapi territories between two countries. Nevertheless, historian Sheila McManus insists that the Niitsitapi were not "passive bystanders" to this division but "used the border for their own purposes, ignoring it when they chose and exploiting its new meanings when necessary."[6] Thus, the Niitsitapi could accurately be described as a transnational community as well as an international one.

Marie Smallface received her early education at a Christian school in nearby Cardston, allowing her to avoid enrolment in a residential school. Frustrated by the racism she encountered there, she convinced her parents to send her to Edmonton to attend high school in Jasper Place.[7] There again, she was struck by the racist attitudes she encountered, not only hostility but also paternalism. She received invitations to speak at "schools and ladies clubs" but felt they were using her as a "token Indian."[8]

As a child, her father encouraged her to fight for Indigenous rights, and she took up that fight from a young age. She became involved in local politics on the Káínai reserve and joined the Indian Association of Alberta at age eighteen.[9] Her father further encouraged her to see education as a means to that end. She later asserted that people "have to inform and empower themselves to facilitate real community development."[10] With that goal in mind, Marie Smallface enrolled in the Department of Sociology and Anthropology at the University of Alberta, between 1962 and 1966.[11]

Smallface's formal introduction to internationalism seems to have begun just before she began university. Beyond the transnational links of the Niitsitapi, she had gained knowledge of the international system when she was one of 160 teenagers sponsored to attend the tenth annual UN Summer School at the Banff School of Fine Arts. The week-long seminar offered students a critical review of the United Nations and its functions and included Canadian diplomats like William Hickson Barton among the speakers. After the seminar, she commented that she now realized "how important the UN is. It always seemed a dream that there were people actually interested in and working for the welfare of the world."[12] Although her words at the time make Smallface seem somewhat dewy-eyed, they nevertheless suggest an early interest in international cooperation.

During her first year at the University of Alberta, Smallface intended to find a career as a social worker, and she covered her university expenses by working at the Charles Camsell Indian Hospital, in Edmonton.[13] While at the University of Alberta, she expanded her participation in Indigenous politics through the National Indian Council (the first well-organized national organization for Indigenous peoples in Canada), attending its July 1964 assembly at Garden River First Nation, near Sault Ste. Marie.[14] She also became involved with the Canadian Indian Youth Council, established in 1965, and formed a friendship with Harold Cardinal, who would soon become a noted Cree political leader.[15] She was also active at the local Canadian Native Friendship Centre in Edmonton and with the Indian Association of Alberta.[16] In January 1966, she attended a two-day conference "on the Canadian Indian" at Trinity College in Toronto.[17] The following May, she joined another panel at the first Alberta Youth Seminar and used the opportunity to call for educational reform, arguing that "our teachers do not know anything of us, our language, culture or religion." She lamented that Indigenous peoples were capable of making intellectual contributions to society but, all too often, they had been convinced that they had nothing to offer. She presciently declared that soon, "Indians will take an active part in Canadian Society and will contribute."[18]

Smallface was the first person from the Káínai to attend the University of Alberta and one of the first Indigenous women to complete a Bachelor of Arts there, but she found that continual reminders of this achievement were tinged with racism. When portrayed as a trailblazer, she could "appreciate the sentiment but not the prejudice behind it. To put it in the context of my race was irritating."[19] On the contrary, the constant emphasis on her role as vanguard at the university only highlighted both the system that made her presence such a rarity and her feelings of isolation on campus.

This sense of separation from the main student body partly encouraged her to expand her social circle beyond Canadian students: "They treated me like a foreign student or they didn't pay any attention to me at all ... That's why I had an affinity for African people."[20] Smallface joined a social group called Club International with members from the wide array of international students at the University of Alberta. Although she associated with people involved in the radical politics of the era, like members of Students for a Democratic Society, Club International became more important to her personally. She eventually served for a year as vice-president.

Club International organized a variety of events and gave Canadian students the opportunity to meet other students from around the world. For Smallface, the organization facilitated friendships with a number of African graduate students who shared her outsider status on campus. Through them, she also became increasingly interested in the politics of imperialism and decolonization. Historical domination, political marginalization, and a desire to regain self-determination linked her experiences as a Káínai person in Canada with what her friends were recounting about Africa and its history.

"The Indian Experience in Canada as Colonial"

Noting Smallface's interest in these topics and her connection with African students, the University of Alberta's dean of women, Mary Saretta Sparling, suggested that she join Canadian University Service Overseas (CUSO) to do work in Africa.[21] Smallface began her first two-year term with CUSO in 1966, working at a girls' camp near Lake Tanganyika in Zambia's Northern Province. Later, she agreed to serve a second term in the county's capital, Lusaka.[22] There, she worked as a senior community officer, working with an official from India tasked with evaluating the government's United Nations Educational, Scientific and Cultural Organization (UNESCO)–sponsored adult literacy program and contributing to a pilot project on literacy radio broadcasts.[23]

As well as noting the "invaluable, intense education" she was receiving as part of her CUSO volunteer work, Smallface also felt a sort of freedom in Zambia that she had not felt back in Edmonton: "At university I was cast as an Indian spokesman. In Zambia my being an Indian is irrelevant." In an international context, the shackles of racism and prejudice were significantly weaker. Interviewed at the time, she expressed a desire to return home and work for the Canadian government's Department of Indian Affairs and to use her "African experience to help bring Canada out of its racial dark ages."[24]

Beyond the work experience with CUSO, Smallface's time living and socializing in Lusaka deeply influenced her perspective. When Zambia gained independence in 1964, it shared borders with some of Africa's few remaining colonial and apartheid strongholds: Angola, Rhodesia, Mozambique, and South West Africa. Zambia's first president, Kenneth Kaunda, adopted a philosophy of African Socialism which resembled that of Julius Nyerere, in Tanzania, Zambia's northeastern neighbour. Kaunda maintained an outward-looking policy that supported decolonization and African liberation. He not only allowed a variety of anti-colonial organizations to establish their headquarters out of Zambia but even helped create a "liberation center" for their work in the capital.[25] Zambia became a prominent member of the international anti-colonial Non-Aligned Movement, hosting the organization's third conference in 1970, at which Kaunda was elected its chairperson.[26] Thus, when Smallface was living in Lusaka, the city's population (and particularly the expatriate community) was enthusiastic about decolonization and Third-Worldist solidarity between newly independent states. While

Zambia was no global superpower, its support for African liberation movements provided a clear demonstration of the ability and responsibility of those with some degree of power and independence to aid those with less.

While abroad, Smallface travelled to Tanzania and became particularly intrigued by Nyerere's ideas of African Socialism. She was impressed that Nyerere believed one "couldn't bring in Marxism to such nations of people, that you had to base their development on their own language, their own culture, their own heritage." In Nyerere's vision of pan-Africanism, she saw the hope that Indigenous culture, language, and history could serve as a source of strength, to build "from the communities upwards" rather than imposing foreign political philosophies from above. Furthermore, she believed that Indigenous traditions of cooperation and solidarity could serve as a basis for unity when organizing Indigenous peoples.[27] These revelations would serve as a spark to help ignite the movement of Indigenous internationalism.

Smallface's experiences in Zambia surely helped reinforce her understanding of the potential benefits (and, indeed, obligations) of international cooperation. She would return home with this strategy in mind, as well as a renewed vision for the decolonization of Canada based on Indigenous culture, language, and tradition. She would later recall, "By observing the African colonial experience, I understood the Indian experience in Canada as colonial. I also saw the structures of Imperialism, neo-colonialism and the limitations of 'paper' independence."[28]

Before she left Zambia, Smallface married Jacob Marule, a South African exile educated in Sweden, and became Marie Smallface-Marule.[29] Marule was an active member of South Africa's African National Congress (although, for her own safety, he did not tell his wife details of his work), and their marriage helped ensure her continued connection to African decolonization.[30]

National Indian Brotherhood and the "Fourth World"

After her second CUSO term ended, Smallface-Marule returned to Canada in the fall of 1970, seeking employment in Ottawa since her husband became a student at the nearby Kemptville College. Through a recommendation from her old friend Harold Cardinal, she met George Manuel, a Secwepemc man who had recently been elected to lead the National Indian Brotherhood (NIB), a lobbying group for Indigenous people included in

Canada's Indian Register. In January 1971, Manuel agreed to hire Smallface-Marule to the body's small staff in Ottawa. As she later recalled with amusement, Manuel "didn't have much in the way of funds at the time so he asked if I would accept a job as his secretary." She agreed on the condition that Manuel accept that she "didn't type and take dictation." Within a few months, the NIB had sufficient additional funding to make Smallface-Marule the organization's executive director.[31]

The position afforded her substantial influence on Indigenous politics and relations with the Canadian state. Among other efforts, she lent her knowledge to the fight against gender discrimination in Canada's Indian Act. At that time, Canadian law required the deregistration of any Status Indian who married someone who did not have Indian Status. For Marie, the struggle for equality was surely a matter of principles, but it was also personal. When members of her band council attempted to remove her from their list for having married Jacob Marule, she replied, "Well, how do you know I'm married?" She had consciously left all the marriage documents behind in Zambia.[32] Cree activist Kathleen Steinhauer, who helped lead efforts to amend the Indian Act, asked for support from her friend at the NIB. Smallface-Marule aided these efforts, travelling to Edmonton to meet with women interested in the problem. With her assistance, they organized as the Ad Hoc Committee on Indian Women's Rights. "If it hadn't been for her, we wouldn't have known how to proceed," recounts Steinhauer, "Marie wrote out a business plan: what to do, when to do it, and who to contact."[33]

The impact of Smallface-Marule's time abroad was immediately apparent in the public statements she made in her new position. She compared Indian reserves to Third World countries but without the control over resources held by African states. Like Africans, young Indigenous children were forced by the Canadian government to attend "a foreign education system, based on alien cultural values."[34] In a series of public talks in 1971, she suggested that Canadian government policies in the Northwest Territories were similar to those found in South Africa and Rhodesia.[35] Smallface-Marule would later recall that, at the time, applying the logic of decolonization to the Indigenous situation in North America was "considered really radical" and that "many of the older Indian statesmen and politicians of the day ... were quite wary of me because they thought I was quite radical [and] worried I was a communist."[36]

Nevertheless, the NIB needed her solid academic skills, and she quickly became friends with Manuel. Before long, he would describe her as "the backbone of the NIB"[37] and his "closest political colleague."[38] Smallface-Marule's interest in African decolonization soon began to influence her boss and, therefore, the direction of the National Indian Brotherhood. In July 1971, just six months after hiring her, George Manuel made reference to African demands for Uhuru (freedom) in his report to the NIB General Assembly.[39] That year, Smallface-Marule facilitated two types of encounters for George Manuel that shifted his perspective toward Indigenous internationalism. First, she helped convince him to attend a government-sponsored trip to Australia and Aotearoa (New Zealand). Manuel had been wary of travelling alongside the then-Minister of Indian Affairs and Northern Development, Jean Chrétien, who had submitted the highly controversial white paper, "Statement of the Government of Canada on Indian Policy," just a couple years earlier.[40] Smallface-Marule and other NIB staff "made it a condition of his participation that he could bear off on his own excursions," which allowed him to make contact with Indigenous leaders abroad. Through these travels, Manuel first noted the strong similarities in circumstances of these diverse peoples, because of their historic and ongoing experience with British colonialism. "Just as much as the Maoris and the Aborigines," he reported, "the Indian people in Canada are dark people in a White Commonwealth."[41]

Second, George Manuel attended a number of Saturday night parties at the home of Smallface-Marule, parties which included a variety of guests from the Third World, including students and diplomatic staff.[42] Such meetings must have supported his rapidly growing interest in the then-blossoming Third-Worldist movement, but Manuel became truly convinced during a trip to Tanzania (organized by Smallface-Marule) toward the end of 1971.[43] While there, he was treated as a VIP and met Julius Nyerere in person.[44] Thereafter, Smallface-Marule and Manuel both shared this first-hand experience in Tanzania and her deep respect for Nyerere's political philosophy. According to Smallface-Marule, "Nyerere's African socialist thoughts were something I held very dearly and George became very interested in that as well."[45] And later, it was a friend of the Marules who would suggest an appropriate way to frame the links of solidarity between Indigenous peoples around the world; Mbuto Milando, executive secretary of the Tanzanian High Commission, asserted that if Indigenous peoples were establishing something like the Third-Worldist movement but distinct, they might best be described as the "Fourth World."[46] Both of these encounters – with other Indigenous peoples and with the Third-Worldist movement – were made possible by Smallface-Marule. It is no surprise, therefore, that in the acknowledgments to his Indigenous political manifesto, Manuel specifically credited her as "the first person to be able to show me, from direct and personal experience, the close relationship and common bonds between our own condition as Indian people, and the struggles of other aboriginal peoples and the nations of the Third World."[47] Her global, anti-colonial perspective had won over the head of the National Indian brotherhood and would soon lead to an entirely new form of internationalism.

The World Council of Indigenous Peoples

Marie Smallface-Marule's contributions to Indigenous internationalism did not, however, end with the inspiration of George Manuel. As executive director of the NIB, she was instrumental in bringing the World Council of Indigenous Peoples into being. Later, as executive director of the World Council of Indigenous Peoples, Smallface-Marule was, in many ways, the primary force behind the organization in its early years.[48]

Following the 1972 United Nations Conference on the Human Environment in Stockholm, Manuel visited the Sámi community in Rensjön, where he agreed to plan an international conference of Indigenous peoples.[49] Much of the organizing work fell to Smallface-Marule. She contacted her friend Robert Moore, the Guyanese high commissioner to Canada, and investigated the possibility of organizing a preparatory meeting for the conference in Georgetown, Guyana.[50] The country's prime minister, Forbes Burnham, had made efforts to link Guyana with the Non-Aligned Movement and hosted the first Conference of Foreign Ministers of Non-Aligned Countries in 1972. Between her contacts in the embassy and the country's Third-Worldist politics, Smallface-Marule felt Guyana was a good candidate to host, so she travelled to Georgetown to formally secure support. The Non-Aligned meeting in 1972 had been held in the Umana Yana, a large version of a traditional Indigenous Wai-Wai thatched hut built specifically for the gathering. The Guyanese government had mobilized the country's Indigenous population as a symbol of an anti-colonial philosophy.[51] After three weeks in Guyana and with the support of Shridath Ramphal (soon to be secretary-general of the Commonwealth of Nations), Smallface-Marule arranged for the first preparatory meeting of the World Conference of Indigenous Peoples to be held in the same building.[52] Its symbolism of anti-colonialism would now be used by Indigenous peoples themselves.

On the same trip, Marie Smallface-Marule travelled to Colombia and Ecuador seeking out Indigenous representatives for the meeting and successfully planned for the attendance of Guambiano leader Trino Morales of Colombia. Her contacts at CUSO again came in handy for networking in Central America.[53]

She attended the first preparatory meeting, in April 1974, and owing to the presence of participants from all four corners of the world, it might be called the first truly global meeting of Indigenous peoples. At the second preparatory meeting, in Copenhagen in May 1974, she suggested the name for a proposed permanent organization, following the style of the World Council of Churches: the World Council of Indigenous Peoples (WCIP).[54] That October, the planned conference welcomed Indigenous guests on the Tseshaht reservation near the town of Port Alberni, British Columbia. Delegates from nineteen different countries and four different continents agreed to establish the WCIP as a formal international organization, with George Manuel as its first president.[55]

When the WCIP was founded, Smallface-Marule was not given any formal role in the new organization. Instead, she left Ottawa early the next year to take a position at the University of Lethbridge.[56] Leroy Little Bear, also from the Káínai people, had invited her to join the university's brand new Native American Studies department, the first of its kind in Canada.[57] By the fall of 1976, however, Manuel was negotiating for the establishment of a WCIP secretariat in Lethbridge under Smallface-Marule's control.[58] In March 1977, the university agreed to allow her to use her academic department as the World Council's offices. At the organization's general assembly in August, delegates opted to eliminate the elected role of secretary-general created at the first meeting and replace it with an unelected chief administrative officer. Marie Smallface-Marule agreed to accept the position in addition to her academic work.[59] Formally, the organization continued to be led by its president, George Manuel, and an elected executive council, but on a day-to-day basis, Smallface-Marule was largely in control.

The secretariat's de facto responsibility for the majority of the World Council's activities was a "somewhat unusual departure" from standard organizational hierarchy, where the elected executive board directs the work of the secretariat.[60] Although unofficial, the structure was effective for the situation. Some matters needed immediate decisions, but the lack of resources made it impossible to stage meetings for the "globally-scattered Executive Council members" on short notice.[61] Thus, Marie Smallface-Marule regularly made significant decisions for the World Council independently, and her importance to the organization in its first decade can hardly be overstated.

Smallface-Marule's stated vision for the WCIP included fostering of mutual self-reliance of Indigenous peoples, but also reaching out to the broader international community for assistance. She hoped the World Council would not only unify Indigenous peoples under a single banner, increasing their strength, but also help Indigenous peoples to learn from each other about different strategies to overcoming similar problems. At the same time, she expected the WCIP would "establish a permanent presence in the United Nations."[62] She believed that a strong position within UN would increase international attention on the primary demands and challenges of Indigenous peoples: their control and protection of lands and resources; their political self-determination; and their cultural and physical survival as peoples.[63] Moreover, a presence at the UN would "give international recourse" when Indigenous peoples failed to find agreement with individual states.[64] This mixture of self-reliance with global solidarity, and the importance placed on the international arena, was undoubtedly connected with Smallface-Marule's understanding of decolonization and internationalism. While recognizing the power of international law to help, she also saw its limitations. "International law is colonial," she argued. "It needs revisions to protect the lands and culture of native people; revisions formulated by the people themselves."[65] The World Council, she hoped, would aim not only to ensure that existing international rights standards were enforced, but also to develop new international standards that served the needs of Indigenous peoples.[66]

During her time at the WCIP, Smallface-Marule was incredibly busy. In just her first two years with the organization, beyond coordinating the WCIP meetings and second general assembly, she was invited to attend the NIB general assembly, the National Congress of American Indians general assembly, the North American Treaty Rights Organization conference, and a preparatory meeting of the Canadian Commission to the UNESCO Conference on Racism and Racial Discrimination. She was also invited to deliver talks at the assembly of the Native Women's Association of Canada, at the University of Manitoba, and at the general assembly of the Union of British Columbia Indian Chiefs.[67]

In her role as chief administrative officer, Marie Smallface-Marule was keen to support Indigenous groups, particularly in Central and South America where they often lacked both political rights and the financial means to organize effectively. In March 1978, she succeeded in securing some funding for a national Indigenous organization in Nicaragua.[68] With her assistance, the World Council quickly helped establish regional branch organizations in Central America (Consejo Regional de Pueblos Indígenas de Centroamérica, México y Panamá, CORPI, in 1977) and South America (Consejo Indio de Sudamérica, CISA, in 1980), both of which grew to have significant political influence of their own. Kolla leader and former CISA president Asunción Ontiveros Yulquila described Smallface-Marule as "the intellectual author of the regional councils of the WCIP."[69] At the very least, it was her work that secured funding for Mapuche leader Nilo Cayuqueo to travel through South America to promote the founding conference of CISA.[70]

In the early 1980s, the WCIP was asked to assist with the efforts to oppose Pierre Trudeau's plan to patriate the Canadian constitution without Indigenous consent.[71] George Manuel, leading the Union of British Columbia Indian Chiefs, organized the "Constitution Express": two chartered trains travelling from Canada's west coast to the capital in Ottawa in order to ensure that Indigenous rights were not threatened by the proposed constitution. Marie Smallface-Marule attempted to reframe allegedly "domestic" Indigenous matters as issues of international law tied to a global history of (de)colonization. Manuel and Smallface-Marule agreed, for instance, that after Ottawa, efforts should continue at the United Nations and in particular, its Special Committee on Decolonization.[72] The WCIP Secretariat assisted by coordinating "extensive lobbying" at the UN.[73]

A report on the topic produced by the WCIP and edited by Smallface-Marule described patriation as "the final stage of colonial imperialism" and made comparisons with other British and French colonies around the world. The report emphasized Indigenous rights to self-determination on the basis of international instruments including Chapters 11 and 12 of the UN Charter (regarding Non-Self-Governing and Trust Territories), and the International Covenant on Economic, Social and Cultural Rights. Given Canada's mistreatment of Indigenous peoples, the report suggested, their administration (held in trust by the Canadian government) should be transferred back to the United Kingdom. It further demanded that following internationally supervised negotiations between Canadian, British, and Indigenous leadership, the United Kingdom and Indigenous peoples should "establish a United Nations authority to oversee a British-First Nations trusteeship."[74] Thus, while Trudeau was arguing for *domestic* control over Canada, Smallface-Marule was helping to argue the exact opposite – increased (albeit temporary) *international* oversight from the United Nations over the administration of Indigenous peoples.

"Solidarity with Oppressed People and Their Struggles for Political and Economic Liberation"

At first, much of Smallface-Marule's time with the WCIP was spent securing funding simply to keep the organization afloat. When she took control, the World Council was at risk of bankruptcy.[75] Initially, it was religious groups that provided funds to keep the WCIP going. In 1977, the Anglican Church of Canada's Primate's World Relief and Development Fund and the Canadian Catholic Organization for Development and Peace covered some operating costs.[76] While appreciated, these limited resources were not enough to maintain the growing organization. In order to obtain increased and more consistent funding, Smallface-Marule would again reach beyond Canada's borders.

In 1978, she travelled to Europe and worked with Ole Henrik Magga of the Nordic Saami Council (a WCIP member organization) to apply for additional funds from Nordic governments.[77] Norway's deputy minister of foreign affairs promised substantial core funding for one year, giving the organization some temporary stability. Norway even assured renewed support on the condition that the Canadian government also agreed to provide funding.[78] This was a substantial obstacle to overcome, since Canada had been hesitant to fully support the organization, but the Norwegian funding acted as a powerful tool. The WCIP ultimately gained traction by playing one country off the other.

The World Council leaned on Flora MacDonald, Canada's new secretary of state for external affairs, who is profiled by former Prime Minister Joe Clark in Chapter 9. MacDonald had built up a good relationship with George Manuel while serving as the opposition critic for Indian Affairs. In 1979, MacDonald wrote a strong letter to the Canadian International Development Agency (CIDA), questioning why the WCIP was receiving funding from Scandinavia but not from the Canadian government.[79] CIDA quickly dispatched the head of its International Non-Governmental Organization division to Lethbridge to collaborate with Smallface-Marule in devising a plan of financial support. The agreement was settled early in 1980.[80] Smallface-Marule and the World Council had used the organization's international network (arguably, its greatest strength) to secure the support of one country, then successfully leveraged that support against another country. Indigenous international cooperation not only established the WCIP, its clever use also ensured the organization's financial survival for the time being.

CIDA continued to fund the World Council until the mid-1990s, but the WCIP's relationship with its funder was not without its challenges. The agency's primary goal was economic development, and this sometimes created tension with the WCIP, an organization focused on political solutions. Smallface-Marule saw economic development as deeply interconnected with political empowerment and resented any efforts to separate them. In Zambia, she had seen that economic aid often came with the price of relinquishing authority over political decisions.[81] She appears to have felt that such a trade-off was not only unfair but ultimately ineffective. In an application for CIDA funding, she expressed support for North-South solidarity. But her submission also referenced *Perpetuating Poverty* – a book deeply critical of CIDA, the Bretton Woods institutions, and international development programs generally – to support her assertion that the purpose of aid should be to secure not only basic needs, but also basic rights. Smallface-Marule quoted directly from the book to emphasize that "authentic development is always a political process as much as an economic and social one" and expressed the hope that Canadian aid policies would be guided by "solidarity with oppressed people and their struggles for political and economic liberation."[82] For Smallface-Marule, decolonization required constant vigilance against colonial attitudes that might restrict self-determination for Indigenous peoples around the world.

Indigenous Internationalism after the WCIP

Early in 1984, the WCIP opted to move its headquarters to Ottawa. Marie Smallface-Marule had been promoted to assistant professor at the University of Lethbridge the previous year, so she opted to stay there and give up her association with the World Council.[83] Although her international activism slowed, it certainly did not cease. Beginning in 1988, she collaborated with other scholars in Alberta to organize a National Symposium on Aboriginal Women in Canada (Past, Present, and Future) at the University of Lethbridge. The forum was intended to bring together "grassroots activists" with academic researchers to exchange ideas, highlight women's strengths, and to generate content for education.[84] Thus, Smallface-Marule continued to combine her Indigenous activism (and support for Indigenous women) with her academic position. While that conference was under way, she evidently had already begun to assist with the next logical step of promoting the perspective of Indigenous women internationally. Smallface-Marule was the lead coordinator for the Second International Indigenous Women's Conference, in Kárášjohka (Sápmi), Norway, from August 5 to 9, 1990. The planning committee included such prominent Indigenous activists from around the world as Maret Sara (Sámi Women's Association), Priscilla Settee (Native Women's Association of Canada), Winona LaDuke (Indigenous Women's Network), Dorothy Davey (Aboriginal Women's Working Party), and Victoria Tauli-Corpuz (Cordillera Women's Education Action Research Center).[85] One hundred delegates from twenty-two countries met under the theme "We Are Indispensable" and discussed a wide range of topics, from sustainable development to "the process of restoration of indigenous women's rights which were destroyed by colonialism and neo-colonialism."[86] Notably, the delegates aimed to establish an International Council of Indigenous Women and issued a list of goals for the organization.[87]

After she started working at the University of Lethbridge, Smallface-Marule's attention to education and teaching pedagogy never wavered. In June 1989, she left the university to take up a position at Mi'kai'sto Red Crow Community College, established on the Káínai reserve to meet the educational needs of the local Indigenous community. According to a colleague, Smallface-Marule's vision for education was to "decolonize by understanding how we were colonized in the first place."[88] To accomplish this, Indigenous peoples needed to seize control of education and to decolonize it, reshaping it to accurately reflect their culture and to meet their needs. Surely, her efforts to do so echoed the National Indian Brotherhood's 1972 policy paper, "Indian Control of Indian Education" and foresaw the content of the United Nations Declaration on the Rights of Indigenous People's Article 14.[89] The influence of Julius Nyerere on her thinking should not, however, be ignored. Beyond framing the problem as colonization and the solution as decolonization, Smallface-Marule held fast to his inspiration (mentioned above) that the development should be rooted in local culture and history not imposed from above. Moreover, there is evidence to suggest that Nyerere's vision of international mutual self-reliance could also be applied in the sphere of education.

In 1991, she became president of the college and worked on designing curriculum that emphasized Indigenous culture over assimilation, including the Kainai Studies Program.[90] She sought to "validate Blackfoot knowledge and encourage mainstream institutions to accept Kainai Studies as accredited courses."[91] Through her efforts, Red Crow College became the first tribally controlled community college in Canada.[92] At Red Crow College, Smallface-Marule also worked to integrate Káínai cultural traditions and knowledge into other educational programs like nursing, agriculture, and science, to "make it part of people's lives in more conscious and academic ways."[93] In 1995, she reached out to the Faculty of Education at the University of Lethbridge to help develop a Niitsitapi Teacher Education Program to be offered jointly with Red Crow College.[94] Despite extensive work, the effort was twice shelved before finally launching as a pilot in 2004, with the first graduates in 2006.[95] After some hiatus, the program started up again in 2018.[96] The college website now boasts that all courses "have been integrated with Niisitapisskska'takssin, the Blackfoot Knowledge Paradigm" and "students are supported in embracing the transformative educational processes of a renewal of Indigenous ways of knowing, the transfer of sacred sciences and practices."[97]

In 1997, Smallface-Marule helped to found the First Nations Adult and Higher Education Consortium, an organization of Indigenous post-secondary institutions in Western Canada.[98] While she served as its first president, the consortium successfully bid to host the 2002 World Indigenous Peoples Conference on Education in Alberta.[99] The meeting resulted in the establishment of a new international organization, the World Indigenous Nations Higher Education Consortium, which envisioned "indigenous peoples of the world united in the collective synergy of self-determination through control of higher education."[100] The aims of international cooperation, mutual self-reliance, and self-determination of Indigenous peoples sound strikingly similar to the goals of the WCIP, though now with a focus on education.

For her contributions to Indigenous education, she won a National Aboriginal Achievement award (since renamed Indspire) in 1995 and a Centennial Medal of Alberta in 2005.[101] She received an honorary Doctor of Letters from Athabasca University in 2006, and an honorary Doctor of Law from the University of Calgary in 2010. Marie Smallface-Marule maintained her focus on education until the end her life, working actively at Red Crow College until the year before her death in December 2014.[102]

Conclusion

Given Canada's long-standing discouragement of Indigenous women's active participation in governance and politics, it should be no great surprise that the personal histories of women like Smallface-Marule have often been ignored and forgotten by scholars of Canada's international history. In the face of powerful sexism, racism, and colonialism, however, this woman was not content to wait patiently for the government to fulfill its treaty promises or its particular obligations to Indigenous women, both of which, despite recent rhetoric, remain largely unmet.

Reflecting on Smallface-Marule's trajectory, Ryan Heavy Head, her colleague at Red Crow College, astutely pointed out that "It's like she started her career backwards ... Most people start locally and work up to national and international work. Marie started internationally and brought back what she had learned there about Aboriginal people and their plights."[103] But perhaps an earlier description of her route told the whole story: "Marie Smallface-Marule has gone full circle from individual and community awareness, to the international level, and back again."[104]

> When I was growing up, I thought the Blood Reserve was the whole world. Being Indian has been very important to me; I am proud of my heritage. I now understand and believe that the real basis for protection and retention of cultural heritage is at the community level. The international work is to give breathing space and time for communities to establish their future as Indian communities.[105]

At the beginning of her life, she had seen education as her primary means to secure the cultural integrity and sovereignty of her people. Throughout her career, she remained deeply committed both to education and to her community. Her life's experience, at home and abroad, simply shifted her understanding of formal education to one based in Káínai knowledge. Her exposure to and work with Indigenous internationalism expanded her world view, without substantially altering her primary goal. All Indigenous communities needed that opportunity to assert their self-determination based on cultural strengths. Ultimately, international cooperation may have been merely a means to that end, but it was a strategy she never abandoned and one that served her well throughout her life.

Acknowledgments

Marie Smallface-Marule was generous with her time, not only agreeing to speak with me on the phone and in person on multiple occasions, but also granting interviews to other young researchers throughout her career. I owe her a personal debt for sharing her time and knowledge with me, in addition to my gratitude for the work she accomplished in her life. I am deeply honoured that Smallface-Marule's daughters, Fee Marule-McLean and Tsuaki Marule, have been supportive of this research and its publication.

Thanks as well are due to Asunción Ontiveros Yulquila for agreeing to share his thoughts on Smallface-Marule's contributions to Indigenous internationalism, as part of a much larger interview, and to Paul McKenzie-Jones at the University of Lethbridge for being so quick to share his collected documents with me. I must thank Doreen Manuel once again for generously sharing access to her father's diaries with me nearly a decade ago. Finally, thanks to Jill Campbell-Miller for her helpful comments on this chapter, among other works of mine over the years.

This chapter relies on work from my doctoral dissertation, some of which was subsequently published in "Another Wave of Anti-Colonialism: The Origins of Indigenous Internationalism," *Canadian Journal of History* 52, 3 (Winter 2017): 533–59, doi:10.3138/cjh.ach.52.3.06.

Notes

1 Ravi De Costa, "Identity, Authority, and the Moral Worlds of Indigenous Petitions," *Comparative Studies in Society and History* 48, 3 (2006): 669–98, doi: 10.1017/S0010417506000260.
2 See, among other examples, Joëlle Rostkowski, "The Redman's Appeal for Justice: Deskaheh and the League of Nations," in *Indians and Europe: An Interdisciplinary Collection of Essays*, ed. Christian F. Feest (Lincoln: University of Nebraska Press, 1989), 435–54; and David Webster, "'Red Indians' in Geneva, 'Papuan Headhunters' in New York: Race, Mental Maps, and Two Global Appeals in the 1920s and 1960s," in *Dominion of Race: Rethinking Canada's International History*, ed. Laura Madokoro, Francine McKenzie, and David Meren (Vancouver: UBC Press, 2017), 254–83. Other early examples of North American Indigenous internationalism are documented in Steven Crum, "Almost Invisible: The Brotherhood of North American Indians (1911) and the League of North American Indians (1935)," *Wicazo Sa Review* 21, 1 (Spring 2006): 43–59, doi:10.1353/wic.2006.0003.
3 Augusto Willemsen-Diaz, "How Indigenous Peoples' Rights Reached the UN," in *Making the Declaration Work: The United Nations Declaration on the Rights of Indigenous Peoples*, ed. Clair Charters and Rodolpho Stavenhagen (Copenhagen: International Work Group for Indigenous Affairs, 2009), 27–28.
4 See, among other examples, Crossen, "Another Wave of Anti-Colonialism"; Rhiannon Morgan, *Transforming Law and Institution: Indigenous Peoples, the United Nations and Human Rights* (Burlington, VT: Ashgate, 2011); and Hanne Hagtvedt Vik, "Indigenous

Internationalism," in *Internationalisms: A Twentieth-Century History* (Cambridge: Cambridge University Press, 2016), 315–39.
5 "Dr. Marie Smallface Marule," obituary, *Lethbridge Herald*, January 9, 2015, https://lethbridgeherald.com/obituaries/2015/01/09/friday-january-9-2015.
6 Sheila McManus, *The Line Which Separates Race, Gender, and the Making of the Alberta-Montana Borderlands* (Lincoln: University of Nebraska Press, 2005), 57. Resistance to the everyday imposition of this international boundary on Niitsitapi people is colourfully depicted in Thomas King's short story, "Borders," in *One Good Story, That One: Stories* (Minneapolis: University of Minnesota Press, 1993), 131–48.
7 Caen Bly, "Marie Small Face," *Kainai News*, December 18, 1968, 9, https://digitallibrary.uleth.ca/digital/collection/sanews/id/18908.
8 "Profile: Marie Smallface-Marule. Is It a Break in Tradition to See Blood Women Take Active Positions in Public Life?," *Kainai News*, December 1, 1980, 10, https://digitallibrary.uleth.ca/digital/collection/sanews/id/23294.
9 Ron Devitt, "Red Crow College Leader Wins National Award," *Windspeaker*, May 1995, S3, http://data2.archives.ca/e/e448/e011197637.pdf.
10 Marie Smallface-Marule, quoted in "Athabasca University Honors RCCC President," *Tribal College* 18, 1 (Fall 2006), https://tribalcollegejournal.org/athabasca-university-honors-rccc-president/.
11 Devitt, "Red Crow College Leader."
12 Smallface, quoted in "Representative Praises Alberta and Alberta Youth," *Lethbridge Herald*, September 28, 1962, 14.
13 "Representative Praises Alberta and Alberta Youth." For more on Camsell Indian Hospital, see Laurie Meijer Drees, "Indian Hospitals and Aboriginal Nurses: Canada and Alaska," *Canadian Bulletin of Medical History* 27, 1 (2016), https://doi.org/10.3138/cbmh.27.1.139.
14 Marie Smallface-Marule, in discussion with the author, May 26, 2011. The National Indian Council (formed in 1961) split into several successor organizations, including the National Indian Brotherhood, which was reorganized as the Assembly of First Nations in the mid-1980s. Her attendance was made possible by her participation in the organization's Princess Pageant as the princess for Alberta. Participants competed "on the basis of education, personality, appearance and speaking ability." "Marie Smallface Named Princess," *Lethbridge Herald*, June 10, 1964, 18.
15 Will Langford describes the origins of the Canadian Indian Youth Council (CIYC) in "Friendship Centres in Canada, 1959–1977," *The American Indian Quarterly* 40, 1 (Winter 2016): 1–37, doi:10.5250/amerindiquar.40.1.0001. Harold Cardinal was elected CIYC president in 1966 but would soon drop out of Carleton University, in Ottawa, returning westward to work for the Indian Association of Alberta, and he was later elected its president. Although the CIYC does not appear to have had much of an international focus to its activities, at least one attendee of its 1966 Canadian Indian Workshop, Willie Littlechild, became a prominent Indigenous internationalist, working with the United Nations for decades. Canadian Indian Youth Council, "Report of the First Canadian Indian Workshop" (1996), Glenbow Archives, M-7655 (James Gladstone family fonds), series 10, folder 84, courtesy of Paul McKenzie-Jones.
16 On these organizations, see Langford, "Friendship Centres in Canada,"; and Laurie Meijer Drees, *The Indian Association of Alberta: A History of Political Action* (Vancouver: UBC Press, 2002).
17 "Discrimination Said a Myth: Indians Must Prove Worth to Take Place in Society," *Lethbridge Herald*, January 24, 1966, 20. Smallface-Marule participated in a panel discussion alongside Anishinaabe activist Fred Kelly, who had organized the prominent protest march

the previous year by Indigenous people in Kenora, Ontario. For more on this march, see Scott Rutherford, "'We Have Bigotry All Right – but No Alabamas': Racism and Aboriginal Protest in Canada during the 1960s," *American Indian Quarterly* 41, 2 (2017): 158–79, doi:10.5250/amerindiquar.41.2.0158.

18 Smallface, quoted in "Education Reform Urged At Alta. Youth Seminar," *Lethbridge Herald*, May 7, 1966, 28.
19 Smallface, quoted in Devitt, "Red Crow College Leader." An interview from 1971 asserts that she was the only First Nations student at the university for two years of her degree. "Compare Canadian Reserves to Undeveloped Countries in Africa," *Kainai News*, April 15, 1971, 24, https://digitallibrary.uleth.ca/digital/collection/sanews/id/19486.
20 Smallface, quoted in Devitt, "Red Crow College Leader."
21 Smallface-Marule, in discussion with the author, May 26, 2011. For a detailed history of Canadian University Service Overseas (CUSO), see Ruth Compton Brouwer, *Canada's Global Villagers: CUSO in Development, 1961–86* (Vancouver: UBC Press, 2014).
22 Smallface-Marule, in discussion with the author, May 26, 2011. Will Langford examined the intellectual exchange between CUSO, the Canadian New Left, and Tanzania (both politically and geographically proximate to Zambia) during this era. Will Langford, "International Development and the State in Question: Liberal Internationalism, the New Left, and Canadian University Service Overseas in Tanzania, 1963–1977," in *Undiplomatic History: The New Study of Canada and the World*, ed. Asa McKercher and Philip Van Huizen (Montreal/Kingston: McGill-Queen's University Press, 2019), 184–205.
23 Part of her work involved producing radio programs for this purpose. A Káínai speaker herself, she worked to include Zambian languages in her radio broadcasts. "Southern Alberta Woman Begins 3rd Year in Zambia," *Lethbridge Herald*, February 3, 1969, 10. See also A.M. Natesh, *Rural Broadcasting (Literacy): Zambia (Mission) December 1969–December 1972*, serial no. 2825/RMO.RD/MC. Paris: UNESCO, 1972, https://unesdoc.unesco.org/ark:/48223/pf0000019833.locale=fr.
24 Smallface, quoted in "Southern Alberta Woman Begins 3rd Year in Zambia," *Lethbridge Herald*.
25 John Hatch, *Two African Statesmen: Kaunda of Zambia and Nyerere of Tanzania* (London, 1976), 228–9; Andy DeRoche, "KK, the Godfather, and the Duke: Maintaining Positive Relations between Zambia and the USA in spite of Nixon's Other Priorities," *Safundi: The Journal of South African and American Studies* 12, 1 (January 2011), 97–121.
26 Hatch, *Two African Statesmen*, 231.
27 Smallface-Marule, in discussion with the author, May 26, 2011.
28 "Profile: Marie Smallface-Marule," *Kainai News*.
29 Nellie Carlson, Kathleen Steinhauer, and Linda Goyette, *Disinherited Generations: Our Struggle to Reclaim Treaty Rights for First Nations Women and Their Descendants* (Edmonton: University of Alberta Press, 2013), 60.
30 Smallface-Marule, in discussion with the author, May 26, 2011.
31 Smallface-Marule, in discussion with the author, May 26, 2011; "National Indian Brotherhood Name Three to New Post," *Kainai News*, September 1, 1971, 8. At the same time, the NIB hired a Trinidadian lawyer, Ramdeo Sampat-Mehta, who also offered the organization a Third World perspective. While working at NIB, he published a book, *The Day After: A Political Guide for the Third World* (Ottawa: Heron Pub. House, 1974).
32 Nellie Carlson, Kathleen Steinhauer, and Linda Goyette, *Disinherited Generations: Our Struggle to Reclaim Treaty Rights for First Nations Women and Their Descendants* (Edmonton: University of Alberta Press, 2013), 60.
33 Smallface-Marule's work to amend the Indian Act is particularly noteworthy, given than the NIB would later oppose these efforts. Carlson, Steinhauer, and Goyette, *Disinherited Generations*, 59–61. For more on this conflict, see Joanne Barker, "Gender, Sovereignty, and

the Discourse of Rights in Native Women's Activism," *Meridians* 7, 1 (2006): 127–61, http://www.jstor.org/stable/40338720.

34 Smallface-Marule, quoted in "Compare Canadian Reserves to Undeveloped Countries in Africa," *Kainai News*, 24.

35 Smallface-Marule, "Treatment of Native People in NWT Not Unlike Those in South Africa," *Kainai News*, November 15, 1971, 18; "Marie Marule Accuses Govt. of Building 'Rhodesia' in N.W.T.," *Kainai News*, December 1, 1971, 2, https://digitallibrary.uleth.ca/digital/collection/sanews/id/19749.

36 Smallface-Marule, in discussion with the author, May 26, 2011.

37 George Manuel Diaries (GMD), April 10, 1972, unpublished, courtesy of Doreen Manuel.

38 GMD, February 1, 1976. An article by Reetta Humalajoki details the transnational work of another woman who worked with the NIB, Anita Gordon. Reetta Humalajoki, "'Yours in Indian Unity': Moderate National Indigenous Organisations and the U.S.-Canada Border in the Red Power Era," *Comparative American Studies* 17, 2 (2020), 183–98, doi:10.1080/14775700.2020.1735920.

39 Peter McFarlane, *Brotherhood to Nationhood: George Manuel and the Making of the Modern Indian Movement* (Toronto: Between the Lines, 1993), 134–35.

40 Chrétien's 1969 white paper had aimed to eliminate any special status for Indigenous people in Canada. Manuel had helped form the Union of British Columbia Indian Chiefs in response to the proposals, which were soon discarded in the face of strong opposition. McFarlane, *Brotherhood to Nationhood*, 114–15.

41 George Manuel, from Report on the New Zealand and Australia tour by George Manuel, 1971, p. 15, quoted in McFarlane, *Brotherhood to Nationhood*, 159.

42 McFarlane, *Brotherhood to Nationhood*, 132.

43 McFarlane, *Brotherhood to Nationhood*, 160–63.

44 GMD, December 11, 1971.

45 Smallface-Marule, in discussion with the author, May 26, 2011.

46 George Manuel and Michael Posluns, *The Fourth World: An Indian Reality* (Don Mills, ON: Collier-Macmillan, 1974), xvi; McFarlane, *Brotherhood to Nationhood*, 160.

47 Manuel and Posluns, *The Fourth World*, xv.

48 To be clear, this is not to undermine or question the vital importance of George Manuel's leadership and wisdom in establishing and running the organization.

49 GMD, June 8 and 9,1972; McFarlane, *Brotherhood to Nationhood*, 166–9.

50 Smallface-Marule, in discussion with the author, May 26, 2011, and June 13, 2012; GMD, August 8, 1973.

51 For more on the Umana Yana, see Roy Elliot Oakley, "Opening the Waiwai *Ewto*: Indigenous Social and Spatial Relations in Guyana" (PhD diss., University of Edinburgh, 2018), 197–227.

52 Smallface-Marule, in discussion with the author, May 26, 2011.

53 Smallface-Marule, in discussion with the author, May 26, 2011 and June 13, 2012.

54 McFarlane, *Brotherhood to Nationhood*, 201.

55 See Douglas E. Sanders, *The Formation of the World Council of Indigenous Peoples* (Copenhagen: International Work Group for Indigenous Affairs, 1977); and *Ha-Shilth-Sa* [newspaper], December 4, 1975, 7–13.

56 "Profile: Marie Smallface-Marule," *Kainai News*.

57 Dianne Meili, "Marie Smallface-Marule: Indigenous Rights Activist Fought Colonialism," *Windspeaker*, February 26, 2017, https://windspeaker.com/news/womens-history-month/marie-smallface-marule-indigenous-rights-activist-fought-colonialism; "Leroy Little Bear: 2003 Distinguished Alumnus of the Year," University of Lethbridge Alumni Relations, https://www.uleth.ca/alumni/awards/2003/leroy-little-bear.

58 World Council of Indigenous Peoples (WCIP), "Four-Year Report (1977–1981)," 3. Courtesy of the Union of British Columbia Indian Chiefs Resource Centre.
59 "Indigenous Conference Draws Attn. to Rights, Self-Determination and Survival," *Kainai News*, September 22, 1977, 2, https://digitallibrary.uleth.ca/digital/collection/sanews/id/21783. Smallface-Marule's published scholarly articles included "The Canadian Government's Termination Policy: From 1969 to the Present Day," in *One Century Later: Western Canadian Reserve Indians since Treaty 7* [Western Canadian Studies Conference proceedings], ed. Ian A.L. Getty and Donald B. Smith (Vancouver: UBC Press, 1978), 103–16; and "Traditional Indian Government: Of the People, by the People, for the People," in *Pathways to Self-Determination: Canadian Indians and the Canadian State*, ed. Leroy Little Bear, Menno Boldt, and J. Anthony Long (Toronto: University of Toronto Press, 1984), 36–45.
60 Rise M. Massey, "The World Council of Indigenous Peoples: An Analysis of Political Protest" (master's thesis, University of British Columbia, 1986), 98, https://open.library.ubc.ca/collections/ubctheses/831/items/1.0096996.
61 Massey, "The World Council of Indigenous Peoples," 98–99.
62 Smallface-Marule, quoted in "Indigenous Conference Draws Attn. to Rights," *Kainai News*.
63 "Indigenous Conference Draws Attn. to Rights," *Kainai News*.
64 "Profile: Marie Smallface-Marule," *Kainai News*.
65 "Profile: Marie Smallface-Marule," *Kainai News*.
66 Brad Teeter, "Indians, Aborigines United in Spirit," *Lethbridge Herald*, April 10, 1981, B1.
67 WCIP, "Four-Year Report (1977–1981)," 7–10.
68 WCIP, "Four-Year Report (1977–1981)," 9.
69 Asunción Ontiveros Yulquila, in discussion with the author, September 15, 2019.
70 At the same time, Smallface-Marule secured funding for "two Indian youth leaders from Canada to visit Tanzania on a UNESCO Youth and Cultural Exchange Program." WCIP, "Four-Year Report (1977–1981)," 9.
71 Union of British Columbia Indian Chiefs, "Minutes" (13th Annual General Assembly of the Union of BC Indian Chiefs, Vancouver, BC, October 28–30, 1981), http://constitution.ubcic.bc.ca/node/138; WCIP, "Four-Year Report (1977–1981)," 31–32.
72 McFarlane, *Brotherhood to Nationhood*, 280. See also, Smallface-Marule, "Traditional Indian Government," 37–39. It was four countries (Tanzania, Cuba, Iran, and Yugoslavia) tied to the Non-Aligned Movement that lent their immediate support to the Union of British Columbia Indian Chiefs and agreed to bring its complaints before the UN Special Committee on Decolonization. Smallface-Marule herself was a delegate to the Cuban mission. "Petition and Bill of Particulars to the Political Standing of Indigenous Tribes and Bands under the Protection of the British Government in the Face of Impending Canadian Independence," Constitution Express Digital Collection, Union of British Columbia Indian Chiefs Resource Centre, http://constitution.ubcic.bc.ca/node/128.
73 WCIP, "Four-Year Report (1977–1981)," 32.
74 Marie Smallface Marule, ed., *First Nations, States of Canada and United Kingdom: Patriation of the Canadian Constitution"* (Lethbridge: World Council of Indigenous Peoples, 1981), 1, 14–15, 21–24.
75 Massey, "The World Council of Indigenous Peoples," 55; GMD, December 24, 1976.
76 WCIP, "Four-Year Report (1977–1981)" 3; WCIP Financial Statements, September 30, 1977, Consultative Arrangements and Relations with the World Council of Indigenous Peoples, United Nations Archives, S-0446-0286-0001.
77 WCIP, "Four-Year Report (1977–1981)," 16.
78 WCIP, "Four-Year Report (1977–1981)," 16.
79 Letter from Flora MacDonald to Martial Asselin (Minister of State for CIDA), September 26, 1979, Library and Archives Canada, RG25, Vol. 14963, 45-13-3-7 Part I.

80 WCIP, "Four-Year Report (1977–1981)," 20.
81 Devitt, "Red Crow College Leader."
82 Correspondence from WCIP to CIDA, Concluding Remarks, March 28, 1983, Library and Archives Canada, RG22, Part I, 45-D140-W1; Robert Carty, Virginia Smith, and the Latin American Working Group, *Perpetuating Poverty: The Political Economy of Canadian Foreign Aid* (Toronto: Between the Lines, 1981), 167.
83 University of Lethbridge Retired Academic Staff Association, "Marule, Marie Smallface" [Obituary], University of Lethbridge, https://www.uleth.ca/retired-faculty/obituaries/marule-marie-smallface.
84 In October 1989, the organizers brought together over three hundred women for a four-day conference. Christine Miller, Patricia Chuchryk, and University of Manitoba Press Staff, *Women of the First Nations: Power, Wisdom, and Strength* (Winnipeg: University of Manitoba Press, 1996), 3–4.
85 Tauli-Corpuz later became the third United Nations Special Rapporteur on the Rights of Indigenous Peoples.
86 "Indigenous Women's Conference Planned," *Kainai News*, May 10, 1990, 2, https://digital library.uleth.ca/digital/collection/sanews/id/29356; Additional information on the conference is from Tromsø Arctic University Museum's "permanent" online exhibit *Sápmi: Becoming a Nation* [online exhibition], particularly the "Topic: Indigenous Women Become Organised" (with translated text from Odd Mathis Hætta, *Samene: Nordkalottens Urfolk* (Kristiansand: Høyskoleforl, 2002). http://sapmi.uit.no/sapmi.%3clink. The online exhibition is currently inaccessible pending reformatting.
87 South and Meso-American Indian Information Center Women's Committee, *Daughters of Abya Yala: Native Women Regaining Control* (Summertown, TN: Book Publishing Co, 1994), 42–46.
88 Meili, "Indigenous Rights Activist Fought Colonialism."
89 Article 14 guarantees "the right to establish and control their educational systems and institutions providing education in their own languages, in a manner appropriate to their cultural methods of teaching and learning." UN General Assembly, Resolution 61/295, United Nations Declaration on the Rights of Indigenous Peoples, A/RES/61/295 (September 13, 2007), 5; National Indian Brotherhood, *Indian Control of Indian Education* (policy paper presented to the Minister of Indian Affairs and Northern Development, Ottawa: National Indian Brotherhood, 1972).
90 "Dr. Marie Smallface Marule," obituary.
91 Tsuaki Marule, quoted in Meili, "Indigenous Rights Activist Fought Colonialism."
92 Meili, "Indigenous Rights Activist Fought Colonialism."
93 Marie Smallface-Marule, quoted in "Dr. Marie Smallface Marule," obituary.
94 Cathy Campbell and Marie Smallface-Marule, "The History and Future of Niitsitapi," *Alberta Teachers Association Magazine* 82, 4 (Summer 2002), https://www.teachers.ab.ca/News Room/ata magazine/Volume 82/Number 4/Articles/Pages/The History and Future of Niitsitapi.aspx.
95 Campbell and Smallface-Marule, "The History and Future of Niitsitapi"; "U of L and Red Crow College to Launch Niitsitapi Teacher Education Program Next Fall," *University of Lethbridge UNews*, August 16, 2017, https://www.uleth.ca/unews/article/u-l-and-red-crow-college-launch-niitsitapi-teacher-education-program-next-fall; "Dr. Marie Smallface Marule," obituary.
96 "U of L and Red Crow College to Launch Niitsitapi Teach Education Program Next Fall."
97 "Academic Programs," Red Crow College, para 2, http://www.redcrowcollege.com/academicprograms.

98 "First Nations Leaders Elected," *Tribal College* 9, 4 (Spring/Summer 1998), https://tribalcollegejournal.org/nations-leaders-elected/. Smallface-Marule also served as vice-chair of the National Association of Indigenous Institutions of Higher Learning. "Dr. Marie Smallface Marule," obituary.
99 Cheryl Petten, "Morley Welcomes World Educators," *Windspeaker*, June 2002, 19, http://data2.archives.ca/e/e448/e011183923.pdf.
100 Merritt Helfferich, "WINHEC Formed at WIPCE," *Sharing Our Pathways* 7, 4 (September/October 2002), 5. http://ankn.uaf.edu/SOP/SOPv7i4.pdf.
101 "Dr. Marie Smallface Marule," obituary.
102 University of Lethbridge Retired Academic Staff Association, "Marule, Marie Smallface" [Obituary].
103 Ryan Heavy Head, quoted in Julie MacIsaac, "Legacy of Trail Blazer Includes Indigenous-Based Studies," *Alberta Sweetgrass* 22, 3 (2015), https://ammsa.com/publications/alberta-sweetgrass/legacy-trail-blazer-includes-indigenous-based-studies.
104 "Profile: Marie Smallface-Marule," *Kainai News*.
105 Smallface-Marule, quoted in "Profile: Marie Smallface-Marule," *Kainai News*.

PART 3

Women in Diplomacy

7

P.K. Page and the Art of Diplomacy
An Ambassadorial Wife in Brazil

Eric Fillion

"What to do about writing? Is it all dead?"[1] Flashes of anxiety swept over Patricia Kathleen Page on April 8, 1957, as she came face to face with her worst fear: writer's block. She had risen to prominence in Canada two years earlier by winning the Governor General's Award for Poetry with *The Metal and the Flower* (1954). At the time, she was in Canberra with her husband, W. Arthur Irwin, the former editor of the Canadian newsmagazine *Maclean's*, who had quit his job as head of the National Film Board of Canada (NFB) to take on new challenges as high commissioner to Australia. That chapter of the couple's life had ended abruptly when Irwin learned, at the end of July 1956, that his new post would be in Brazil.[2] "We had been told that Rio is the most beautiful city in the world, and it *is* beautiful," Page wrote in her diary upon arriving there six months later.[3] The city's disorienting noisiness and topography, however, stupefied the poet so much that it rendered her speechless and incapable of writing more verses. That Portuguese was difficult to learn did not help matters.

Page was the first to theorize about her own silence. Indeed, the literature that explores the poet's experience of Brazil derives from works that she penned herself: a 1969 essay titled "Questions and Images" and *Brazilian Journal*, a significantly edited version of the diary she kept while overseas. In the former, she omitted any mention of her diplomatic status in South America. This better framed her time there as the transformative odyssey of a "mute observer" who learned to draw, to take in the vastness and diversity of the land.[4] Having just returned to Canada, the traveller's trope was a

Figure 15 The artist-ambassadress Patricia Kathleen Page in May of 1957, shortly after she had settled into her new life in Rio de Janeiro. | Courtesy Library and Archives Canada, PA-214248 and the Estate of P.K. Page

potent device for rejoining the Canadian literary scene. Published in 1987, *Brazilian Journal* provided a more elaborate picture of Page's efforts to negotiate the interplay between her private and public personas, her "Brazilian self" and "Canadian self," and her double status as an artist and a diplomatic wife.[5] Both publications foregrounded the idea that Brazil was just a stage on her aesthetic journey, providing a compelling narrative arc for both her travel memoir and her decades-long career.[6]

To her later critics, Page may have appeared "curiously absent" due to the "language shock" that she experienced in Brazil, but her withdrawal into a silent stare was in appearance only.[7] The notion that the writer's arrival in Rio de Janeiro catalyzed a "decade of silence" fails to adequately account for the voice that she claimed for herself within the context of Canada-Brazil relations.[8] As a diplomatic wife, she performed her numerous duties – from hosting and entertaining to accompanying Irwin on endless rounds of social functions – while asserting her presence through informal networks of artists and intellectuals. Not only did Page turn to visual art to communicate her impressions, she also accorded interviews and gave speeches, in both

English and Portuguese, in which she reflected on her work and that of her compatriots. As an artist-ambassadress alongside her husband, she acted as an independent agent, engaging critically, in public and in private, with Canada's image in Brazil. She was neither silent nor invisible.

Much of the scholarship around *Brazilian Journal* focuses on questions of exoticism, positionality, and the power asymmetry that is embedded in the "tourist gaze."[9] Although important, these approaches neglect the explicitly gendered dimension of Canadian international relations and, more importantly, Page's own efforts to transcend her diplomatic role through aesthetic modes of communication. The poet's so-called decade of silence thus doubles here as a decade of invisibility.

Page's invisibility is also a function of the marginal status assigned to women in the study of Canadian diplomatic history.[10] She was not the only wife to offer knowledge about life abroad by putting pen to paper, only for it to be overlooked. Rae Hardy and Tova Clark, who each spent close to thirty years in the foreign service with their husbands, George Hardy and Lorne Clark, also chronicled their experiences (from philanthropic endeavours to cocktail parties and official outings), which they characterized unequivocally as a challenging job that required creativity and adaptability.[11] Historical news sources are replete with references to the important work accomplished by women like Page, Hardy, and Clark, who set aside or reassessed their career goals to find fulfillment in their roles as diplomatic wives. Their travel memoirs can, and should be, read against the official and private correspondence of their husbands. As the feminist scholar Cynthia Enloe explained, taking this material seriously "enables one to lift the curtain on government's reliance not only on a certain kind of marriage but also on those women willing to adopt a certain kind of wifely role."[12]

Moreover, much of Page's invisibility must also be attributed to a dearth of writing on the place of culture in Canada's pursuit of an international identity. Until recently, few works had explored, in a Canadian context, diplomatic historian Akira Iriye's contention that all international relations are in fact intercultural relations.[13] Culture, the postcolonial scholar Edward Said insisted, is always enmeshed with power and resistance; it offers a "largely common although disputed terrain" where individual and collective identities are defined, performed, opposed, and reimagined.[14] Combined insights from cultural studies, communications, and Canadian international history are now examining this terrain and shedding light on the "complicated partnerships," which state and non-state actors entered into abroad.[15] This was especially true in Brazil, the country that enticed Canada to sign its first bilateral cultural agreement in 1944.[16]

This chapter situates Page vis-à-vis her Canadian precursors in Brazil by drawing together her diverse and complex range of experiences, which stemmed from her double status as artist-ambassadress as well as from the relationship of complicity and trust that she maintained with Irwin. At the same time, it examines Page's efforts to resist hierarchies of gender (even as she asserted those of race and class) in order to validate her sense of place in the world.

Backdrop

Australia was the farthest a Canadian diplomat could go in the early 1950s. Still, some of it felt familiar. Like Canada, the country was a former settler colony with membership in the predominantly white "Old Commonwealth."[17] Brazil, in contrast, was on the periphery of the English-speaking world. Irwin was evidently not enthusiastic about the prospect of relocating there. Neither was Page, who asked him to decline the assignment. "Send a letter to [Under-Secretary of State for External Affairs] Jules [Léger], ... I'll draft it," she urged her husband.[18] Irwin did not seem to think much of Brazilians and their country's geopolitical importance when he indicated, in a letter to his superiors in Ottawa, that he "might be most useful" in another country where there is "substantive political work" to be done.[19] Whether or not Irwin and Page wrote the letter together is difficult to say. Either way, the couple was needed in Brazil. There were no other options.

Born in England on November 23, 1916, Patricia Kathleen Page grew up in and around Calgary, where her father, a military officer, had purchased land. He was an avid reader who let his daughter devour his books when he was done with them. According to biographer Sandra Djwa, Page's childhood experience in the Canadian hinterland "fostered the development of her literary and artistic imagination."[20] It motivated her to seek what lay beyond her immediate horizon. Dissatisfied with the education she was receiving at St. Hilda's School for Girls, Page spent the greater part of her free time at the Calgary Public Library. There, she discovered Frances Winwar's *Poor Splendid Wings: The Rossettis and Their Circle* (1933), which tells the story of a group of poets and painters who sought to transform Victorian England with their art.[21] It convinced her that an artistic life was possible. After completing high school in 1934, Page travelled to England, where she immersed herself in the city's cultural life. She read Dante Gabriel Rossetti's poetry and marvelled at his paintings in the Tate Gallery, but she also ventured into bookstores and art venues in her search for modernist art.[22]

Although Page had been writing poetry for many years, she had never done so professionally. The publication of "The Moth" in the London *Observer*, on December 2, 1934, was a seminal moment. Page, however, still lacked confidence, which might explain why she hid behind her initials and signed "P.K. Page."[23] What the emerging poet lacked in self-confidence, she made up for in discipline and sense of purpose. When she returned to Canada late in the summer of 1935, Page found herself living in Saint John, where her father was now commanding officer. Although she continued to publish and was active in local theatre and writing groups, she was under no illusion that she could have a future there as a poet. With the support of her family, she moved to Montreal in the fall of 1941 to make a career out of writing.

As the site of a small but thriving artistic modernism, the booming city was being transformed by then-premier Adélard Godbout's brand of liberalism and the influx of both exiled artists and expats returning from war-torn Europe, including the Mannheim-born cellist Lotte Brott and the French Canadian painter Alfred Pellan. Once settled, Page found a group of like-minded writers, poets such as Abraham Klein and F.R. Scott, who helped find outlets for her work, among others, the modernist anthology *Unit of Five* (1944) and the poetry magazine *Preview*. She also secured a publisher for her first novel, *The Sun and the Moon* (1944).[24] In Montreal, Page and her colleagues "argued with equal exuberance over the potential of an emphatically Canadian modern writing" while trying to imagine the life that awaited them after the war.[25] There was "*muito entusiasmo* [much enthusiasm]" and "*muita vontade de fazer* [lots of goodwill]," she later recalled in Brazil during an interview with a reporter from *Correio da Manhã*.[26] However, the death of her father in 1944 and financial considerations eventually compelled her to move to Ottawa and accept a job as a scriptwriter at the NFB, where she met Irwin. The two married on December 16, 1950.

Arthur Irwin had joined the NFB earlier that year to deal with the aftermath of Igor Gouzenko's defection from the Soviet Union's embassy in 1945. The cipher clerk exposed a Soviet spy ring at the heart of the Canadian state, plunging Canada in the escalating Cold War confrontation between the communist Soviet Union and the US-led western democracies. As a climate of national insecurity gripped the country, the NFB and its progressive workforce became a target of the Royal Canadian Mounted

Police and a government royal commission investigating leaks of confidential information. In the fall of 1949, Norman Robertson, clerk of the privy council, recruited Irwin to head the battered institution and restore its morale.[27] Although not a staunch anti-communist, he did have a "strong feeling for the country and strong views of what it meant to be Canadian."[28] Irwin, his biographer David Mackenzie explained, "exhibited a dynamic and definite brand of Canadian nationalism" that had allowed him to shape "*Maclean's* into a successful and important player in Canadian life."[29] He invested the same efforts into restructuring the NFB and giving it the additional autonomy needed to bounce back.

By 1953, Irwin had accomplished his mission and was now ready to "try his hand at interpreting his own people to others" after years of "telling Canadians about themselves" from behind his desk at *Maclean's* and the NFB.[30] Secretary of State for External Affairs Lester B. Pearson knew that Irwin, a long-time acquaintance who had developed a sustained interest in foreign policy, was contemplating a career in diplomacy. In fact, the former editor had accepted the NFB job with the implied understanding that a posting overseas would follow.[31] In recognition for his service, Pearson offered Irwin three options to choose from in 1953: Australia, Mexico, or Seattle.[32] The aspirant diplomat chose the first for his ambassadorial debut. He and his wife expected to be given a similar choice of assignments in 1956, but it was not to be.

The couple was reluctant to leave Australia because they saw Brazil as both too foreign and too irrelevant to Canada's international priorities. "I find it hard now to remember why Brazil fell on my heart with so heavy a thud," remarked Page in 1987.[33] She continued: "Perhaps it was the memory of the Latin-American diplomatic wives in Ottawa who had looked like a cross between women and precious stones; perhaps an unformulated wish for a European post after Australia; perhaps ... who knows?"[34] In Canberra, she proved herself to be an exceptional ally to Irwin in "social affairs" without having to set aside her writing career.[35] She became a "semi-public figure, both as Mrs. Arthur Irwin and as poet P.K. Page," after the publication of her award-winning collection, *The Metal and the Flower*.[36] Would life in Brazil afford her the latitude and opportunities to pursue her artistic ambitions? Irwin, who found his work in Australia both stimulating and enjoyable, was also apprehensive about starting a new job whose primary focus, he thought, was on diplomacy's wearisome and uninspiring "representational side."[37]

Conceding that "Brazilian politics were not easily understandable from abroad," Léger reassured Irwin that his mandate in Brazil was broad and that it included the kind of political work for which he felt most qualified.[38] The diplomat arrived with a detailed list of Canadian priorities: keeping abreast of communist inroads; providing updates on the country's foreign policy; collating information regarding the "rather delicate subject" of Canada's relationship to the Organization of American States; generating interest in increased bilateral trade; and keeping an eye on domestic policies that might harm Canadian business interests in Brazil, notably those of Brazilian Traction, Light and Power Company (nicknamed "The Light") – Canada's largest overseas corporation.[39]

Political life in 1950s Brazil was unpredictable and difficult to understand. The country had gone from empire to republic to dictatorship and republic again in a little less than seven decades, most of which were marred by coups of one kind or another. And though it branded itself as a racial democracy, Brazilian society was heavily divided along ethnic, class, regional, and political lines.[40] The South American giant plunged into an unprecedented crisis in 1954 when President Getúlio Vargas, the former dictator who had returned to power through legitimate elections, committed suicide rather than be ousted from power by the military. From August 1954 until January 1956, Brazilians watched as a succession of presidents sought to wrest control of a volatile political environment.

Juscelino Kubitschek's presidency ultimately brought some stability and hopefulness. His economic plan, branded as fifty years of progress in five, called for modernization, diversification, and territorial integration through education, energy reforms, and the expansion of the country's transportation network. His lasting contribution would be the construction of a new capital: Brasília, a feat of urban design whose skyline would juxtapose modern architectural wonders against the surrounding tropical scrubland and savannahs.[41]

There was optimism in the air. On the eve of Irwin's arrival, Canadian Henry Borden, president of The Light, confidently assured English-speaking industry leaders in Toronto and Rio de Janeiro that the twentieth century belonged to Canada and Brazil.[42] He added somewhat condescendingly: "Believe me, in Brazil you will find any number of very able men in business, in government, in the profession. And not only do you find *able* men, you also find men who are cultured, intelligent, and charming."[43] Borden, of course, operated within male-dominated elite spaces where androcentric discourses and practices prevailed. Irwin soon joined him in claiming that "things both economic and political in Brazil are rarely, if ever, as bad as they look."[44] Standing by his side, Page kept diligent and incisive notes from her vantage point as both a woman and an artist-ambassadress.

Precursors

Canada-Brazil relations were framed in gendered terms since the first exchange of diplomatic representatives in 1941. The opening of the legation and its subsequent upgrade to an embassy, a little over two years later, were responses to profound changes brought about by the outbreak of war in Europe. With the conflict disrupting their respective transatlantic trade networks, the two aspiring middle powers hoped to consolidate their bilateral economic ties in the shadow of the United States' increasing political and cultural dominance of the hemisphere.[45] Brazilians celebrated this rapprochement by welcoming Canadians within the "*família Americana* [American family]" and placing high hopes in the possibility of further ties between the two "*pátrias irmãs* [sister nations]."[46]

Jean Désy pioneered diplomatic relations in Brazil, first as minister plenipotentiary (1941–43) and then as ambassador (1943–47). Taking his cues from his Brazilian hosts, including Vargas, who projected "paternalistic competency" to depict his dictatorship as a benevolent one, Désy carefully honed his own image as a fatherly figure to draw attention to his leadership qualities and caring abilities.[47] Pictures of him with his wife, Corinne de Boucherville, and two children, Mariel and Jean Louis, revealed paternal attributes that presumably qualified him for diplomatic work, especially since it involved managing relations between two sister nations.[48] His masculine sense of self was a composite of his domestic and civic identities (as a devoted father and as a diplomat), both of which derived from his relationship to his wife.

De Boucherville played a variety of crucial roles, starting with helping her husband mould his public image. A descendant of ennobled aristocrat Pierre Boucher, founder and seigneur of Boucherville, she added substance to the notion that Désy's intimate connections to elite cultural and social circles reached deep into the past. The ambassadress herself projected a friendly image through charitable projects and various social events, one of which involved facing off against other diplomatic wives in an amicable horse-riding competition.[49] Participation in such initiatives was a means of nurturing harmonious relations and generating both goodwill and gratitude among the city's diplomatic community.[50] However, the bulk of her work consisted of hosting and entertaining at the official residence to help foster conversations and people-to-people interactions between Désy and his male interlocutors. This domestication of diplomacy, to borrow Enloe's expression, revealed the importance of "feminized domestic settings" for the "manly sort of trust-building" that diplomatic activity entailed.[51]

Désy was, in many respects, an unorthodox diplomat, particularly when it came to using culture to project an engaging image of Canada to make it better known. His many experiments in cultural diplomacy, however, did not translate into a less androcentric world view. One of the high points of his years in Rio de Janeiro was the signing, in 1944, of a far-sighted bilateral cultural agreement, the first of its kind for Canada, aimed at facilitating closer relations between the two countries.[52] As official envoys, cultural ambassadors were expected to impress and inform while helping create a climate conducive to reciprocal understanding and productive exchanges, most notably within elite milieux where decision makers and people of influence congregated. Those who travelled south during the first decade of Canada's cultural rapprochement with Brazil formed an impressive cohort: among others, the painter Jacques de Tonnancour, the composer Ernest MacMillan, and the four singers of Quatuor Alouette. Soprano Muriel Tannehill, who was accompanying her husband, the pianist Jean Dansereau, was the sole woman's voice in this.

Although the spotlight was on Dansereau, Tannehill's presence did not go unnoticed when they arrived in Rio de Janeiro, in June of 1943. The image of an artistic couple made for great headlines in the effort to promote more intimate relations between Brazilians and Canadians. "The Dansereau couple, with their artistic prestige, is one more link in the strong chain of friendship that unites the two sister nations," affirmed H. Coutinho in *Jornal do Brasil*.[53] A colleague from *A Noite* added: "It is now the hearts that intertwine in a common affection, a feeling made more refined and more harmonious through the art of Jean and Muriel Dansereau."[54] The trope of family spoke of closeness and intimacy, which the artists both embodied and projected on stage, in the press, and during outings with Désy and de Boucherville. Tannehill did not perform as often as her husband did, but she unquestionably helped set the musical mood for this rapprochement, even if only by her presence.[55]

The pianist Ellen Ballon was the only Canadian woman to travel solo to Brazil. That she did so on her own initiative, with next to no support from Désy or his staff, was a testament to her agency as an impromptu cultural ambassadress in a male-dominated world.[56] The Montreal-born prodigy had distinguished herself on world stages, including in the United States where she had met the renowned Brazilian composer Heitor Villa-Lobos. Taking advantage of Canada's closer relations with Brazil, she astutely commissioned him to write a piano concerto, which he promptly accepted out of recognition for her talent. On October 11, 1946, Ballon travelled to Rio de Janeiro as a guest of the Brazilian government to perform the world premiere of Villa-Lobos' new composition, *Concerto de Piano e Orquestra No. 1*, which he dedicated to her.[57] She went on to present the first performance of the work in the United States and in Canada to pursue the twin goals of advancing her career and promoting Canadian culture. On September 1, 1956, she asked External Affairs for help in bringing the concerto to London to "establish a musical entente cordiale between Canada, Brazil, and England."[58] The department, which had yet to focus attention on cultural matters, had little to offer beyond endorsement by Canada House in London, but it did recognize Ballon as a "formidable lady."[59]

Artist-Ambassadress

The stage had been set, so to speak, by the time Page disembarked in Rio de Janeiro. The official and impromptu ambassadresses that had come before her had developed the diplomatic and cultural terrain that had been reserved for them. Ballon had gone a step further by demonstrating surprising resourcefulness in using newly established channels to move centre stage and represent Canada in ways that could bolster her personal and professional ambitions.[60] An award-winning poet with close to four years of foreign service experience in Australia, Page was exceptionally qualified to build on the work of her predecessors.

The stage metaphor is an apt one considering that diplomatic wives, notwithstanding their privileged status as *personae gratae* in elite circles abroad, performed a variety of roles in shaping Canada's international image. Christine Hantel-Fraser, a former "Canadian foreign-service wife" with a PhD in political science, explained that "stage management" was at the heart of what she and her female colleagues did.[61] In other words, these women were the "true power behind the official hospitality scene" and an "invaluable asset to their husband's official endeavours."[62] Their efforts did not just complement the work of their male partners, but were also essential for the overall success of the diplomatic mission. Page made that point when she began work on *Brazilian Journal*. I was "[i]mmensely privileged," she wrote, but "despite what might be taken as evidence to the contrary, it was also hard work."[63]

The opening pages of her published diary take us inside the official residence, a *palacete* [mansion], as Page and Irwin called it, acquired by Canada in March of 1955. Considerable work awaited the couple since they were the first occupants. Page noted:

> Despite generous help from embassy staff, moving into a fifty-seven-room house never before equipped as an official residence requires endless patience – doily-counting patience. I check inventories, make lists of needed supplies – those to be purchased locally, those which can't be obtained here and must be requested from Ottawa. I write endless letters to the Supplies and Properties Division [of the Department of External Affairs].[64]

Learning Portuguese to communicate with her ever-rotating staff also required its share of patience and considerable effort.

All this work was not just about making the *palacete* habitable. It was also about making it an inviting place since it "symbolized the national space of Canada."[65] This was notably true when it came to entertaining Brazilian politicians or local heads of mission and their wives, as was the case during the November 1958 visit of Secretary of State for External Affairs Sidney Smith. Official reports of the trip provide little indication of the magnitude of the work that had to be accomplished and the stress it caused Page. "At one point I panicked," she confided in her diary.[66] "I was not afraid of the minister, heaven knows, but of the organization and planning, the tug and pull and strain of dozens of different people and events, with us the analgesic, the oil, the man in the middle."[67] In the first five days of Smith's visit, the ambassadress entertained on four occasions for a total of more than six hundred guests.

At the same time, Page's work was not confined to the residence's domestic space. She followed in the footsteps of de Boucherville by joining other diplomatic wives on cultural outings or at charity events, from Girl Guides to Pioneiras Sociais, an organization that provided medical and educational assistance to women living in poverty-stricken communities. While Irwin announced his presence to his male counterparts in Rio de Janeiro, Page connected with the wives (there were more than fifty missions in the city) as a necessary first step before entertaining or being invited to dinner. Getting to know other women in this way had its advantages, because they were "all sources of information of one kind or another."[68] Yet the flow of intelligence went both ways. For example, Page once found herself needing to speak about Canada at a "Pan-American Round Table" composed of women representing fifteen countries.[69] Such "female sociability networks" were an integral part of the information-gathering that took place in diplomatic circles.[70]

These networks of women extended beyond Rio de Janeiro and they were not all connected to the diplomatic corps. In her role as ambassadress, Page brought encouragement and inspiration to the wives of engineers who had travelled to the northern city of Belém to work in the oil industry.[71] She also enlivened the spirit of a group of Quebec nuns who had been doing missionary work for three years in Alcântara, also in the north, with no contact whatsoever with the embassy. Page noted in her diary that they were "all obviously happy to see faces from home."[72] She was impressed by their dedication and benevolence in providing educational training and medical services to the impoverished community. "In this isolated corner of tropical Brazil, the ambassadors of Canada wear ... cornet[te]s; witnessing their work and measuring their qualities, we were proud to be Canadians," Irwin reported to External Affairs.[73]

It was not unusual for the ambassador to write in the first-person plural. His report on their trip to the interior is a case in point. Manaus, the capital of Amazonas, left a deep impression on the couple. "The city is like a faded, middle-aged women living in genteel poverty in a sagging mansion built by *nouveau riche* parents on the edge of a forest jungle," Irwin wrote.[74] This impressionistic description of the city was uncharacteristic of his otherwise dispassionate reports. No doubt, he and Page openly discussed their impressions, some of which found their way into documents destined for the staid East Block headquarters of the Department of External Affairs. "We shall not soon forget the special [piano] performance offered us" at the "golden-domed opera house ... a mixture of magnificent extravagance and atrocious *fin de siècle* taste," he added.[75]

Page had her own briefing book for this trip and, unlike her husband, she kept meticulous notes on it. She too wrote about the distressing performance on the "incredibly out of tune ... theatre piano" in a city whose "hey-day" was long over.[76] She also kept a log of the places they visited, the people they met, and the hospitality afforded to them during their stay. The fact that Irwin held on to her annotated brief suggests that he might have relied on it when preparing his "Close-Up of the Amazon" report.

It is fair to assume that the two also discussed their shared experience of the Bienal Internacional de Arte de São Paulo before writing down their thoughts about the event. External Affairs and the National Gallery of Canada had collaborated to put together what they hoped would be a stellar display of Canadian achievements in the arts. The painting exhibit centred on the works of Jean Paul Lemieux, Takao Tanabe, and Harold Town. Also included in the biennial's fourth edition were a series of architectural photographs, Inuit sculptures, and a theatre display. There were obvious echoes of Page's diary in Irwin's report and vice versa: the theatre props were great, but the photographs were too small, the Inuit sculptures were badly displayed, and Lemieux's landscape paintings, which were placed side by side, unfortunately emphasized the country's flatness. Whereas Irwin's official reports implicitly affirmed that Canada's contribution paled compared to those of Italy and France, among others, Page bluntly noted in private: "Somehow we ought to know that this was not a pipsqueak Brazilian show but an international show of considerable size and merit."[77] An artist herself, she was conceivably more attuned to the importance of culture as an instrument of diplomacy and, thereby, more critical of Ottawa's apparent half-hearted interest in the matter.

Brazilian reporters encouraged Page to take on the role of cultural ambassadress by welcoming her as an eminent representative of the Canadian cultural elite, rather than just a diplomatic wife. Not since Dansereau and Tannehill had they been that excited about a Canadian couple. Reporters invariably referred to Page's achievements as a poet to the extent that she occasionally eclipsed her husband. For example, *Diário Carioca* published a photo of the couple the day after they arrived, omitting Irwin's name from the caption, which focused on the artist-ambassadress.[78] *Revista da Semana*, *Última Hora*, *O Jornal*, and *Correio da Manhã* all published interviews with her.[79] Page reminisced about her childhood and the years she spent in Montreal. She spoke of her travels and the writers that were transforming cultural life back home, many of whom were women: among others, Anne Wilkinson,

Ethel Wilson, Kay Smith, Miriam Waddington, and Anne Hébert. In championing her female colleagues, Page sought to elevate and broaden the reach of their collective voice. The image of Canada put forward in these interviews was that of a youthful and modern country with a soulful, dynamic culture that spoke of authenticity, democracy, and inclusion.

If External Affairs could not capitalize on Page's artistic reputation to further the two countries' rapprochement, the Brazilian intelligentsia would. On March 24, 1959, Austregésilo de Athayde, president of the Academia Brasileira de Letras (ABL), informed Page that his organization planned to honour her along with two other women: the historian Courtney Espil and the novelist Stella Zilliacus, wives of the Argentinian and British ambassadors, respectively.[80] Modelled on the Paris-based Académie française, the ABL's membership was restricted to a select group of men known as the "immortals." Although they were breaking with tradition by recognizing, albeit only symbolically, "*a inteligência feminina* [female intelligence]," Page confided in her diary that she felt somewhat bothered that no Brazilian women had been extended that honour.[81] The morning of the May 7 ceremony, *Jornal do Brasil*'s Maria Rita published a scathing critique of the ABL's exclusionary practices but encouraged all women to attend the event in support of the three torchbearers.[82] That night, Page nervously took the stand and delivered her speech, which included a subtle and polite protest: "I am immensely proud to be received by the immortals here ..., yet humble to appear before you – mortal, a woman."[83]

Ever skilful in navigating between worlds, Page assumed the role of impromptu cultural ambassadress at the ABL by using literature as a means of mediating new connections to her host society. Seeking inspiration in the Brazilian canon, she spoke warmly of her travels throughout the country and translated her awe into a series of stanzas written in the Portuguese language, a first for the artist. Her performance elicited much applause and praise. The event was front-page news in Rio de Janeiro the following day.[84] *O Jornal* celebrated the speech as a "beautiful message of faith, affection, and love to Brazil" while *Jornal do Commercio* reproduced it for its readers.[85] Robertson, who had succeeded Léger as under-secretary of state for external affairs, even wrote to Irwin asking him to congratulate Page "on the honours she has won in Brazil for herself and for Canada."[86] It would have been difficult for External Affairs not to notice her under the spotlights.

Page was clearly not invisible. Neither was she silent even as she retreated from poetry and embraced the visual art as her preferred means of capturing not only the lush and colourful vegetation that surrounded the *palacete* and greeted her everywhere she travelled, but also the ceremonial practices of the Brazilian elites and lower classes. Given her limited knowledge of the Portuguese language, drawing and painting allowed her to communicate her impressions of Brazil in the "*arguably* ... more universal language" of the visual art.[87] It provided the incentive to go on urban excursions to discover more of the country's cultural life, including the work of the painter Candido Portinari, whom Page admired. Page's evolving artistic practice was an opportunity to explore, expand, and transgress sociability networks. In addition to repeatedly soliciting the advice of Arie Aroch, an Israeli painter and diplomat, she took lessons with Frank Schaeffer, an "attractive" Brazilian artist who nearly trapped her in a "relationship as binding as marriage."[88] The poet-turned-painter navigated single-mindedly through male-dominated cultural circles to reinvent her artistic self and escape the confines of the official residence.

Brazilian Journal opens an unexpected window into Page's wide-ranging experiences. She spent two decades rewriting sections of her diary, some of it with the help of Irwin, fashioning a narrative arc out of her artistic journey before publishing it. Yet, she chose to be unusually transparent and honest about her impressions of Brazil by greeting the reader with the following disclosure: "This is a period piece."[89]

A white artist writing from the standpoint of a diplomatic wife, Page positioned herself in relation to – and against – an exoticized Brazilian Other, particularly in her description of Afro-Brazilian expressive cultures and slum neighbourhoods:

> We drove today up over the hills and through the *favela*, which should make any sensitive, decent person devote his life to social reform, but I'm afraid my initial reaction was one of fierce pleasure in its beauty. Turning a corner we saw a group of vividly dressed people against a great fortress of square gasoline tins painted every conceivable colour. Water, of course. And socially distressing. But my eyes operate separately from my heart or head – or at least in advance of them – and I saw, first, the beauty.[90]

If the couple's recollection of Manaus in the annotated brief and External Affairs report referred to above did not make their white privilege apparent, the published diary certainly did.

In Rio de Janeiro, Page circulated within elite cultural and political milieux where whiteness operated as a gatekeeper. "Social note: have never met a Negro at a party," she wrote in her diary.[91] Distance and detachment characterized her encounter with the Afro-Brazilian Other, whom she observed through a car window or from the balcony of an apartment overlooking Ipanema Beach, as was the case on New Year's Eve, 1959. The Afro-Brazilian *macumba* ceremony unfolding on the beach, with its sea of white candles and flowers, captivated her imagination. At the same time, the participants' "self-induced [deliriums]" and their syncretic appropriation of Catholic symbols repulsed her.[92] In these moments (and many others), Page felt ambivalence, attraction, and contempt in the face of cultural practices and social realities that she could not understand. On the one hand, she uncritically attributed "to Brazil a seductive exoticism," but on the other hand she expressed unease with regard to its "unsettling, even threatening alterity."[93]

A critical reading of *Brazilian Journal* reveals the cultural values, biases, and assumptions that informed Page's – and by extension her husband's – lofty ways in projecting Canada abroad. The presence of Irwin's voice in the pages of *Brazilian Journal* was not incidental. Page purposely pulled material from his notes to add detail and colour to the manuscript, "using such ruses as 'A. tells me that …' or such phrases."[94] For example, "A. was up to his neck in last-minute detail … to witness the inauguration of a new highway to Brasília."[95] Or in the case of the infamous piano from Manaus: "'Tropics-tortured,' A. called it."[96] This cyclical give-and-take relationship is more evidence of their complicity and the porosity of the line that separated the gendered domestic and public realms of diplomacy in 1950s Brazil.

Farewell

Their Brazilian adventure ended in the summer of 1959 with the news that the Canadian delegation to the United Nations needed Irwin's services in New York. The couple would then resume their ambassadorial duties in Mexico in the winter of 1960 until retirement four years later. The South American giant had grown on them, so leaving it was bittersweet. "We have, my wife and I, too much to be grateful to Brazil for," Irwin told the fifty or so people who assembled for a farewell luncheon, on August 5, in the large banquet hall of the Ministry of Foreign Affairs.[97] He was speaking in the first-person plural, as he frequently did when referring to their experience of the country.

As was often the case in the past, the gendered trope of family proved a convenient one to celebrate Canada-Brazil relations. Horácio Lafer, Brazil's foreign minister, echoed his predecessors when he spoke of the two countries as "sister nations" who shared a destiny.[98] More striking, however, was the homage he paid to Page in his response to Irwin's speech:

> Understanding and cooperation between nations depend largely on the activities of their diplomatic representatives, of their professional and cultural stature. Especially so, Mr. Ambassador, when they can count on the help ... of wives who understand so well the mission assigned to their husbands. And here, I wish to refer ... to Ambassadress Arthur Irwin, because, with her "simpatia," intelligence and culture, she has known how to win the friendship and admiration of the Brazilian society.[99]

That Page elicited positive feelings of closeness and esteem was no doubt a function of her double status as a diplomatic wife and an impromptu cultural ambassadress. Yet despite all the interest and prestige that she independently brought to Canadian diplomacy, "Ambassadress Arthur Irwin," to use Lafer's form, was still cast by those in power as a lady engaging in delicate work on behalf of her husband.

Today, we can see Page as something much more than this gendered description suggests. She may have been working in a separate realm as an artist, within intercultural relations rather than the state-to-state domain of international relations, but emphasizing that contrast obscured her contributions to the art of diplomacy. Likewise for the distinction between state actors and those who, like Page, acted independently both within the power apparatus and parallel to it. Her use of culture to mediate new connections to the world, irrespective of External Affairs' tepid efforts to instrumentalize the practice, was consequential, even if only in the ways that it influenced how Brazilians perceived Canadians. Page's ability to shape the trajectory of Canada's relationship with the South American giant was arguably augmented by the wide-ranging and important work that she accomplished as a diplomatic wife. Her unwavering presence alongside Irwin clearly complicates the idea of separate spheres in the conduct of diplomacy. It speaks to the fact that the place Page and her predecessors occupied on the margins of political power was not – is not – outside history.

Notes

1 P.K. Page, *Brazilian Journal* (Toronto: Lester and Orpen Dennys, 1987), 34.
2 Jules Léger to W.A. Irwin, July 28, 1956, Library and Archives Canada (LAC), W. Arthur Irwin fonds, MG31-E97, vol. 26, Appointment to Brazil.
3 Page, *Brazilian Journal* (emphasis in original).
4 P.K. Page, "Questions and Images," *Canadian Literature* 41 (Summer 1969): 19.
5 Page, *Brazilian Journal*, 238.
6 This explains, in part, why Page was not inclined to have "Memoirs of an Ambassador's Wife" as the subtitle of the book. P.K. Page to Gena K. Gorrell, February 24, 1987, LAC, P.K. Page fonds, MG 30-D311, vol. 27, *Brazilian Journal* – Lester and Orpen Dennys (2 of 2).
7 Denise Adele Heaps, "P.K. Page's *Brazilian Journal*: Language Shock," *Biography* 19, 4 (Fall 1996): 355, 369.
8 For a discussion of Page's "decade of silence," which is also known as her "prolonged middle silence," see Brian Trehearne, *The Montreal Forties: Modernist Poetry in Transition* (Toronto: University of Toronto Press, 1999), 41; Sandra Djwa, *Journey with No Maps: A Life of P.K. Page* (Montreal/Kingston: McGill-Queen's University Press, 2012), 171; and Diane Stiles, "'The Person You Call I': Configurations of Identity in the Poetry of P.K. Page" (PhD diss., University of British Columbia, 2001), 160.
9 See Heaps, "P.K. Page's *Brazilian Journal*"; Suzanne Bailey, "Ethics, Aesthetics, Modernism, and the Primitive in P.K. Page's *Brazilian Journal*," *Mosaic* 46, 1 (March 2013): 53–75; Kevin McNeilly, "Toward a Poetic of Dislocation: Elizabeth Bishop and P.K. Page Writing 'Brazil,'" *Studies in Canadian Literature* 23, 2 (1998): 85–108; and Hannah McGregor, "Troping the Foreign in P.K. Page's 'Questions and Images,'" *University of Toronto Quarterly* 82, 2 (Spring 2013): 185–97.
10 According to Claire Turenne Sjolander and her colleagues, "the gendered nature of foreign policy is the marginalization of women's experiences as other, as outside the 'real' Canadian foreign policy." Claire Turenne Sjolander, Heather A. Smith, and Deborah Stienstra, "Taking Up and Throwing Down the Gauntlet: Feminists, Gender, and Canadian Foreign Policy," in *Feminist Perspectives on Canadian Foreign Policy*, eds., Claire Turenne Sjolander, Heather A. Smith, and Deborah Stienstra (Don Mills, ON: Oxford University Press, 2003), 9. See also Edna Keeble and Heather Smith, *(Re)Defining Traditions: Gender and Canadian Foreign Policy* (Halifax, NS: Fernwood, 1999); Deborah Stienstra, "Can the Silence Be Broken? Gender and Canadian Foreign Policy," *International Journal* 50, 1 (1994–95): 103–27; Cynthia Enloe, *Curious Feminist: Searching for Women in a New Age of Empire* (Berkeley: University of California Press, 2004); Judith Papachristou, "American Women and Foreign Policy, 1898–1905: Exploring Gender in Diplomatic History," *Diplomatic History* 14, 4 (Fall 1990): 493–509; Molly M. Wood, "Diplomatic Wives: The Politics of Domesticity and the 'Social Game' in the U.S. Foreign Service, 1905–1941," *Journal of Women's History* 17, 2 (Summer 2005): 142–65; and Molly M. Wood, "Wives, Clerks, and 'Lady Diplomats': The Gendered Politics of Diplomacy and Representation in the U.S. Foreign Service, 1900–1940," *European Journal of American studies* 10, 1 (2015): 1–12, doi.org/10.4000/ejas.10562.
11 Rae Hardy, *Distaff Diplomacy: My Elegant Life as a Diplomat's Wife* (Victoria, BC: Trafford on demand, 2001), 70–72. See also Tova Clark, *Compartments* (Manotick, ON: Penumbra Press, 2005), 90–99.
12 Cynthia Enloe, *Bananas, Beaches, and Bases: Making Feminist Sense of International Politics* (Berkeley: University of California Press, 2014), 104.
13 Akira Iriye, "Culture and Power: International Relations as Intercultural Relations," *Diplomatic History* 3, 2 (Spring 1979): 115–28. One of the earliest studies of Canadian cultural

diplomacy is Andrew Fenton Cooper, ed., *Canadian Culture: International Dimension* (Toronto: Centre on Foreign Policy and Federalism, University of Waterloo/Canadian Institute of International Affairs, 1985).
14 Edward W. Said, *Culture and Imperialism* (New York: Vintage Books, 1994), 200.
15 Lynda Jessup and Sarah E.K. Smith, "Introduction: Curating Cultural Diplomacy," *Journal of Curatorial Studies* 5, 3 (2016): 284. Other noteworthy works include Sarah E.K. Smith, "Art and the Invention of North America, 1985–2012" (PhD diss., Queen's University, 2013); Graham Carr, "'No Political Significance of Any Kind': Glenn Gould's Tour of the Soviet Union and the Culture of the Cold War," *Canadian Historical Review* 95, 1 (March 2014): 1–29; and Kailey Miller, "'An Ancillary Weapon': Cultural Diplomacy and Nation-Building in Cold War Canada, 1945–1967" (PhD diss., Queen's University, 2015). The following edited collections also contribute to a rethinking of the field of diplomatic history by bringing into focus the agency of non-state actors and the importance of alternate channels of communication in the making of international relations: Luis René Fernández Tabío, Cynthia Wright, and Lana Wylie, eds., *Other Diplomacies, Other Ties: Cuba and Canada in the Shadow of the US* (Toronto: University of Toronto Press, 2018); and Asa McKercher and Philip Van Huizen, eds., *Undiplomatic History: The New Study of Canada and the World* (Montreal/Kingston: McGill-Queen's University Press, 2019).
16 Portions of this chapter build on the author's doctoral dissertation. Eric Fillion, "Experiments in Cultural Diplomacy: Music as Mediation in Canadian-Brazilian Relations (1940s–1960s)" (PhD diss., Concordia University, 2019).
17 Srdjan Vucetic, *The Anglosphere: A Genealogy of a Racialized Identity in International Relations* (Stanford, CA: Stanford University Press, 2011), 57.
18 Page, *Brazilian Journal*, 1.
19 Arthur Irwin to Secretary of State for External Affairs, July 30, 1956, LAC, W. Arthur Irwin fonds, MG31-E97, vol. 26, Appointment to Brazil.
20 Djwa, *Journey with No Maps*, 22.
21 Djwa, *Journey with No Maps*, 31.
22 Djwa, *Journey with No Maps*, 39.
23 Sandra Djwa, "P.K. Page: Discovering a Modern Sensibility," in *Wider Boundaries of Daring: The Modernist Impulse in Canadian Women's Poetry*, ed. Di Brandt and Barbara Godard (Waterloo, ON: Wilfrid Laurier University Press, 2009), 79.
24 Published under the pseudonym, Judith Cape.
25 Trehearne, *The Montreal Forties*, 3.
26 Mauricio Caminha de Lacerda, "Na Antiga Mansão da Gávea a Embaixatriz Faz Poesia," *Correio da Manhã*, February 9, 1957, 10.
27 Gary Evans, *In the National Interest: A Chronicle of the National Film Board of Canada from 1949 to 1989* (Toronto: University of Toronto Press, 1991), 12.
28 David Mackenzie, *Arthur Irwin: A Biography* (Toronto: University of Toronto Press, 1993), 3.
29 Mackenzie, *Arthur Irwin*, 3. For a detailed account of the "red scare" at the National Film Board of Canada, see Reg Whitaker, Gregory S. Kealey, and Andrew Parnaby, *Secret Service: Political Policing in Canada from the Fenians to Fortress America* (Toronto: University of Toronto Press, 2012), 192–95.
30 Mackenzie, *Arthur Irwin*, 263.
31 Mackenzie, *Arthur Irwin*, 233. See also Reg Whitaker and Gary Marcuse, *Cold War Canada: The Making of a National Insecurity State, 1945–1957* (Toronto: University of Toronto Press, 1994), 252.
32 Mackenzie, *Arthur Irwin*, 263.
33 Page, *Brazilian Journal*, 2.

34 Page, *Brazilian Journal*, 2.
35 Mackenzie, *Arthur Irwin*, 268.
36 Djwa, *Journey with No Maps*, 150.
37 Arthur Irwin to Secretary of State for External Affairs, July 30, 1956, LAC, W. Arthur Irwin fonds, MG31-E97, vol. 26, Appointment to Brazil.
38 Jules Léger to W.A. Irwin, January 22, 1957, LAC, W. Arthur Irwin fonds, MG31-E97, vol. 26, Appointment to Brazil.
39 Jules Léger to W.A. Irwin, January 22, 1957.
40 On this topic, see Darién J. Davis, *Avoiding the Dark: Race and the Forging of a National Culture in Modern Brazil* (Aldershot, UK/Brookfield, VT: Ashgate, 1999); and Thomas E. Skidmore, *Black into White: Race and Nationality in Brazilian Thought* (Durham, NC: Duke University Press, 1993).
41 For concise histories of Brazil, see Thomas E. Skidmore, *Brazil: Five Centuries of Change* (New York: Oxford University Press, 1999); and Joseph Smith, *A History of Brazil, 1500–2000: Politics, Economy, Society, Diplomacy* (London, UK: Pearson Education, 2002).
42 Henry Borden, *Modern Brazil*, 1956, in LAC, W. Arthur Irwin fonds, MG31-E97, vol. 26, General Interest – Articles, Correspondence, Notes, Pamphlets, & Reports. Printed in Rio de Janeiro in December 1956, this pamphlet contains the entirety of a speech Borden delivered earlier that year to Canadian industrial leaders in Toronto.
43 Henry Borden, *Modern Brazil* (emphasis in original).
44 Arthur Irwin, "Brazil – Final Draft," n.d., LAC, W. Arthur Irwin fonds, MG31-E97, vol. 26, Despatches and Drafts of Despatches (2 of 2).
45 Rosana Barbosa recently published a survey of Canadian-Brazilian relations in which she argued that the two countries' "position as satellite economies" of the United States determined the nature of their interactions. To a great degree, her synthesis of the relationship between the two aspiring middle powers reproduces the top-down, state-centric motifs that characterize traditional Canadian diplomatic history, although it also successfully brings to the fore a neglected history worth pursuing. Rosana Barbosa, *Brazil and Canada: Economic, Political, and Migratory Ties, 1820s to 1970s* (London: Lexington Books, 2017), xv.
46 "Brasil-Canadá," *A Notícia*, November 21, 1940, in LAC, Brascan Limited fonds, MG28-III112, vol. 76, 011.4 pt. 20, Brazil: Politics & Elections; "Dois Grandes Povos, Duas Pátrias Irmãs," *Jornal do Commercio*, July 18, 1943, 10.
47 Robert M. Levine, *Father of the Poor? Vargas and His Era* (Cambridge: Cambridge University Press, 1998), 61.
48 For example, "Chegou o Primeiro Ministro Canadense no Brasil," *A Noite*, September 11, 1941, 1; and "Uma Entrevista com o Ministro do Canadá no Brasil," *Correio da Manhã*, July 1, 1942, 1.
49 See "Inaugurado Mais um Posto de Trabalho da Organização das Voluntárias," *Vida Doméstica* 26, 345 (December 1946): 3; "Pró Aliados," *Careta*, December 13, 1941, 24; "Legião Brasileira de Assistência," *A Manhã*, September 23, 1942, 7; and "Cavaleiros Paulistas e Cariocas em Novo Cotejo," *Gazeta de Notícias*, August 13, 1944, 8.
50 Christine Hantel-Fraser, *No Fixed Address: Life in the Foreign Service* (Toronto: University of Toronto Press, 1993), 189.
51 Enloe, *Bananas, Beaches, and Bases*, 96.
52 *Exchange of Notes between Canada and Brazil Constituting an Agreement for the Promotion of Cultural Relations between the Two Countries*, Canada-Brazil, May 24, 1944, Treaty Series 1944, no. 15, 3.
53 H. Coutinho, "Uma Oferta de Arte do Canadá ao Brasil," *Jornal do Brasil*, July 18, 1943, 2. Unless otherwise noted, all translations are by the author. The original quotations in Portuguese have been reproduced in the footnotes for reference purposes: "O casal Dansereau,

54 Ariel, "Brasil-Canadá," *A Noite*, July 7, 1943, 4. In Portuguese: "Agora são os corações que se entrelaçam em um sentimento comum, a que a arte de Jean e Muriel Dansereau, deu um requinte maior e uma harmonia mais pura."
55 Fillion, "Experiments in Cultural Diplomacy," 69–78.
56 The evidence – or lack thereof – suggests that the embassy provided nothing more than basic logistical support. P.W. Cook to Saul Rae, September 15, 1947, LAC, Department of External Affairs (DEA) fonds, RG25, vol. 2215, CBC I/S S/W Service to Latin America.
57 Ellen Ballon to Heitor Villa-Lobos, March 3, 1945, Museu Villa-Lobos, Heitor Villa-Lobos Collection, Correspondencia – Ellen Ballon.
58 Ellen Ballon to J.B.C. Watkins, September 1, 1956, LAC, DEA fonds, RG25, vol. 7271, Miss Ellen Ballon – Canadian Pianist – Tours of various countries.
59 J.B.C. Watkins to High Commissioner for Canada in London, October 4, 1956, LAC, DEA fonds, RG25, vol. 7271, Miss Ellen Ballon – Canadian Pianist – Tours of various countries.
60 Fillion, "Experiments in Cultural Diplomacy," 178–80.
61 Hantel-Fraser, *No Fixed Address*, xii, 173.
62 Hantel-Fraser, *No Fixed Address*, 173.
63 Page, quoted in Early draft of foreword, n.d., LAC, P.K. Page Fonds, MG 30-D311, vol. 25, *Brazilian Journal* – Mss. Revised Pages.
64 Page, *Brazilian Journal*, 12.
65 McGregor, "Troping the Foreign in P.K. Page's 'Questions and Images,'" 190.
66 Page, *Brazilian Journal*, 181.
67 Page, *Brazilian Journal*, 181. See also Arthur Irwin to Secretary of State for External Affairs, "Visit of the Honourable Sidney E. Smith," December 8, 1958, LAC, W. Arthur Irwin fonds, MG31-E97, vol. 26, Despatches and Drafts of Despatches (1 of 2).
68 Page, *Brazilian Journal*, 31.
69 Page, *Brazilian Journal*, 97.
70 Gemma Allen, "The Rise of the Ambassadress: English Ambassadorial Wives and Early Modern Diplomatic Culture," *The Historical Journal* 62, 3 (2019): 623.
71 Page, *Brazilian Journal*, 229.
72 Page, *Brazilian Journal*, 224.
73 Arthur Irwin to Secretary of State for External Affairs, "A Close-Up of the Amazon," July 27, 1959, LAC, W. Arthur Irwin fonds, MG31-E97, vol. 27, Trips to Brazilian States – Official Visit to Amazonas.
74 Arthur Irwin to Secretary of State for External Affairs, "A Close-Up of the Amazon."
75 Arthur Irwin to Secretary of State for External Affairs, "A Close-Up of the Amazon."
76 "Ambassador's Official Visit to the States of Pará, Maranhão, and Amazonas," April 1–13, 1959, LAC, W. Arthur Irwin fonds, MG31-E97, vol. 28, Trip to Pará, Maranhão and Amazonas – Mrs. Irwin's Brief.
77 Early draft, n.d., LAC, P.K. Page fonds, MG 30-D311, vol. 25, *Brazilian Journal* – Mss. Early Transcripts. See also Arthur Irwin to Under-Secretary of State for External Affairs, "The São Paulo IVth Bienal of Modern Art," October 18, 1957, National Gallery of Canada Library and Archives, National Gallery of Canada fonds, vol. 151, file 3, Canadian Exhibitions – Foreign (São Paulo, 4th, 1957).
78 "Diplomacia, Energia, e Poesia Juntos Chegam no Brasil," *Diário Carioca*, January 18, 1957, 12.
79 See Mauricio Caminha de Lacerda, "Na Antiga Mansão da Gávea a Embaixatriz Faz Poesia," *Revista da Semana*, July 19, 1958, 31–33; Edouard Bailby, "Patricia Kathleen Page, Poetisa e

Embaixatriz," *Última Hora*, April 1, 1957, 7; "Escritora e Poetisa a Embaixatriz do Canadá," *O Jornal*, June 4, 1957, 2; and Caminha de Lacerda, "Na Antiga Mansão da Gávea a Embaixatriz Faz Poesia," *Correio da Manhã*, 10.
80 Austregésilo de Athayde to Patricia Irwin, March 24, 1959, LAC, P.K. Page fonds, MG 30-D311, vol. 17, Speeches – Brazilian Academy.
81 Page, *Brazilian Journal*, 149. See also "Homenagem à Inteligência Feminina O Sentido da Recepção na Academia," *Diário da Noite*, May 8, 1959, 6; and "Casa de Machado Quebra Tradição Homenageando Mulheres Ilustres," *Diário Carioca*, May 10, 1959, 13.
82 Maria Rita, "Festa de Gala," *Jornal do Brasil*, May 7, 1959, 3.
83 Draft of speech [with English translation], n.d., LAC, P.K. Page fonds, MG 30-D311, vol. 17, Speeches – Brazilian Academy.
84 "Embaixatrizes São Uma Trindade Augusta," *Diário Carioca*, May 8, 1959, 1.
85 "Casa de Machado de Assis Recepciona 3 Embaixatrizes," *O Jornal*, May 8, 1959, 5. In Portuguese: "... belíssima mensagem ao Brasil, mensagem de fé, de carinho e amor." See also "Embaixatriz na Academia," *Jornal do Commercio*, July 19, 1959, 1–2.
86 Norman Robertson to W.A. Irwin, July 14, 1959, LAC, W. Arthur Irwin fonds, MG31-E97, vol. 27, Removal – Brazil to Ottawa.
87 Heaps, "P.K. Page's *Brazilian Journal*," 365 (emphasis in original). For a discussion of Page's visual art, see Michèle Rackham Hall, *The Art of P.K. Irwin: Observer, Other, Gemini* (Erin, ON: The Porcupine's Quill, 2016); and Barbara Godard, "Kinds of Osmosis," *Journal of Canadian Studies* 38, 1 (Winter 2004): 65–75.
88 Page, *Brazilian Journal*, 237.
89 Page, *Brazilian Journal*, xi.
90 Page, *Brazilian Journal*, 70.
91 Page, *Brazilian Journal*, 76.
92 Page, *Brazilian Journal*, 193.
93 McNeilly, "Toward a Poetic of Dislocation," 86; McGregor, "Troping the Foreign," 188.
94 P.K. Page to Gena K. Gorrell, October 3, 1986, LAC, P.K. Page fonds, MG 30-D311, vol. 27, *Brazilian Journal* – Lester and Orpen Dennys (2 of 2).
95 Page, *Brazilian Journal*, 181.
96 Page, *Brazilian Journal*, 230.
97 Arthur Irwin to Under-Secretary of State for External Affairs, "Farewell Calls and Functions," August 14, 1959, LAC, W. Arthur Irwin fonds, MG31-E97, vol. 26, Despatches and Drafts of Despatches (1 of 2).
98 Arthur Irwin to Under-Secretary of State for External Affairs, "Farewell Calls and Functions," August 14, 1959. See appendix for the English-language version of the foreign minister's speech.
99 Arthur Irwin to Under-Secretary of State for External Affairs, "Farewell Calls and Functions," August 14, 1959.

8

Jean Casselman Wadds
Patriation, Dinner Party Wars, and a Political Diplomat

Steve Marti and Francine McKenzie

MOST HISTORICAL ACCOUNTS OF Canada's decolonization from Britain end around the Second World War. While Canada fought alongside Britain in the war, it decisively affirmed sovereignty over its foreign policy, foreign governments recognized Canada's authority, and wartime officials articulated a distinctive international identity for Canada. But the story did not end there. Decolonization was a multilayered and ongoing process and Canadian governments still lacked sovereign authority in one fundamental area: only Westminster, the British parliament, could amend Canada's constitution, the British North America Act.[1] Patriating the constitution was a priority for Liberal prime minister Pierre Trudeau, who entered his final term in office following his surprising re-election in 1980. The Canadian high commission in London would be critical in securing British support for patriation. At the head of the high commission was Jean Casselman Wadds, recently appointed as high commissioner by the short-lived Progressive Conservative government of Prime Minister Joe Clark. She was a political appointment, not unprecedented, and the first woman to be Canada's high commissioner to London.

Casselman Wadds had considerable experience as a politician and public official, but she was new to diplomacy and international affairs. Nonetheless, it fell to her to develop and implement the tactics and strategy to see through a high-stakes and high-profile diplomatic challenge that was politicized in both Canada and Britain. Casselman Wadds has received much praise for her efforts. Mark MacGuigan, the secretary of state for external affairs, described her as "our single most effective lobbyist in London."[2] Trudeau singled out Casselman Wadds, along with Queen Elizabeth and British prime minister Margaret Thatcher, as the three women responsible for patriation.[3] And yet, very little has been written about how Casselman Wadds organized and carried out this diplomatic campaign which has been described, perhaps dismissively, as a dinner party war. Nor have many scholars considered why she was so well-suited to the task. Was she a typical Canadian diplomat or was there something about her personality, background, or experiences that allowed her to manage this particular diplomatic challenge?

To date, the history of Canadian foreign relations revolves around small groups of mostly English-speaking, white, male diplomats.[4] Studies of women in the Canadian foreign service and of the influence of gender on foreign policy and foreign relations are scarce. The official history of the Department of External Affairs (DEA) identifies some of the structural impediments facing women. It tracks the number of women who joined the diplomatic service (in far smaller number than their male counterparts), examines the impact of equity legislation on the employment and advancement of women diplomats (the DEA lagged behind other government departments), and discusses support (of which there was very little) for women, especially women with families, which compounded the disincentives to the recruitment and retention of women diplomats and foreign service officers.[5]

There are a few studies of trailblazing Canadian women in international affairs. The biographies of Margaret Meagher (the first Canadian woman to be appointed as head of a diplomatic mission – Sweden, Austria, and Israel) and Mary McGeachy (who had a long and distinguished career as an international civil servant which included working for the Information Section of the League of Nations, 1928–40; being the Director of Welfare for the United Nations Relief and Rehabilitation Administration, 1944–46; and serving as President of the International Council of Women, 1963–73) explored how these two women navigated the gendered terrain of international affairs and "managed their femininity" so that they could be effective in their positions.[6] Nonetheless, the achievements of these exceptional women did not automatically bring about structural change or have long-lasting effects. As political scientist Claire Turenne Sjolander concluded in her study of Meagher, "Her success did not translate into any systematic effort to recruit a greater number of women" into Canada's foreign service.[7]

Casselman Wadds fell into the exceptional category and she had several firsts to her name. She was elected as a Member of Parliament (MP) in the late 1950s, when few women achieved such success; she was the national secretary to the Conservative Party; and she served as a royal commissioner. She was the first woman appointed as a principal secretary (to the Minister of Health and Welfare) and first woman appointed to head a senior diplomatic post for Canada.[8] Her professional success would be noteworthy at any time, but it was especially remarkable because it occurred from the late 1950s to early 1980s, when women in Canada had to overcome numerous disadvantages that prevented or limited their professional opportunities.

Historians have not entirely overlooked Jean Casselman Wadds. She is visible, acknowledged, and praised in historical accounts of the patriation of the constitution. But she has also been relegated to a domestic role – as hostess of dinner parties – placing her contribution in the same league as the unpaid but valuable work done by diplomatic wives (a subject David Webster and Eric Fillion take up in their chapters). In their history of Trudeau's foreign policy, Jack Granatstein and Robert Bothwell briefly described Casselman Wadds as "loyal, indefatigable, and possess[ing] the necessary social skills to join enthusiastically in the 'dinner party war,'" before focusing on the male political envoys sent by Trudeau to hasten negotiations in London.[9] Even though Casselman Wadds was present, *her work* has been invisible or understood primarily in terms of gendered expectations. Her marginalization is especially curious because diplomatic work often takes place at social gatherings and in the domestic spaces of embassies and high commissions. As Australian historians Carolyn James and Glenda Sluga pointed out, "sociability" has always been an important aspect of diplomatic practice.[10] Clearly, Casselman Wadds' role in developing and implementing the strategy to ensure that Westminster supported patriation is worth re-examining. Was diplomatic work being done during the dinner party wars? What other diplomatic work did Casselman Wadds do? That she was a woman in a senior diplomatic posting and entrusted with one of the most important files in Canadian history makes gender a crucial factor to examine. How Casselman Wadds used gender to navigate in politics and diplomacy – two fields regularly described as being a man's world – is at the centre of this chapter.

A Life of Politics and Privilege

Casselman Wadds was one of a small group of women Members of Parliament in the 1950s and 1960s. Although she said that she never expected to have a political career, she was born (in 1920) into a political family. Her parents were William Earl Rowe and Treva Lennox. Her father was a prominent local politician (county councillor and reeve), later member of the legislative assembly of Ontario, leader of the Conservative Party of Ontario, and, finally, lieutenant-governor of Ontario. As a child, she accompanied her father to political functions, including county council meetings. She knew and admired leading Conservative politicians including R.B. Bennett, Robert Manion, George Drew, and Robert Stanfield, many of whom she met during her annual weekly holiday at Ottawa's fabled Château Laurier hotel.

Casselman Wadds was at ease in political circles and familiar with the nature of politics. As an undergraduate student at the University of Toronto, she was aware of politics on campus and she could tell everyone's political allegiance from their last names. But by her own account, she was not involved in political activities. After university, she "drifted[ed] along pretty happily."[11]

In 1946, she married Arza Clair Casselman, a senior Conservative party member and MP for Grenville-Dundas. She had known Casselman since she was a child. Casselman was a widow with two teenage sons. Before long, she and Casselman had two more children, Nancy and William. Jean moved to Prescott after her marriage, a town that she loved. She recollected the busyness of married life, including attending the children's sporting events (rugby, hockey, and cricket) and she and the children skied, bowled, and curled.

When her husband died in 1958, she was asked to run in the by-election to replace him as Member of Parliament. Casselman Wadds stated on numerous occasions that she had never aspired to a political career,[12] but she agreed to run in the by-election because she liked meeting people and wanted to keep busy.[13] Wives replacing deceased husbands as MPs was not unknown. But her political success was not pro forma. There were several men vying for the nomination. In the hard-fought nomination race, she did not criticize the other candidates because she recognized that after the race they would still be fellow members of the Progressive Conservative Party. The importance that she attached to a civil style of politics did not detract from her determination to win the nomination. She did on the fourth ballot by three votes. Casselman Wadds subsequently ran a tireless election campaign, waking up early to meet people throughout the riding. She was elected with a majority of fifty-one hundred votes and became the tenth female MP. In a 1962 profile written by New Democratic Party MP Walter Pitman, he observed that some men might see Casselman Wadds as a "sweet young thing," but he advised that "competing with a knowledgeable, intelligent woman with a life-long interest and experience in politics would be a worthy challenge for any man."[14] Although most women who replaced their husbands as MPs sat for only one term, Casselman Wadds was re-elected four times, finally losing in 1968.

As an MP, Casselman Wadds developed her political principles and refined her political practices. Despite spending a lot of time in the House of Commons, she did not enjoy Parliament. She preferred meeting people. She liked "the conviviality of ... assemblies of people and get-togethers and groups."[15] In addition, Casselman Wadds believed that meeting people was a form of research.[16] In 1961, she was a delegate to the Social, Humanitarian and Cultural Committee of the United Nations. The task of this committee was to draft the international covenant on human rights. While in New York, Casselman Wadds attended many diplomatic social events; she saw it as part of her job and she wanted to meet as many delegates as possible. Her focus was always on people and she took seriously the cultivation of personal relations.

Casselman Wadds was a member of the Progressive Conservative Party, and she embraced conservative political values of free enterprise, competition, and individual initiative. She described herself as "anti-Socialistic," but she was quick to distinguish between her opposition to government intervention that assumed responsibilities better left to individuals and her support for "social legislation" to assist people in need.[17] She was a staunch supporter of lifelong learning as the key to individual success and for the betterment of humankind. She believed education was a progressive force that nurtured "sympathy, respect for one another, understanding," values she clearly embraced. Education was also the means to achieve individual and national standards of excellence. She called for government support for high educational standards in Canada, but this did not detract from her belief in individual responsibility and effort. As she observed, when things were too easy, it undermined the "all-out effort" needed to sustain "ambition for excellence."[18] The privilege that she enjoyed in her own life informed her confidence that education and application would lead to success as well as her belief in a circumscribed role for government in people's daily lives.

While she was loyal to her party, she did not endorse divisive politics and readily acknowledged the good work done by politicians in other parties. For instance, she admired Liberal cabinet minister C.D. Howe and she recalled Liberal prime minister Mackenzie King as "very friendly and amiable" with a "flashing white smile."[19] Above all, she prized Canadian unity. She once admitted that she would rather see the Progressive Conservative Party end than see the country divided.[20] She recommended that all MPs should go on a cross-country tour within six months of taking their seats. By understanding the country better, they would work more constructively for the good of all. Better understanding of the bigger picture would facilitate compromise and cooperation, essential to effective federal politics. She also accepted uncritically a progressive national narrative; she took pride in "what our forefathers have created out of most forbidding surroundings," and she celebrated the pioneers whose "warmth and humanity [had] brought our many regions together."[21] These views reflected her position of power and privilege in a settler society.

Casselman Wadds' public partisan loyalty hid her political savvy and actions. In the leadership challenge to Progressive Conservative leader John Diefenbaker in 1967, Casselman Wadds supported Dalton Camp, the president of the Conservative Party who had instigated the leadership review and seriously considered running himself. Diefenbaker bitterly named her in his memoirs as a member of the duplicitous faction that packed the front rows with Camp supporters during the televised speeches at the party convention, creating the appearance that Diefenbaker walked on stage to face a silent, stone-faced audience.[22] In characteristic fashion, Casselman Wadds was circumspect about her opposition to Diefenbaker and her work to remove him as leader.

After her electoral defeat in 1968, she became national secretary of the Progressive Conservative Party. In this position, she refined her skills as a shrewd operative. Michael Meighen, another supporter of Camp's leadership bid, challenged Don Matthews for the presidency of the party in 1974. When the incumbent Matthews attempted to block votes from some thirty unelected conference delegates, Casselman Wadds quickly gathered petitions to call a meeting of the party's executive committee without Matthew in the chair and secured a motion to rescind Matthews' attempt to block votes. Her intervention proved decisive: Meighen won the presidency with a margin of fewer than thirty votes.[23] Yet her role in Meighen's success remained invisible. Family connections and sociability did much to establish Casselman Wadds in partisan politics, but she secured her position as a prominent member of the Progressive Conservative establishment with her ability to wield influence and maneuver the party's rules and procedures to get results.

Although Casselman Wadds insisted that she was not "internationally sophisticated in any way at all,"[24] she had decided ideas about global politics and Canada's role in world affairs. She supported the UN and an internationalist approach to international relations. Hinting at world federalist ideas that were not common at the time, she talked about how the UN could become a parliament for the world and expressed the belief in a common humanity and desire for peace that transcended the nation-state approach to world affairs. She also observed that the pressing problems that affected peoples – war, hunger, disease, the need for international law, nuclear weapons, and the space race – made the UN essential.[25] She was able to square her internationalist outlook with her commitment to the Western cause in the Cold War, for example, by distinguishing between the actions of governments and the conditions of people.

Casselman Wadds' views about Canada's role in world affairs were far more conventional; indeed, she could be called a small *p*–Pearsonian. She believed that Canada was a constructive and internationally minded middle power that made positive contributions to world affairs. She praised Canada's efforts at promoting development through the United Nations International Children's Emergency Fund (UNICEF), the Colombo Plan (a collaborative Commonwealth program that promoted the development of South and Southeast Asia), and educational programs in Africa. She characterized Canadian foreign policy as "humane" and "reasonable," which she contrasted with the "imperialistic and aggressive" foreign policies of other (unnamed) countries. In the 1960s as European empires collapsed in Africa, Asia, and the Caribbean, she held up Canada as a model for newly independent nations: "We are an inspiration to these new countries, an example of the civilized way in which widely divergent races, divergent religions, divergent geographical parts can be welded together voluntarily without force or bloodshed into a nation."[26] Almost twenty years later, she described Canada as having an unblemished past which made it a model for other Commonwealth countries to emulate: "We have no colonial past for which to reproach ourselves, no ambitions toward conquest."[27] Such claims rested on a selective interpretation of Canada's development as a nation, particularly with respect to the treatment of Indigenous peoples. Nonetheless, she subscribed to an international politics based on common interests and cooperation where smaller countries with good ideas and good intentions could make their mark and make a difference.[28]

Her conservatism impressed itself on her admiration for Britain, whose historic and contemporary role in world affairs she celebrated. Following the Suez Crisis of 1956, then-Prime Minister Diefenbaker made it a priority to repair relations with Britain. His first diplomatic visit was to Britain to attend a Commonwealth meeting only five days after his election in 1957. He followed this up with an unexpected announcement that he wanted to shift 15 percent of Canadian trade back to Britain. In 1958, he embarked on a seven-week Commonwealth tour during which he praised the Commonwealth's past and evinced confidence in its future. Despite Diefenbaker's enthusiasm for Britain and the Commonwealth, relations were strained by his opposition to Britain's application to join the European Economic Community and his role in South Africa's withdrawal from the Commonwealth.[29] Although Diefenbaker's pro-British policies backfired, support for close relations with Britain remained strong across the Conservative party, and Casselman Wadds made many favourable references to Britain, praising the wartime leadership of Prime Minister Winston Churchill and the resolve of Britons during the blitz. She associated the Commonwealth with freedom, an association based on a selective reading of the history of the British empire.[30]

Her privileged personal circumstances prepared her for, and opened to her, a career in politics, but she could not evade sexism on the campaign trail. One constituent interviewed in 1958 insisted that the riding did not want "another Charlotte," a clear reference to Charlotte Whitton from nearby Renfrew who had been mayor of Ottawa from 1951 to 1956, the first woman to head a major Canadian city. He added, "Let them stay where they belong."[31] As a public figure, Casselman Wadds was often asked how she dealt with the challenge of being a woman in male-dominated professions. She denied that her gender had hindered her. This is a surprising claim. Political debates and discourse were replete with gendered notions and prejudices. Even her most devoted mentor and champion – her father – complained to Diefenbaker about her appointment as parliamentary secretary because there were men who needed the stipend that went along with the job more than his daughter. Diefenbaker replied that she was the only person, other than himself, who reported for work before 8 a.m.[32] Casselman Wadds claimed that she did not think of herself as a woman MP but as an MP who happened to be a woman.[33] As high commissioner, she again insisted that gender was irrelevant: "When I walk into a roomful of men, I just don't think of myself as being the only woman there. I'm only conscious that I'm there for a purpose and that there is a job to be done."[34]

Casselman Wadds was not the only female diplomat to deny that gender influenced their work. Mary McGeachy's biographer noted that she wanted to be seen as feminine but not a feminist.[35] British historians Helen McCarthy and James Southern also pointed out that women in the British foreign service did not support "a woman's agenda" into the 1970s.[36] As McCarthy observed elsewhere, women in the British Foreign Office did not want to be called "women diplomats"; they just wanted to get on with the work.[37] Margaret Thatcher, with whom Casselman Wadds got along well, also emphasized ability as the only relevant criteria for assuming a leadership position. When asked in 1973 if she would like to see a woman as prime minister of Britain, Thatcher replied: "I don't think it depends so much whether it's a man prime minister or a woman prime minister as whether that person is the right person for the job."[38]

Casselman Wadds' decision to detach gender from her professional life reflected her own unease with second-wave feminism. Although Casselman Wadds' political and diplomatic career overlapped with the second-wave feminist movement that challenged entrenched ideas about the roles and abilities of women, she acknowledged in a 1979 interview that the "so-called woman's movement [was] a little foreign to me."[39] In 1985, she took part in a panel discussion on the advances of women, along with three other women receiving honorary doctorates from Dalhousie University.[40] While the other women discussed prejudice, glass ceilings, lower pay and "structural inequality for women," Casselman Wadds admitted that she was bewildered by the feminist movement. In her own life, she had never felt disadvantaged: it was assumed that she could do everything that her brothers did. Socio-economic circumstances, a well-connected family, and her particular family dynamic meant that she did not confront the kinds of prejudice, social barriers, and power dynamics that perpetuated female disadvantage and oppression.[41] Her experience informed her ideas about social policy; she did not endorse affirmative action policies and quotas to end gender discrimination. Instead, she repeatedly emphasized that hard work, doing a job well, and education were the real keys to success.

Although she distanced herself from feminism, Casselman Wadds supported mothers and working mothers. In 1966, she insisted that homemaking was the toughest job of all.[42] In 1968, she argued that the money spent on the Royal Commission on the Status of Women would have been better spent in creating more child care for working mothers and supporting women to attend university.[43] Twenty years later, in the panel at Dalhousie, she talked about the challenges that confronted working mothers and called for "society ... to be more compassionate in its treatment of working mothers."[44] Her numerous statements about women and equality align with some of the core views of first-wave feminism which emphasized maternal roles and responsibilities. She opposed discrimination, arguing that gender should not be a factor in determining suitability for any position. As she put it in 1966, a brilliant mind is a brilliant mind; it should not matter what body the mind belonged to.[45] She believed in equality between men and women, but she did not conclude that equity was needed to bring it about. Her views on women, mothers, and working mothers placed her, sometimes awkwardly, between the first and second waves of feminist thought.

Despite repeated statements to the effect that being a woman did not affect her professional life, no one she met could overlook her gender. Casselman Wadds was known for her beaming smile, trademark red lipstick, and impeccable fashion sense. She owned her femininity. For example, she deliberately dressed fashionably and there were many admiring descriptions of her chic outfits. Attention to appearance was important for Casselman Wadds, who understood the value of a well-constructed public persona. But she also downplayed her achievements and embraced qualities that made her less threatening to the men around her.

She also valued good manners in politics and she sometimes linked civil politics to feminine qualities. For example, she praised British prime minister Margaret Thatcher for behaving as "an attractive, feminine woman" rather than "in a nasty, hard-headed, mannish way."[46] She had displayed her own practice of civil politics during her nomination race in 1958. Just as she denied having experienced sexism in her life, she also denied that gender influenced interpersonal relations. For example, she insisted that her positive relationship with Thatcher had nothing to do with the fact they were both women.[47] Despite Casselman Wadds' public disavowal of the impact of gender on her professional success, her deliberate feminine political style, along with her privileged and political life experience, allowed her to navigate effectively in professional environments where women were under-represented so that she was liked and respected and reaped opportunities. That she was seen as highly capable was clear when she was appointed Canada's first woman high commissioner to London, in 1979. That she did not underestimate her own abilities was evident when she accepted the post.

Patriating the Constitution

The process of patriating the constitution embroiled British-Canadian relations in a diplomatic morass that combined the complexity of constitutional law with the obstinacy of partisan deadlock. Relations between Canada and the United Kingdom were cordial but grew evermore distant during the 1970s. Canadian exports to Japan and the European Economic Community gradually overtook trade with Britain, which lost its status as Canada's second-largest trading partner. Bilateral relations chaffed over multilateral commitments such as the Commonwealth, which Trudeau sought to preserve as Edward Heath predicted its decline, and NATO, where the British delegation increasingly withheld intelligence from their Canadian counterparts.[48]

Prime Minister Trudeau's effort to bring home the constitution required closer bilateral cooperation than Canada or Britain had found necessary in the preceding decade. So long as Westminster retained the power to amend the British North America Act, patriating the constitution required an act of British Parliament. During Trudeau's visit to London in June 1980, Thatcher vaguely assured him that her government would table any constitutional legislation drafted by the Canadian government. But Trudeau's long-held ambition to draft a new constitution with an amending formula and a Charter of Rights and Freedoms soon became mired in quarrels with provincial governments. Unable to reach consensus by September 1980, Trudeau announced his intention to pass constitutional reform unilaterally. Working only with support from the premiers of Ontario and New Brunswick, and from the federal New Democratic Party (NDP), Trudeau's resolve to push his constitutional package through Westminster threatened to ensnare British parliamentarians in a web of Canadian political entanglements.[49]

While Trudeau postured and asserted his mandate to forge ahead without the support of provincial premiers, Thatcher bristled at the prospect of taking on Canadian constitutional reform amid an economic crisis. Facing inflation and Britain's highest unemployment since the 1930s, Thatcher's budget of March 1981 raised taxes in the face of public criticism from leading economists. As riots broke out in major cities and commentators anticipated a reversal in policy, Thatcher weathered open calls for her resignation and maintained control of her cabinet and backbenches.[50] Unruly backbenchers were unlikely to defeat a Canadian constitutional package, but they could embarrass the government by stalling the bill in debate, amending the legislation, or narrowing its margin of support. Labour MP Austin Vernon Mitchell warned high commission staffers that the House had been "'whipped' too often," and a Canadian patriation bill would allow members to "act up" on an issue that did not affect their constituents.[51] With Thatcher presiding over a precarious government and Trudeau impatient to outmaneuver dissenting premiers, the bilateral cooperation required to patriate the constitution became increasingly politicized.

Competing interests on both sides of the Atlantic exploited the patriation process for their own gains. Previous amendments to the British North America Act established a precedent requiring provincial consent before amending the constitution. To counter Trudeau's decision to patriate the constitution unilaterally, provincial representatives in London organized an aggressive lobbying campaign asking British politicians to uphold the provinces' right to play a role in patriation.[52] This lobbying turned the question of Thatcher's support for Trudeau into a source of embarrassment. Moreover, Trudeau's brash posturing did little to win British support. His suggestion that British lawmakers should "hold their noses" and pass whatever legislation he drafted only encouraged disruptive MPs, who accused Trudeau of using Westminster to outflank provincial opposition.[53] While Trudeau remained determined to repatriate the constitution unilaterally, Thatcher was equally determined to avoid a patriation bill that would exacerbate the political turmoil generated by the economic crisis. The need to cooperate with British parliamentarians added an additional burden to the already arduous patriation process and placed Canada's high commissioner at a critical juncture on the path to a new Canadian constitution. Fortunately, her career in party politics provided Jean Casselman Wadds with the skills needed to help bring the constitution home.

With neither prime minister inclined to back down, it fell to Casselman Wadds and her staff at the high commission to maintain cordial bilateral relations while making the case for Trudeau's patriation package to British parliamentarians. Practised in the craft of mingling with social and political elites, Casselman Wadds had eased her way into the exclusive circles of London society with a confident charm developed while growing up in a political household and with an eye-catching wardrobe. Casselman Wadds likened the social side of diplomatic work to running a political campaign on behalf of her country.[54] She approached Liberal leader David Steel and Shadow Foreign Secretary Peter Shore at a state function and secured commitments from both to do what they could to help pass the constitutional package. She later met Lord Charteris, former private secretary to Queen Elizabeth II, and Labour leader Michael Foot at business lunches hosted by British and Canadian firms. While chatting with Casselman Wadds, Charteris identified himself as a willing champion of Canadian patriation and the two discovered they shared a long list of mutual friends.[55] Foot showed more caution, and Casselman Wadds knew not to apply too much pressure.

Like many diplomats, Casselman Wadds coordinated meetings, luncheons, and dinner parties to cultivate goodwill. The work of arranging social events to facilitate diplomatic conversations, as David Webster explains in his chapter, often fell to the wives of diplomats and this is the role that Casselman Wadds has been cast as playing during the patriation campaign. Reeves Haggan, one of the aides Trudeau sent to London to negotiate the process, recalled that Casselman Wadds said, "My house, my table are at your disposal."[56] Such recollections suggest that Casselman Wadds' main contribution was to support the work of male envoys from Ottawa as they secured deals with their British counterparts. But Casselman Wadds eagerly took up the work of winning the support of British parliamentarians. While the work of lobbying British politicians over lunch was usually left to political operatives, Casselman Wadds played a coordinating role by selecting invitees whose influence would benefit the patriation campaign. David Collenette was parliamentary secretary to the president of Trudeau's privy council and spent several weeks in London in the spring of 1981 lobbying British MPs. He described the "genius" of Casselman Wadds' skill in selecting guests with compatible personalities to ensure that High Commission lunches remained cordial and constructive.[57]

In some cases, Casselman Wadds met with prominent British politicians herself and curated the guest list to her advantage. While pursuing support from the Labour front bench, she invited Michael Foot to a dinner at the high commission along with the dissenting provincial representatives – to maintain the appearance of impartiality. The seating arrangement, however, gave Casselman Wadds access to Foot throughout dinner while isolating her provincial opponents. Foot continued to keep his cards close to his chest, and Casselman Wadds did not pressure him to state his position on patriation.

The high commissioner's reluctance to press Foot on his stance reflected Casselman Wadds' civil approach to politics and diplomacy. Throughout the patriation campaign, she remained careful not to sacrifice cordial relations by making her case too aggressively. Trudeau advisor Michael Kirby, who visited London to assess the situation in November 1980, reassured Trudeau that Casselman Wadds knew to keep things slow and subtle.[58] At a meeting with elder Labour statesman Denis Healey, Casselman Wadds learned that the provincial agents were losing the support of opposition MPs by trying to do "too much too soon."[59] Though provincial representatives made headlines in Britain, their persistence wore on the patience of parliamentarians. Labour and Co-operative Party MP Laurie Pavitt complained that he was inundated with material from the provincial offices.[60] In her cables back to Ottawa, Casselman Wadds showed her disdain for this forward approach when she criticized Quebec agent general Gilles Loiselle for "continually pressing himself on" Thatcher during a dinner at the high commission. Loiselle's "embarrassing" behaviour, Casselman Wadds concluded, did more harm than good.[61]

The dinner party war required much more than food, wine, and place settings. Casselman Wadds also orchestrated a lobbying campaign of her own. Working with a steering committee of senior diplomats, Casselman Wadds monitored the campaign of provincial agents and distributed information packets to provide British parliamentarians with evidence to support the case for patriation. Staff compiled detailed estimates of undecided backbenchers that might be swayed by a meeting with a high-profile delegate from Ottawa.[62] In their studies of patriation, historians Jack Granatstein and Robert Bothwell focused on the extra help that arrived from Ottawa. Political operatives, such as Reeves Haggan, set up residence in London, while federal cabinet ministers, including MacGuigan and Justice Minister Jean Chrétien, flew in to sell Trudeau's constitutional package in after-dinner speeches at the Canadian Club of London.[63] But the success of these visits depended on information gathered by the high commission, and Casselman Wadds provided sound tactical advice. She warned MacGuigan, for instance, to soften the tone of his speech to the Canadian Club because British politicians were irritated at Trudeau's insistence that Westminster had to pass whatever legislation he concocted.[64] The information gathered by Casselman Wadds and the advice she offered based on her assessments of the situation ensured that these Ottawa men made the most of their visits to London.

The campaign of well-mannered dinner parties and Casselman Wadds' tactful advice to delegates from Ottawa were necessary to smooth over an increasingly bitter battle of wills between the Canadian and British governments. In Ottawa, the British high commissioner, Sir John Ford, waged his own lobbying campaign to pressure Trudeau to drop the Charter of Rights from the patriation package. Ford leaked details of Trudeau's early meetings with Thatcher to prove that the Canadian had not mentioned the Charter of Rights, nor the prospect of entrenched provincial opposition, when asking for Thatcher's support.[65] Ford famously attempted to undermine the federal NDP's support for Trudeau at an Ottawa skating party by confiding to an NDP MP that the patriation package would never pass Westminster.[66] NDP leader Ed Broadbent protested Ford's attempt to undermine his party's support for Trudeau's minority government, which resulted in Ford's recall to London. Ford's recall highlights the importance of Casselman Wadds' measured approach during this volatile political battle. Leaked cables from the high commission in London, however, made a sensation of her shrewd, and sometimes scathing, appraisal of British ministers. Casselman Wadds' suspicion of wiretapping at the high commission, likewise leaked to the press, revealed a growing distrust between the two governments.[67]

The campaigns orchestrated by Indigenous activists in London added another layer of acrimony to the patriation campaign. In addition to legal challenges launched in British courts by several provincial First Nations associations, hundreds of delegates arrived in London to urge British parliamentarians to entrench treaty relationships into Canada's patriated constitution. Their campaign won the support of the British press, the public, and several Members of Parliament. Canadian and British lawmakers struggled to recognize or understand the concept of Indigenous governance, and Casselman Wadds became uncharacteristically flustered when faced with this issue.[68] Known for her calm composure, she recalled getting "angrier and angrier" when confronted by young Conservative MPs who challenged her about redressing Canada's treatment of Indigenous peoples. Her frustration revealed how a lifetime immersed in party politics framed Casselman Wadds' understanding of patriation. She dismissed her British interlocutors' accusations of Canada's historic mistreatment of Indigenous peoples by arguing that "there had never been any ill will towards our native people from the Canadian government."[69] These views certainly demonstrated Casselman Wadds' ignorance of Canadian policies of dispossession and assimilation, but she also showed little sympathy for social movements that relied on public protest and legal challenges, rather than on the rules and conventions of party politics that she was accustomed to.

By the summer of 1981, the main obstacle to patriation came from legal challenges launched by the dissenting provinces.[70] Much to Trudeau's frustration, Thatcher insisted on waiting for the Supreme Court of Canada to rule on these challenges before tabling a patriation package in Westminster. In September 1981, the Supreme Court justices agreed that the federal government must seek substantial provincial support for constitutional reform. Pushed back to the negotiating table, Trudeau organized another conference to gain the consent of provincial premiers. Late on the third night of the conference Chrétien struck a deal, popularly known as the Kitchen Accord, which established a threshold of provincial consent for further amendments and inserted the Notwithstanding Clause into the proposed constitution. As the premiers were roused to learn of the late-night agreement, Quebec premier René Lévesque, who lodged at a separate hotel, on the Quebec side of the Ottawa River, was left out of the discussions until the deal was presented to him the following morning. Though nine premiers agreed to the new constitutional package, Lévesque remained defiantly opposed and vowed to pursue the matter in court. A spate of new legal challenges launched by Lévesque, women's groups, and a handful of First Nations communities threatened to lock the constitution in further court battles. Trudeau hastily included provisions to entrench gender equality and Indigenous rights into the constitution and rushed to pass the new package through Westminster. The British House of Commons passed the constitutional package on March 9, 1982, with 177 votes to 33 against. The bill sailed through the House of Lords two weeks later.[71]

Passing the patriation package through Westminster brought an end to a difficult moment between Canada and Britain. With rebellious backbenchers threatening to disrupt Thatcher's government and stubborn provincial premiers throwing up obstacles for Trudeau, the bilateral cooperation needed to pass the constitution devolved into a battle of wills, mired by suspicion and leaked documents. In the tense aftermath, Casselman Wadds continued her work as high commissioner trying to repair the damage done to British-Canadian relations. Although Queen Elizabeth II would represent the Crown at the patriation ceremony in Ottawa, Casselman Wadds made the case for inviting a delegation to represent Westminster. She reminded Trudeau that the patriation campaign had frayed relations with both the Thatcher government and opposition parties. To mend British-Canadian relations, she recommended inviting Thatcher, the Speaker of the House of Commons, and Lord Chancellor, as well as the leaders of the Labour and Liberal Parties. Most accepted the invitation. With a British naval task force setting sail for the Falkland Islands, Thatcher declined to attend the ceremony on April 17, 1982.[72]

Though she had devoted herself to ushering Trudeau's patriation package through Britain's divided parliament, Casselman Wadds reflected with dismay on the changes that the Constitution Act had brought to Canadian politics and society. She was particularly apprehensive that the Charter of Rights and Freedoms empowered Canadians to seek change by working outside of party politics and anticipated a proliferation of protesters "running up and down noisily" to Parliament Hill or taking their complaints directly to the Supreme Court.[73] For Casselman Wadds, the Constitution Act meant that Canadians could challenge the status quo without engaging with the political system that she had learned to navigate so well.

Conclusion

Jean Casselman Wadds should figure prominently in accounts of the patriation of the constitution. She was already an accomplished public figure when she was appointed high commissioner in the UK. She only added to her accomplishments while there. She developed and implemented the vital diplomatic campaign in London, shaping its tactics and organization, offering advice, and lobbying hard. Her political style – civil, amiable, charming – was an asset when dealing with mutinous British backbenchers with their own agendas, recalcitrant party leaders, and an irritated prime minister who had problems enough of her own without having to steer patriation through a restive Westminster. Framed in the broader history of Canadian diplomacy, Casselman Wadds managed a lobbying effort of curated social events and coordinated ministerial visits that bore many similarities to the public diplomacy, or "new diplomacy," widely attributed to Allan Gotlieb's pioneering approach to his tenure as ambassador to the United States.[74]

Casselman Wadds repeatedly explained her successes in politics and diplomacy as a product of hard work and dedication. Though she highlighted her femininity in her manners and appearance, she consistently downplayed the role of gender as either an advantage or impediment to her work in politics and diplomacy. Nevertheless, her gender defined a political style that allowed her to be successful and effective in both. Casselman Wadds' many achievements depended on her ability to navigate around barriers in male-dominated spheres at a time when gendered expectations worked against her. Her success also owed much to her privileged background and status as a political insider. She acknowledged this advantage without ever fully recognizing the larger structural implications that held other women back.

Did gender have an influence beyond her diplomatic style? Did it also influence her views on foreign policy and international affairs? Scholars like Sylvia Bashevkin have examined the link between gender and foreign policy. She identified a slate of "core transnational feminist issues" and found that "gender matters in important ways to international aid practices and to foreign policy language."[75] Casselman Wadds' foreign policy priorities and rhetoric map onto some transnational feminist issues like hunger, disease, poverty, and aid; she also spoke up about the challenges that affected working mothers. But Casselman Wadds' foreign policy views were also shaped by her conservatism and partisan allegiances, inherited settler colonial assumptions, generation, and contemporary global conditions. An intersectional approach that integrates gender, class, race, family, region, and time offers a more compelling understanding of her views about domestic and global politics.

Jean Casselman Wadds' experience as high commissioner and her work on the patriation of the constitution confirm the importance of gender to understanding her work and the way her work has been remembered. Indeed, gender should be folded into studies of all participants in Canada's international activities, whether they worked in or out of government, in embassies, community-development projects, emancipatory movements, or within family structures. Including gender results in a more complete history that challenges entrenched ideas about the motivations and consequences of Canadian involvement in world affairs and questions established ideas about the purpose of Canada's diplomatic history. It will also produce histories that are reflexive, where the spotlight turns in to explain international policies, activism, and relations as products of domestic circumstances rather than simply as a response to external activities and conditions. When gender is integrated into the historical methodology, the subject and object are reversed, the historian's gaze is redirected, and her purpose is redefined.

This volume focuses on exceptional individual women – women of firsts – and asks whether and how they broke down barriers for other women. Their accomplishments did not automatically lead to seconds, thirds, and fourths.[76] In the case of senior diplomatic appointments to the largest embassies, barriers persisted after Casselman Wadds' appointment. It was not until 2016 that Janice Charette became the second woman to serve as high commissioner in London. In 2017, Isabelle Hudon became the first woman ambassador to Paris, and in 2020, Kirsten Hillman became the first woman ambassador to Washington. Nonetheless, Casselman Wadds' story tells us how one thoughtful, savvy, and well-connected woman defined a public demeanour that was conducive to success in male-dominated worlds of politics and diplomacy. In Casselman Wadds' case, that never involved headlong confrontations or explicit challenges to gendered norms and structures of power in life, politics, or diplomacy. Her career also conformed to patterns revealed in the experiences of other women. Individual agency alone does not explain the successes of women in Canadian diplomacy. Their stories highlight how larger forces – including social norms, international contexts, and institutional structures – created barriers for them. In some cases, women confronted those barriers directly. Casselman Wadds navigated around them, a tactic that worked for her and that women continue to employ today.

Notes

1 See, for instance, P. Buckner, ed., *Canada and the End of Empire* (Vancouver: UBC Press, 2005).
2 Mark MacGuigan, *An Inside Look at External Affairs during the Trudeau Years: The Memoirs of Mark MacGuigan*, ed. P. Whitney Lackenbauer (Calgary: University of Calgary Press, 2002), 97.
3 Pierre E. Trudeau, *Memoirs* (Toronto: McClelland and Stewart, 1993), 311.
4 Recently, political scientists have examined Canadian foreign policy through a feminist lens. See C. Turenne Sjolander and Heather A. Smith, eds., *Feminist Perspectives on Canadian Foreign Policy* (Don Mills, ON: Oxford University Press, 2003). The literature on gender and American foreign policy is better developed. See Emily S. Rosenberg, "Gender," *The Journal of American History*, 77, 1 (June 1990): 116–24. Two recent contributions are: Carolyn James and Glenda Sluga, eds., *Women, Diplomacy and International Politics since 1500* (London: Routledge, 2016); and Jennifer Cassidy, ed., *Gender and Diplomacy* (London: Routledge, 2017).
5 John Hilliker, Mary Halloran, and Greg Donaghy, *Canada's Department of External Affairs*, vol. 3, *Innovation and Adaptation, 1968–1984* (Toronto: University of Toronto Press/Institute of Public Administration of Canada, 2017), 71–72, 300–5.
6 C. Turenne Sjolander, "Margaret Meagher and the Role of Women in the Foreign Service: Groundbreaking or Housekeeping?," in G. Donaghy and K.R. Nossal, eds., *Architects and*

Innovators: Building the Department of Foreign Affairs and International trade, 1909–2009 (Montreal/Kingston: McGill-Queen's University Press, 2009), 223–36; Mary Kinnear, *Woman of the World: Mary McGeachy and International Cooperation* (Toronto: University of Toronto Press, 2004). McCarthy discusses managing femininity in her study of women diplomats in the UK. Helen McCarthy, "Gendering Diplomatic History: Women in the British Diplomatic Service circa 1919–1972," in James and Sluga, eds., *Women, Diplomacy and International Politics*, 179.

7 Sjolander, "Margaret Meagher and the Role of Women," 230.
8 She described herself as leading a "traditional Canadian life." Mrs. Jean Casselman Wadds (JCW, interview with Tom Earle, March 20, 1985, in Library and Archives Canada (LAC) R1026–63–2-E-vol-2564-file-3, 20.
9 J.L. Granatstein and R. Bothwell, *Pirouette: Pierre Trudeau and Canadian Foreign Policy* (Toronto: University of Toronto Press, 1991), 355.
10 James and Sluga, *Women, Diplomacy and International Politics*, 6.
11 JCW, interview with Tom Earle, 6.
12 JCW, interview with Tom Earle, 4.
13 "Jean's at Home in the House," *Weekly Magazine* 8, 46, 1958, 13–15, LAC MG26-N11-C2, vol. 136, file 355–8C Wadds, Mrs. J. Casselman. All other magazine and newspaper articles are also from this file, unless indicated. See also S. Sharpe, *The Gilded Ghetto, Women and Political Power in Canada* (Toronto: HarperCollins 1995), 77.
14 W. Pitman (MP), "An MP Who Happens to Be a Woman," *Peterborough Examiner*, March 29, 1962.
15 JCW, interview with Tom Earle, 1; "Says Jean Casselman: Politics Perfect Place to Meet People," *Toronto Star*, March 13, 1961.
16 G.J. Inwood, *Continentalizing Canada: The Politics and Legacy of the MacDonald Commission* (Toronto: University of Toronto Press, 2005).
17 JCW, interview with Tom Earle, 31–32.
18 Canada, *Hansard*, 24th Parl., 4th Sess., Vol. 2 (January 24, 1961) at 1354–55.
19 JCW, interview with Tom Earle., 4, 13.
20 "I Would Rather See Our Historic Party Dismembered," *Ottawa Journal*, February 4, 1969.
21 "The Making of Foreign Policy," George C. Nowlan Lecture (1), given by Her Excellency Mrs. J. Casselman Wadds, Canadian High Commissioner to the United Kingdom, October 14, 1981, Acadia University Archives, 1–2.
22 J.G. Diefenbaker, *One Canada: Memoirs of John G. Diefenbaker*, vol. 3, *The Tumultuous Years, 1962–1967* (Toronto: Macmillan, 1977), 276; Peter Stursberg, *Diefenbaker: Leadership Lost, 1962–1967* (Toronto: University of Toronto Press, 1976), 171.
23 G.C. Perlin, *The Tory Syndrome: Leadership Politics in the Progressive Conservative Party* (Montreal: McGill-Queen's University Press, 2006), 121–22.
24 JCW, interview with Tom Earle, 20.
25 Canada, *Hansard*, 24th Parl., 5th Sess., Vol. 1 (February 19, 1962) at 1014–1015.
26 Canada, *Hansard*, 24th Parl., 5th sess., Vol. 1 (February 19, 1962) at 1014, 1015.
27 "Partners in Freedom 1980," an Address by The Honourable Jean Casselman Wadds, Canadian High Commissioner to the United Kingdom, to the Empire Club, October 16, 1980.
28 As high commissioner, she repeated that smaller states had more freedom of maneuver than great powers and could take the lead on global initiatives. Mrs. J. Casselman Wadds, "The Making of Foreign Policy," 23–24.
29 F. McKenzie, "A New Vision for the Commonwealth: Diefenbaker's Commonwealth Tour of 1958," in *Reassessing the Rogue Tory: Canadian Foreign Relations in the Diefenbaker Era*, ed. J. Cavell and R. Touhey (Vancouver: UBC Press, 2018), 25–44.

30 See John Hilliker and Donald Barry, *Canada's Department of External Affairs*, vol. 2, *Coming of Age, 1946–1968* (Montreal/Kingston: McGill-Queen's University Press/Institute of Public Administration of Canada, 1995), 322–26.
31 "Jean's at Home in the House."
32 "Family Background Key to Success Panelists Say," *Dal News* 16, October 23, 1985, p. 3, Dalhousie University Archives, MS-1-Ref, box 222, folder 3, item 4, https://findingaids.library.dal.ca/dal-news-volume-16-issue-no-4.
33 Pitman, "An MP Who Happens to Be a Woman."
34 "Lady in London Thrives on Hectic Pace," *Ottawa Citizen*, February 5, 1980, 53.
35 Mary Kinnear, *Woman of the World: Mary McGeachy and International Cooperation* (Toronto: University of Toronto Press, 2004), 254.
36 Helen McCarthy and James Southern, "Women, Gender and Diplomacy: A Historical Survey," in *Women and Diplomacy*, ed. Jennifer Cassidy (London: Routledge, 2017), 27.
37 Helen McCarthy, "Gendering Diplomatic History: Women in the British Diplomatic Service, circa 1919–1972," in *Women, Diplomacy and International Politics since 1500*, ed. C. James and G. Sluga (London: Routledge, 2016), 179.
38 Margaret Thatcher, quoted in Kate Maltby, "Margaret Thatcher Gave Britain's Female Politicians the Freedom to Fail," *Guardian*, May 3, 2019, https://www.theguardian.com/commentisfree/2019/may/03/margaret-thatcher-success-britain-female-politicians-fail.
39 J. Rusk, "An Old Friend of Clark's Family Named Commissioner to UK," *Globe and Mail*, October 13, 1979, 11.
40 The other women were Anna Laing, ophthalmologist; Margaret Doody, novelist and professor at Princeton; and Kathryn Sullivan, astronaut.
41 "Family Background Key to Success Panelists Say," 3.
42 B. Sarsfied, "Jean Wadds MP Says Investment in Bright Minds Greatest Value for the Dollar," *Ottawa Journal*, March 10, 1966.
43 "MP Claims Commission Funds Could Have Gone Elsewhere," *Ottawa Journal*, March 6, 1968.
44 "Family Background Key to Success Panelists Say," 3.
45 Sarsfied, "Jean Wadds MP Says Investment in Bright Minds Greatest Value for the Dollar."
46 JCW, interview with Tom Earle, 38.
47 "Canada's High Commissioner Says She Doesn't Find the Job a Strain," *Leader-Post*, May 7, 1980, 16.
48 J.L. Granatstein and R. Bothwell, *Pirouette: Pierre Trudeau and Canadian Foreign Policy*, 337–38; J.L. Granatstein and R. Bothwell, *Trudeau's World: Insiders Reflect on Foreign Policy, Trade, and Defence, 1968–84* (Vancouver: UBC Press, 2006), 322.
49 Frédéric Bastien, *The Battle of London: Trudeau, Thatcher, and the Fight for Canada's Constitution*, trans. J. Homel (Toronto: Dundurn Press, 2014), 68–75.
50 R. Vinen, *Thatcher's Britain: The Politics and Social Upheaval of the Thatcher Era* (London: Simon and Schuster, 2009), 103, 113–14.
51 Notes from meeting with Austin Vernon Mitchell, March 1981. "Views of British Members of Parliament about the Canadian Constitution," LAC, RG 25, vol 27042, file 20-CDA-16-1-4 (part 2).
52 Bastien, *Battle of London*, 185.
53 J. Hay, "The Constitution: A Rough Passage Home," *Maclean's*, April 5, 1982, 21–22.
54 "Canada's High Commissioner Says She Doesn't Find the Job a Strain," 16.
55 Transcript of memo by Jean Casselman Wadds, November 12, 1980; Telegram from LDN XNGR2579 to BH FPOTT/KIRBY DE OPM December 2, 1980, LAC, RG 25, vol 8723, file 20-CDA-16-1-4 (part 7).

56 Casselman Wadds, quoted in Granatstein and Bothwell, *Trudeau's World*, 336.
57 Francine McKenzie interview with David Collenette, November 5, 2019.
58 Memorandum for the Prime Minister from Michael Kirby, November 25 1980, LAC, RG25, vol. 8723, file 20-CDA-16-4-1 (part 5).
59 Telegram from LDN PATR0013 to EXTOTT GEB, February 19, 1981, LAC, RG 25, vol. 11077, file 20-CDA-16-1-4 (part 17).
60 Notes re: Mr. Lauire Pavitt, MP, "Views of British Members of Parliament about the Canadian Constitution," LAC, RG 25, vol. 27042, file 20-CDA-16-1-4 (part 3).
61 Note for the Minister, October 31, 1980, LAC, RG 25, vol. 8872, file 20-CDA-16-1-4 (part 3).
62 Telegram from LDN PATR0024 to EXTOTT GEB, March 2, 1981, LAC, RG 25, vol. 11078, file 20-CDA-16-1-4 (part 19).
63 Granatstein and Bothwell, *Pirouette*, 355-56.
64 Telegram from LDN NXGR0394 to EXTOTT MIN, February 13, 1981, LAC, RG 25, vol. 11077, file 20-CDA-16-1-4 (part 16).
65 Bastien, *Battle of London*, 180.
66 Granatstein and Bothwell, *Pirouette*, 358.
67 Hilliker, Halloran, Donaghy, *Canada's Department of External Affairs*, 3: 371.
68 K. Ladner, "An Indigenous Paradox: Both Monumental Achievement and Monumental Defeat," in *Patriation and Its Consequences: Constitution Making in Canada*, ed. L. Harder and S. Patten (Vancouver: UBC Press, 2016), 269.
69 JCW, interview with Tom Earle, 52.
70 Bastien, *Battle of London*, 218.
71 Bastien, *Battle of London*, 317.
72 From LDN PATR0027 to BH FPROOTT / KIRBY de OPM EXTOTT / GEM, March 15, 1982; From LDN XNGR1092 to PCOOTT / FOWLER / CHEARY PCOOTT / PITFIELD, April 2, 1982; From LDN XNGR1094 to PCOOTT / CHEARY PCOOTT / PITFIELD, April 2, 1982; LAC, RG 25, vol. 11478, file 20-CDA-16-1-4 (part 34). Though these documents do not state a reason for Thatcher's decision not to attend, it should be noted that a Royal Navy task force was preparing to sail for the Falklands.
73 JCW, interview with Tom Earle, 57.
74 Hilliker, Halloran, Donaghy, *Canada's Department of External Affairs*, 3: 407.
75 S. Bashevkin, "Numerical and Policy Representation on the World Stage: Women Foreign Policy Leaders in Western Industrialized Systems," *International Political Science Review* 35, 4: 416-17, 425.
76 Rebecca Tiessen, "Canada's Longstanding Commitments to Gender Equality: An Overview" (paper presented at Breaking Barriers, Shaping Worlds: Women and the Search for Global Order, 1919-2019, Ottawa, March 2019).

9

Flora MacDonald
Secretary of State for External Affairs, 1979–80

Joe Clark

THIS COLLECTION ON WOMEN breaking barriers and changing worlds shines an overdue light on the experiences of courageous and accomplished individuals – quite different from one another – who drove change and set new standards for Canada's international contributions, in its diplomacy and in its foreign ministry. This volume encourages and allows us to reflect on how and why the contributions of women were constrained and the ways in which some of those constraints were overcome. That reflection itself allows a clear-eyed consideration of the most effective lessons about how barriers might be broken and the world changed in our challenging future.

We all recognize the profound impact on the improvement of conditions in the world by women who work outside ministries, such as in nongovernmental organizations – responding as citizens to crisis, promoting respect and assertion of rights, demonstrating eloquent and courageous advocacy, and driving transformative initiatives and innovation. One encouraging characteristic of contemporary times is the increasing prevalence and range of practical partnerships between governments and citizens – partnerships within which women play leading roles.

My observations here are about Flora MacDonald, whose significance lies not just in the fact that she was the first female secretary of state for external affairs (or foreign minister) in Canada's history but also, more significantly, in the transformative way she performed that role. She was practical, innovative, and interested in tangible results. She personified and pioneered the benefits of combining the instincts, understanding, and experience of the "professional" and those of the "citizen," reinforced by a determined disposition to assist and include individuals whom ordinary practice might exclude.

This will not be a dispassionate or objective assessment of Flora MacDonald. Flora and I were friends, allies, partisans, leadership candidates, ministerial colleagues, and lucky Canadians together.

One of my first paying jobs, in the early 1960s, was on the tiny Ottawa staff of the national headquarters of the Progressive Conservative Party of Canada. The nominal boss was a smart and gifted man, Allister Grosart, later a senator. But the person who made the place run – made the party run – was Flora. That was not what she came to Ottawa to do. She had applied for a position as a secretary at the Department of External Affairs and – in the long wait for a response – took a "temporary" job as a typist with the political party that she and her family had long supported.

I will focus on Flora the barrier-breaker, at home and abroad, and offer a view on some of the factors which made her both an exceptional individual and a contemporary model for others interested in changing the world.

Did it matter that she was a woman? Of course it did. Did it matter that she grew up in a Cape Breton mining town in the midst of the Great Depression of the 1930s? Unquestionably. Because growing up a girl, in North Sydney, in an economy where only one in twenty miners was working full-time taught her about both exclusion and aspiration.

Formidable Flora was a notably effective minister in three complex departments – External Affairs, Employment and Immigration, and Communications – in two governments, always prepared and persuasive in cabinet, eloquent and usually successful in defining issues that some colleagues might consider "soft" or intangible, and knowing when to fight and when to wait.

Why was that? One of the most important reasons was her experience and skill at the beating heart of Canadian party politics. For a formative decade in the nation as a whole and in most of its provinces and territories, her constant and essential role was to respect and reconcile the often deep differences that are inescapable in a huge country and in political parties, which – at their best and in their time – sought to bring and keep Canadians together. Among the destructive recent changes in Canada's political system has been the serious erosion of the role of national political parties as brokers of legitimate interests. Robert Stanfield, who served as premier of

Nova Scotia, federal Progressive Conservative leader, and Leader of Her Majesty's Loyal Opposition, observed long ago that Canada has enough natural divisions without political parties creating new ones. For years, the major national political parties – including at critical times the Co-operative Commonwealth Federation/New Democratic Party – drew differences together and reconciled them. And in that process, the Canadians who worked in political parties themselves became skilled at finding common ground. Certainly, Flora did. It helped make her a better and more effective minister and leader of change. She broke barriers.

That was her most significant legacy – as a change-maker. In a very real sense, she started with herself. Without resentment, or anger, or even a specific ambition, she changed her own course first. Her springboard was not material wealth, nor family prominence nor privilege, and certainly not gender. Cape Breton was like most of Canada in the Depression of the 1930s and the Second World War years when Flora was growing up there. She later recalled that in that community, in that era, "education for a son was a [family] investment, for a daughter ... an expense." She topped her classes, but was encouraged to stop high school at grade eleven, go to business college, and then to work – first as a teller at the Bank of Nova Scotia. She followed her constant instinct to learn, finding ordinary opportunities to work across the country, travelling whenever she could throughout North American and Europe.

Yet she was always anchored. Cape Breton is a community which one never leaves emotionally, and Flora never did. But being rooted there also means learning that often you have to move to grow. For Flora and many others, Cape Breton is the opposite of insular – bound together by history, by clan, by identity; the mythic connections to Scotland persist and can be deeply personal – Flora proudly shared the name of the eighteenth century Scottish heroine. Her great-grandfather had been a seafaring captain, more often away from Cape Breton than at home. Her grandfather went to sea himself at age twelve, and when he married her grandmother, she voyaged with him, gave birth to three sons at sea, then brought them "home" to North Sydney. Her father was a reader, their house full of books, often travel books; during the Second World War, when Flora was in her teens, he ran the Western Union Telegraph Company terminus in North Sydney, receiving the dots and dashes which connected Canada and the world – and Canada and the war in Europe – and he brought those stories home to Flora every night.

No organization helped her. There was no National Association for the Advancement of Bright Young Women from North Sydney. So, confident of her roots but not prepared to be confined by them, she soon set out to see the wider world, coming back to Nova Scotia in 1956 and then, fatefully, looking for opportunity and adventure in her nation's capital.

So the young Flora may have been briefly confined by gender and geography, but from her earliest days she was connected to the world, first via the experience of others, and later by travelling and asking questions wherever she landed, in villages as well as cities, hard places as well as landmarks, visiting more than one hundred countries in her life, literally learning from experience at every stop.

One of her real strengths in elected office was a capacity to link human problems and local communities to the otherwise distant realms of national government and international affairs and theory. In that sense, no Canadian political leader went to a better school, with a better attitude – except perhaps for that other Macdonald, from Kingston.

Flora did not have much time as foreign minister – that was not her fault – but in her eight months there she led remarkable and durable change, including in treating international engagement as a partnership between Canadian citizens and their government. She did not invent that idea, but she mobilized and dramatized it throughout her life, perhaps most influentially by empowering, with our colleague Ron Atkey, the instinct of thousands of Canadians to respond, including through private sponsorship, to the crisis of Southeast Asian refugee "boat people" cast adrift in the late 1970s to die. She admired profoundly the innovation and dedication of Canada's front-line public servants who made that Canadian generosity work, often in near-impossible circumstances.

Then, of course, in her life after high office, while so many of us glided into first-class cabins and corporate boards, she walked the talk of Canadian citizen engagement in the dusty villages and dangerous backroads of the developing world. In those later years, she was more often in the world's Kabuls than in our Kingstons, still an inspiring symbol of Canada.

For a century or more, there has been an influential minority of Canadians who are keenly interested in international affairs, deeply informed, and often engaged, but public discussion of foreign policy has not been as intense or frequent as in many comparable countries. That probably goes with the territory of being an effective "middle power," often influencing events but only occasionally determining them. It has often occurred to me that, with the exception of the Suez Crisis in 1956, the celebrated "golden age" of Pearsonian diplomacy owed a lot to the fact that the fine minds of External Affairs – the fine male minds – did not have to worry very often about parliamentary or public scrutiny. Their work was respected but not much known, and that relative invisibility was bound to end, for better or for worse.

Among other things, Flora gave foreign affairs visibility, a human connection to the country and an understanding that what we did in the world – this former colony; this neighbour to a superpower; this community of immigrants – could make a tangible difference.

She had an instinct for the essence of an issue and its significance. Robert Stanfield said that "Flora can see around corners" – and she had an ability to express, even personify, what made an issue or an opportunity significant. Flora could lift her argument above the details in her briefing book. In Marshall McLuhan's terms, she was the medium who became the message. It is not accurate to say that she "did it on her own." Although she sometimes seemed solitary, I think Flora was never really on her own. She could be demanding – she could be insensitive – but, even in the most unlikely places, and at her worst times (and she had them), she struck true chords with others. This was as true for remote villagers in Afghanistan as it was for instinctive and sophisticated skeptics here at home, and it was also true for the diverse and vibrant clusters of friends who cared about her. She was transparent. She was real, in realms where that was not easy. She was honest.

And she was disciplined. I asked Senator Lowell Murray, my good friend and Flora's, whether her ability and willingness to compromise was learned or instinctive. He replied emphatically, "Learned, not instinctive!" Some External Affairs officials from 1979 might argue that her capacity to compromise was still being learned when she came to the Foreign Ministry. But they too had things to learn. Flora certainly had things she believed in, fervently, but she was also practical, able to build and accept and defend compromises and to understand – and usually respect – other perspectives. In two governments – and in the often more challenging environment of opposition – she was one of my most effective colleagues. Flora was not just a voice, but a force. She also understood, innately, the concerns and perspectives of people who were often not on the radar of governments and consequently easy to overlook. In that important sense, she was an "outsider" on the inside, determined to make change.

There had been outstanding women diplomats shaping and implementing Canadian foreign policy before 1979, but they had been the eloquent exception, not the rule, just as women had been in the corporate world and in universities presidencies, senior public service, most professions, and the House of Commons. No woman had been the foreign minister before (and it took the United States until 1997, when Madeleine Albright became secretary of state – eighteen years later – to catch up). It is an intriguing footnote that it was an earlier Progressive Conservative government that had appointed Canada's first female cabinet minister, Ellen Fairclough – the first after ninety years of Confederation. And it is worth speculating whether that party's long minority status – twenty years out of national government before the Progressive Conservative Party won a minority government in 1957 and Prime Minister John Diefenbaker appointed Fairclough – might have created a more positive disposition toward ending the exclusion of women from high elective office.

It is also worth noting that in the precedent-setting cabinet of 1957, Fairclough's portfolio as secretary of state had been among the most junior until she was moved to the more thorny portfolio of Citizenship and Immigration. It is equally worth considering that Flora was one of only two women elected to the House of Commons as Progressive Conservatives in the 1979 election. There was one woman NDP MP and seven Liberal women MPs, a total of ten women in a House of Commons of 262 MPs. Flora, naturally, was a major advocate of Jean Casselman Wadds' appointment in 1979 as the first woman high commissioner to the United Kingdom, a step that also broke precedent. So, while Flora did not shatter the mould of women in high office in Canada, her performance created a new model, with all the challenges that being a precedent-maker involved. And she relished those challenges.

I will draw three positive lessons from the example of Flora MacDonald, foreign minister.

First, what Canada does best in the world can sometimes be driven by and embodied in the instincts and initiatives of engaged citizens as much as by the skill and wisdom of excellent diplomats; those two forces should be combined and harnessed as frequently as possible.

Second, experience in national party politics can be a unique and instructive preparation for the understanding and accommodation of differences and the identification and pursuit of common purposes that are essential to successful foreign policy. What Flora learned in her years at the heart of the national Progressive Conservative Party, before election to the House of Commons, was both a constant crash course and a guide in how to respect and reconcile Canada's distinct, deep, and legitimate differences. That party experience helped her broaden the departments that she led, most emphatically External Affairs, and the governments in which she served.

Third, Flora's formal education ended at grade eleven ("because she was a girl"), but her informal education was constant and conscious throughout her life. She was always genuinely interested in things that were new to her – her range of knowledge and experience of domestic and international events was among the broadest of the MPs elected in 1972 – she had often actually "been there," whether through civic organizations like the John Howard Society at home or through extensive reading and visits abroad. She had talked and listened directly to people with problems and with aspirations, travelled outside her range, learned from observation and experience, and been guided more by curiosity than convention.

Her life and success demonstrate that an able, outward-reaching woman, given determination and the opportunities that are routinely accorded to men, can both break barriers and lead the field.

Conclusion
Breaking Historiographic Barriers

Dominique Marshall

CANADIAN HISTORIANS HAVE BEEN late to the study of women, gender, and transnationalism, but this inaugural collection on this theme offers an opportunity for a few answers.[1] It is hardly surprising that the impetus for this volume came from the Historical Section of Global Affairs Canada (GAC). Over the past decade, Canadian governments have adopted a growing number of pro-women policies and plans. Building on earlier Conservative government initiatives in the maternal health and defence sectors, Liberal prime minister Justin Trudeau's government has been especially active in pursuing a feminist foreign and defence agenda. In 2016, his newly elected government was already actively exploring increased opportunities for Canadian women to participate in global peace operations, addressing the "disproportionate" and "specific" impact of wars on women in order to build societies that are "more stable, inclusive, and just."[2] Within a year, the Department of National Defence had launched the Elsie Initiative for Women in Peace Operations, named after Canadian women's rights pioneer Elsie MacGill. At the same time, GAC announced the Feminist International Assistance Policy, an idea dismissed as far-fetched when the Canadian non-governmental organization MATCH International brought it forward forty years ago. The policy claims to reorient Canada's development assistance efforts toward "empowering women" to help "families and countries become more prosperous," using the word "barrier" as a leitmotif.[3] These efforts were later folded into a broader National Action Plan on Women, Peace and Security, which targeted ninety-three programs across Canada's development assistance, humanitarian action, and peace and stabilization efforts. Meanwhile, pressed by civil society groups in Canada, GAC diplomats joined officials from Crown-Indigenous Relations and Northern Affairs Canada to work with other governments on the National Inquiry into Missing and Murdered Indigenous Women and Girls at the United Nations Permanent Forum on Indigenous Issues.[4]

The ambitions of this volume are not unlike those of the government, as the introduction indicates: "In the past, Canada's search for a global order was limited by its adherence to strict gender roles that constrained its ability to solve diplomatic problems, increase trade, and address poverty." By documenting the multiplicity of situations where women, as individual actors and as subjects of inquiry, figured in Canada's international past, historians can explore the relationship between women's issues and larger questions of justice, inclusivity, prosperity, and peace and stability.

First, why were women mostly absent from the highest positions in Canadian international relations in the past?

The explanations offered in this collection for the success of women who did break barriers in reaching for positions of global influence are wide-ranging and complicated. They include the efforts by individual women, the work of women's movements and their allies, the importance of socioeconomic privilege, international differences in gender norms, as well as political circumstances. The sectors criss-crossed by the itineraries documented in this collection were varied and porous: the biographical approach adopted by most authors traces the movements of individual women between UN agencies, transnational churches, and non-governmental organizations; it also follows their paths between international and domestic theatres.

The goals of the transnational actions of these women occupied a whole "continuum," to use the notion of American historian Ellen Carol DuBois.[5] As Sharon Anne Cook and Lorna McLean demonstrate in Chapter 4, at one end of the spectrum are "emancipatory actions" that "altered or expanded existing understandings of women's place," such as those of the American political thinker Emily Greene Balch. These efforts called for extraordinary determination, often resulting in isolation and loneliness. At the spectrum's other end, the kinds of "social reform" actions undertaken by the wives of Canadian UN technical assistance advisors in Indonesia, Jamaica, the Soviet Union, and New York "relied on and expanded women's authority." As

David Webster's chapter reveals, these efforts were often facilitated by the existence of spheres from which men were excluded: embassy kitchens, gynecology practices, women's missions, convents, and same-sex sociability. Even for women with privileged upbringings and advanced education, gender norms often played the largest role in determining their place and function as change-makers.

Yet, context did matter, and intensifying global nationalist movements in the twentieth century sometimes gave women unexpected opportunities. In only a few years at the turn of the 1950s, as Jill Campbell-Miller demonstrates, the newly independent government of India diverted the meaning of the work of two Canadian health care practitioners with ties to the mission movement from evangelicalism to the strengthening of an autonomous and modern health system. Similarly, Kim Girouard's study of Jessie MacBean explores how the rising Chinese nationalism of the 1930s gave one Canadian woman doctor, also imbued of Christian ideals, a seminal role in the development of maternal medicine in the south of the country.

The contingent nature of most changes uncovered in this volume warns against the idea of a cumulative transformation toward gender equality. Similarly, the advances heralded by recent federal plans have been accompanied by new problems, in sequences that will need historical scrutiny. During thirteen years of war in Afghanistan, a policy aimed in part at freeing Afghan women might have badly underestimated the counter-influences wielded by women in the segregated quarters of the fundamentalist Taliban.[6] Elsewhere, the rise of women in the Canadian armed forces occurred in conjunction with the rise of Canadian private companies in security missions abroad. In the absence of legislated requirements for diversity, the hiring of women in such businesses is likely the consequence of lower wages and poorer educational prerequisites.[7]

It is always difficult to delineate the influence Canadians had in the search for a global order or to detect elements of exceptionalism in Canada's foreign policy. But there are hints about the impact of Canadian women and women's issues in this volume. Marie Smallface-Marule, a woman of the Káínai First Nation, travelled to northern Zambia in the late 1960s and occupied administrative positions in Canadian Indigenous political organizations thereafter. This goes a long way to explain the rise, and the anti-colonial nature, of Indigenous rights in Canada. It also helps make understandable the influence of Indigenous people from the area now called Canada in transnational Indigenous politics since then.

Second, why have women who participated in the history of Canadian international relations been so easily forgotten?

The role of women in the history of Canadian international relations has never been slight, and historians risk perpetuating undeserved exclusions if they do not reflect on the causes of women's absences in past accounts. Steve Marti and Francine McKenzie restore the role of Jean Casselman Wadds, Canadian high commissioner in London, during the debate over the patriation of the Canadian constitution in the early 1980s. Her efforts were largely forgotten, they suggest, not because her role was minor, but because the quiet diplomacy she practised did not impress contemporary reporters and colleagues as much as the forceful maneuvers of other diplomats. Like Casselman Wadds, several Canadian women who achieved a measure of authority abroad steered away from the "culture of aggression" prevalent in international affairs to foster consensus and understanding.[8] As Cook and McLean show in Chapter 4, Quebec-born Julia Grace Wales, who devised the the Continuous Mediation without Armistice Peace Plan, of 1915, deliberately chose positions that did not attract fame.

The invisibility of these women in studies of Canada's foreign relations might be the effect of a similar tendency by historians to equate power with assertive pursuits and to favour more masculine definitions of leadership. Some of the young Canadian men and women of the Student Union for Peace Action who travelled south to register rural African American voters during the civil rights drives of the early 1960s, for instance, ended up working under the guidance of black women of their mothers' age. The students were surprised by the command that these women held over those around them. As the doctoral thesis of Victoria Campbell Windle shows, the energy of female leaders was spent on a "personal approach in community interactions, and communication networks" best performed at an intermediary level of public life. These informal networks were as vital for success as more formal types of authority.[9]

This volume also confirms and illustrates the larger shift in the focus of Canadian political history over the past two decades. Traditional diplomatic history has given way to a new focus on religious missions, technical assistance, aid and development, and transnational movements of solidarity. Attention has shifted from the reporting of male diplomats' lives to their families, office work, and relations in local fields, spaces, and cultures, and from the figures of women's movements to multitudes. The most striking purpose of the portraits of transnational lives offered here is not so much the restoration of women's place in heroic accounts of "rebels and victims," to use the phrase of French historian Michelle Zancarini-Fournel. It is rather the affirmation of the significance of "intermediary" places where most women can be found at all levels of international relations. What strikes former prime minister Joe Clark about the achievements of his colleague and friend Flora MacDonald, the first woman to serve as secretary of state for external affairs, was her ability to bring to high politics the "experience and skill" she garnered in work "at the beating heart of Canadian party politics."

Many of the themes running through this collection, including the connections between Canadian families abroad and local women and children, the roles of teachers and domestic servants, the political discussions between husband and wives, and the transmission of values between fathers and daughters (as in the case of Marie Smallface-Marule), benefit from the approaches of labour and family history, which have a long-standing affinity with women's history.[10] Moreover, the "grandeur and condescension" of high-class families posted on foreign missions is demystified when the tools of the cultural historian of public life are critically deployed.[11] Matrimonial metaphors are prevalent in the descriptions of Canada-Brazil relations penned by P.K. Page, a Canadian ambassador's wife and an artist in her own right. As Eric Fillion suggests in Chapter 7, Page's writings were part of an idiom that expressed at once equal social relations with Latin American elites and patronizing superiority not only toward Afro-Brazilian ceremonies but also for Canadian missionary nuns labouring in the Amazon.[12]

The collection also reflects an important shift in the way women's history is increasingly written, the value of studying women "within historical problems in general," to again use the words of Zancarini-Fournel, and away from the isolation in which early historians of women have tended to understand them. For instance, as Susan Colbourn and Jonathan Crossen each show in their chapters, the peace movement of the 1950s and 1960s and the early Canadian Indigenous rights movement involved dynamic relations between men and women. It is interesting that, with a remarkable regularity, and regardless of their position on the continuum of motivations mentioned above, these movements gravitated around promoting of education and opposing violence.

Third, how does the presence of women, and the attention to women's issues, change the history of Canada's international relations?

The changes brought about by the women depicted in this collection were not necessarily long-lasting or structural. Indeed, most protagonists pursued issues traditionally associated with women's concerns: child welfare, maternal health, and the nationality of married women. And several of them broke barriers because of their place on the margins of officialdom. So, do these transnational itineraries of women's inclusion hold out the prospect of more prosperous "families and countries" and of societies that are more "stable," "inclusive," and just, as the Canadian Feminist International Assistance Policy of 2017 demanded?[13] The link between women and justice appears complicated, but the cumulative impact of women's work on daily lives, at home or away, in birth control, or on Indigenous rights is incontestable, as Chapters 1, 2, and 6 in this collection indicate.

Is the prognosis similar for the historiography of international relations? In other words, can a history more mindful of issues associated with women construct a more equitable history in its practice as well as in its content? The juxtaposition of essays in this collection is partly the result of auspicious new ways of conducting historical research: the increased training and involvement of Canadians from the "Third" and "Fourth" Worlds; a rising number of scholars who are familiar with multiple languages; the promotion of South-North and South-South collaborations led by questions from the South; the collection of documents associated with the words and deeds of everyday life; and the co-construction of archives by Canadian women's groups in partnership with groups abroad.[14]

The recent warnings to Northern humanitarian policy-makers by Belgian political scientist Frédéric Thomas may well apply to historians of Canadian foreign relations. To avoid the cycle of virtuous ambitions to abandonment requires opening one's practice to "other power relations hidden" in international operations. This is done by looking especially at aspects of foreign relations that are less glittering: "time and money invested in the building of infrastructures, civil protection, public services, anticipation of catastrophes."[15] It is also necessary to allocate a larger share of attention to the role of Southern populations in the making of Northern transnational policies, the implementation of international norms, and the running of transnational initiatives. Finally, if the research leads to this conclusion, it is perhaps time to abandon the very idea that foreign interventions matter. Despite international aid efforts, the vast majority of labour on humanitarian issues and economic development occurs domestically.

I will conclude with one extraordinary example of Canadian transnational history that embodies the problems and solutions listed by Thomas, discovered by chance as I followed avenues opened by this volume. In 1946, the UN included a Commission on the Status of Women in its Economic and Social Council; in 1952, the UN adopted a Convention on the Political Rights of Women, a topic the League of Nations had hitherto refrained from codifying out of respect for national traditions.[16] The Commission on the Status of Women was to host four global conferences on women, on issues of "equality, development and peace" and reproductive rights: Mexico City in 1975, Copenhagen in 1980, Nairobi in 1985, and Beijing in 1995. Much remains to be learned about the history of these international institutions and Canadians' role in them. Anthropologists show that "femocrats," staffers, and their allies have often worked in a downward direction, to implement restrictive ideas of femininity.[17] The Nairobi edition of the World Conference, dubbed the "Third World Conference on Women," might have been the first where priorities were informed by women from the South, and the Conference might have included several recommendations on Indigenous women. Yet the Canadian delegation did not include Indigenous women, for the kind of "colonial" reasons that were becoming the core of Marie Smallface-Marule's preoccupations at the time.[18]

In 2006, the Canadian International Development Agency and its Gender Equity Support Project contributed to the funding of an initiative to commemorate and archive the history of the Nairobi Conference. The money was used by the African Woman and Child Feature Service to organize an Alumni Workshop and a Forum, and to assemble a compact disc of press clippings from seven Kenyan newspapers documenting the local dimensions of the 1985 conference and its impact on the country. A conference held that year, Nairobi+21, gathered one thousand women of the region to keep the "Nairobi Forward-Looking Strategies" vigorous and to communicate them to the younger generation.[19] The 2017 Feminist International Assistance Policy, which did not invoke enough precedents, could do worse than support the discovery of such rich and forgotten alternatives and honour them.

Notes

1. For the Canadian practitioners of the field of International Political Economy, Heather A. Smith, "Unlearning: A Messy and Complex Journey with Canadian Foreign Policy," *International Journal* 72, 2 (June 2017): 203–16. For a much earlier program from Canadian geographers, see Simon Dalby, "Gender and Critical Geopolitics; Reading Security Discourse in the New World Disorder," *Environment and Planning D: Society and Space* 12, 5 (October 1994): 595–612, doi:10.1068/d120595.
2. Canada, House of Commons Standing Committee on Foreign Affairs and International Development, *An Opportunity for Global Leadership: Canada and the Women, Peace and Security Agenda*, 42nd Parl., 1st Sess., October 2016, 1, 7, 9, https://www.ourcommons.ca/Content/Committee/421/FAAE/Reports/RP8433298/faaerp03/faaerp03-e.pdf.
3. McLeod Group Blog, "Canada's Feminist International Assistance Policy: Can GAC Deliver?," *McLeod Group Blog*, June 20, 2017, https://www.mcleodgroup.ca/2017/06/canadas-feminist-international-assistance-policy-can-gac-deliver. See also Beth Woroniuk, "A Feminist Foreign Policy? What about Women, Peace and Security?" *McLeod Group Blog*, June 27, 2016, https://www.mcleodgroup.ca/2016/06/a-feminist-foreign-policy-what-about-women-peace-and-security. On the history of MATCH, see MATCH International Centre, *An UnMATCHED Partnership, 25 Years of Working with Women* (Ottawa: author, 2001); the archives of the non-governmental organization are at Carleton Archives and Special Collections. See also "Chronology of CIDA's Commitment to Gender Equality," in Canadian International Development Agency, *CIDA's Policy on Gender Equality* (Hull: Minister of Public Works, 1999), 30. MATCH, now called the Equality Fund, is the main distributor of federal grants under the new policy.
4. Canada, Department of Crown-Indigenous Relations and Northern Affairs Canada, *Crown-Indigenous Relations and Northern Affairs Canada: Departmental Plan 2020–21*, https://www.rcaanc-cirnac.gc.ca/eng/1581457623099/1581457696303.
5. Ellen Carol DuBois, "Women's Movements," in *The Palgrave Dictionary of Transnational History*, ed. Akira Iriye and Pierre-Yves Saunier (Basingstoke, UK: Palgrave Macmillan, 2009), 1114–21.
6. Stephen Azzi and Richard Foot, "Canada and the War in Afghanistan," in *The Canadian Encyclopedia*, Historica Canada, article published June 4, 2009; last edited February 5, 2021, https://www.thecanadianencyclopedia.ca/en/article/international-campaign-against-terrorism-in-afghanistan; Patricia Sellick, "The Impact of Conflict on Children in Afghanistan," 1998, UNICEF, Save the Children Federation Inc. Save the Children UK. http://repository.forcedmigration.org/show_metadata.jsp?pid=fmo:3225.
7. Ruth Montgomery and Curt Taylor Griffiths, "The Transformation of Policing and Growth of Private Industry,": The Use of Private Security Services for Policing, Public Safety Canada, last modified November 14, 2017, https://www.publicsafety.gc.ca/cnt/rsrcs/pblctns/archive-2015-r041/archive-index-en.aspx#01; and Canada, Department of National Defence, "Statistics of Women in the Canadian Armed Forces," https://www.canada.ca/en/department-national-defence/services/women-in-the-forces/statistics.html.
8. Andrew M. Johnston, "Jeanne Halbwachs, International Feminist Pacifism, and France's Société d'Études Documentaires et Critiques Sur La Guerre," *Peace and Change* 41, 1 (January 2016): 22–37.
9. Victoria Campbell Windle, "'We of the New Left': A Gender History of the Student Union for Peace Action from the Anti-Nuclear Movement to Women's Liberation" (PhD diss., University of Waterloo, 2017), 346, http://hdl.handle.net/10012/12406. In the sixth chapter, Campbell Windle uses the definitions of authority summarized in Vicki Crawford, "African

American Women in the Mississippi Freedom Democratic Party," in *Sisters in the Struggle: African-American Women in the Civil Rights Movement*, ed. Bettye Collier-Thomas and V.P. Franklin (New York: New York University Press, 2001), 121–38.
10 Michelle Zancarini-Fournel, "Histoire des femmes, histoire du genre," in *Historiographies, Concepts et débats*, 1 (Paris: Gallimard, 2010), 209–10.
11 See also Bruce Curtis, "'The Most Splendid Pageant Ever Seen': Grandeur, Condescension, and the Domestic in Lord Durham's Political Theatre," *Canadian Historical Review* 89, 1 (2008): 55–88; and Veronica Jane Strong-Boag, *Liberal Hearts and Coronets: The Lives and Times of Ishbel Marjoribanks Gordon and John Campbell Gordon, the Aberdeens* (Toronto: University of Toronto Press, 2015). Sonya Grypma's work on the influence of these mixed loyalties among children of Canadian medical missionaries born and raised in China before the Revolution points at extraordinary consequences in the public life of the next generation. Sonya Grypma, *Walls Fall Down: Canadian Missionary Kids Return to China* (Langley, BC: Sonya Grypma, 2012 c2017), DVD.
12 See, for instance, Janice Cavell, "Like Any Good Wife: Gender and Perceptions of Canadian Foreign Policy, 1945–75," *International Journal* 63, 2 (June 2008): 385–403. Glenda Sluga offers an important retrospective and program in "Women, Feminisms and Twentieth-Century Internationalisms," in *Internationalisms: A Twentieth-Century History*, ed. Glenda Sluga and Patricia Clavin (Cambridge: Cambridge University Press, 2017), 61–84.
13 Global Affairs Canada, "Canada's Feminist International Assistance Policy," Canada.ca, https://www.international.gc.ca/world-monde/issues_development-enjeux_developpement/priorities-priorites/policy-politique.aspx?lang=eng&wbdisable=true.
14 See Andriata Chironda, "Narrators, Navigators and Negotiators: Foreign Service Officer Life Stories from Canada's Africa Refugee Resettlement Program, 1970 to 1990" (PhD diss., Carleton University, 2020). Chironda, a Canadian refugee from Zimbabwe, interviewed Canadian immigration officers stationed in Africa who developed the very programs of refugee resettlement which she experienced first-hand, to discover significant differences in the storytelling of men and women occupying the same positions in the federal government. See also Sonya DeLaat's study of the contrast between official pictures of Canadian development work and the in-house training pictures of CIDA fieldwork destined to convince families that their lives would be familiar: "Pictures in Development: The Canadian International Development Agency's Photo Library," in *A Samaritan State Revisited: Historical Perspectives on Canadian Foreign Aid*, ed. Greg Donaghy and David Webster (Calgary, AB: University of Calgary Press, 2019), 223–44. The ambition "to forge an equal partnership for justice and development between Canadian women and those in the South" was the goal of the founders of the MATCH International Centre in 1975. MATCH International, *An UnMATCHed Partnership* (Ottawa: author, 2001), 1.
15 Frédéric Thomas, "Taking the World without Changing Power," *Le Monde diplomatique*, English edition, April 2020, 7.
16 Leanne Dustan, "Convention on the Political Rights of Women," *Encyclopedia of Women and American Politics*, ed. Lynne E. Ford (New York: Facts on File, 2008), 131. See also UN Women, "World Conferences on Women," UNWomen.org, https://www.unwomen.org/en/how-we-work/intergovernmental-support/world-conferences-on-women.
17 See, for instance, the anthropology of the World Bank "institutional practices" by Kate Bedford, *Developing Partnerships: Gender, Sexuality, and the Reformed World Bank* (Minneapolis: University of Minnesota Press, 2009). See also Amanda Ricci, "Making Global Citizens? Canadian Women at the World Conference of the International Women's Year, Mexico City 1975," in *Undiplomatic History: The New Study of Canada and the World*, ed. Asa McKercher and Philip Van Huizen (Montreal-Kingston: McGill-Queen's University Press, 2019), 206–29.

18 Agnes Grant, "Feminism and Aboriginal Culture: One Woman's View," *Canadian Women Studies/Cahiers de la femme* 14, 2 (1994), 56–57.
19 African Woman and Child Feature Service, *Nairobi+21: Commemorating the Third UN World Conference on Women*, 2007, https://ke.boell.org/sites/default/files/nairobi_21_-_commemorating_the_3rd_un_world_conference_on_women.pdf.

Greg Donaghy
An Appreciation

Patricia E. Roy

ALAS, THIS IS ONE of the last collections to appear with Greg Donaghy's name on the title page as an editor. Greg conceived the project, then consulted with his coeditors to select topics and contributors, edit submissions, and submit the manuscript to the press. The book was in its penultimate stages when, on Canada Day 2020, as the result of a heart attack, Greg left us. These essays represent his broad interests in Canadian history as it relates to the world, reflect his high standards of scholarship, and reveal his skill in bringing together practitioners of diplomacy and scholars of varied vintages.

Greg's monographs, *Tolerant Allies: Canada and the United States, 1963–1968*[1] and *Grit: The Life and Politics of Paul Martin Sr.*,[2] demonstrate that he was a gifted solo performer, but he also excelled as a concertmaster, a role he truly enjoyed. He was a researcher for the second volume of the official history of the Department of External Affairs (now Global Affairs), coauthor of the third,[3] and leader of the team that produced six volumes of *Documents on Canadian External Relations*. At the same time, he shared his talents as concertmaster beyond the Pearson Building, the headquarters of the Department of Global Affairs in Ottawa, by organizing thematic conferences and editing related publications that often included essays of his own.

In his first edited collection, *Uncertain Horizons: Canadians and Their World in 1945*,[4] Greg noted the beginning of historical interest in the experiences of Canadian women during the war.[5] The collection had an article on children's rights and four female authors but no papers specifically on women. Nevertheless, Greg realized the need to consider women's role in Canada's external relations. When Global Affairs decided "that women were to be a main focus of interest, particularly in the realm of international development, under then Minister Chrystia Freeland,"[6] Greg seized the opportunity. This volume is the result.

Family was important to Greg. Both his single authored monographs and many of his edited works carry acknowledgments and/or dedications to his wife, children (whose names were added as the family grew), and sometimes to both. He also thanked his parents and other family members for their moral and practical support. When an appointment as visiting professor of Canadian Studies at Kwansei Gakuin University took him to Kobe, Japan, for a semester in 2015–16, he brought his two sons, settled in an old missionary house, and enrolled the boys in a Marist International School.[7]

Few of the many memorial tributes to Greg refer to his strong religious faith. His Roman Catholicism informed his understanding of Paul Martin Sr. He presented a talk on Martin's faith and politics at St. Jerome's University in the fall of 2012 to remind his audience "a) that Martin was once hailed as a progressive and b) that Catholicism can be a wellspring of progressive activism."[8] Yet, Greg was ecumenical in his approach, and his awareness of the importance of religion in international relations linked nicely with his appreciation of "soft power." This collection, for example, includes papers on Dr. Jessie MacBean, a physician who worked in Presbyterian hospitals in China, and on two Canadian women, engaged in health care in India, who respectively had Presbyterian and Anglican connections.

Contradictory Impulses: Canada and Japan in the Twentieth Century, the book that Greg and I coedited, includes essays on both Protestant and Catholic missionaries, many of whom were women. It was in organizing the 2004 Conference and the subsequent book that I worked most closely with Greg. The theme was Greg's suggestion; like many of his conferences and publications, it fit the mandate of the Department of Foreign Affairs and International Trade. A conference and a publication were appropriate means of commemorating the seventh-fifth anniversary of the establishment of diplomatic relations between Canada and Japan. With his understanding of the Ottawa bureaucracy, Greg found the funding. Enthusiastically, I joined the project. Like the editors of this volume, we began by sharing ideas about possible topics and contributors.

After the conference in Victoria, we edited the submissions. Again, we shared the task. Our authors were generally very cooperative in submitting their manuscripts on schedule and responding to peer reviewers in a timely and effective way. When one author was a bit difficult, Greg exercised his natural diplomatic talents (no doubt enhanced by knowledge gained from delving into the formal practice of diplomacy), dealt with that scholar, and eventually secured a fine contribution.

Later, as associate editor of *Historical Studies*, the journal of the Canadian Catholic Historical Association, I had the pleasure of editing Greg's article on Paul Martin.[9] The journal editor had noticed an announcement of Greg's talk to the Ottawa Historical Society on H-Can. She thought the topic was appropriate for the journal but knew nothing of Greg so asked if I did. I was happy to inform her that Greg was a friend and a first-class scholar. Greg immediately replied to my email that his text was designed for an oral presentation, but he sent it along. The editor and I agreed that it was sufficiently advanced to be sent out for peer review. The reviewers were positive in their assessments (one made comments only to make "a good paper even better") but all agreed that the "chatty" introduction, ideal for a talk, did not transfer well to print. Although somewhat disappointed by the need to recast the introduction, Greg quickly revised it, made some minor refinements proposed by the reviewers, and provided clear explanations of why some suggestions were impractical. As editors, we had little to do since Greg was an elegant writer, but he generously thanked us for our efforts when reporting his delight at receiving congratulations from a Jesuit historian for the article.[10]

Greg's published contributions to knowledge of Canada's international history will be read for many years. Alas, there will be no more contributions. Sadly too, a new generation of scholars will not have the benefit of his gentle encouragement and wise counsel. We are grateful for having known him and of learning from him.

Notes

1   Greg Donaghy, *Tolerant Allies: Canada and the United States, 1963–1968* (Montreal/Kingston: McGill-Queen's University Press), 2002.
2   Greg Donaghy, *Grit: The Life and Politics of Paul Martin Sr.* (Vancouver: UBC Press, 2015).
3   John Hilliker, Mary Halloran, and Greg Donaghy, *Canada's Department of External Affairs*, vol. 3, *Innovation and Adaptation, 1968–1984* (Toronto: University of Toronto Press/Institute of Public Administration of Canada, 2017).

4 Greg Donaghy, ed., *Uncertain Horizons: Canadians and Their World in 1945* (Ottawa: Canadian Committee for the History of the Second World War, 1997), xvii.
5 Dominique Marshall, "Reconstruction Politics, the Canadian Welfare State and the Ambiguity of Children's Rights, 1940–1950," in *Uncertain Horizons: Canadians and Their World in 1945*, ed. Greg Donaghy (Canadian Committee for the History of the Second World War, 1997), 261–83.
6 Jill Campbell-Miller and Stacey Barker to Patricia Roy, personal email, October 7, 2020.
7 Greg Donaghy to Patricia Roy, personal emails, September 10 and 15, 2015.
8 Donaghy to Roy, personal emails, April 3, 2013.
9 Greg Donaghy, "A Catholic Journey: Paul Martin Sr., Politics and Faith," *Historical Studies*, 79 (2013): 25–40.
10 Donaghy to Roy, personal email, November 19, 2013.

Bibliography

Archival Sources

Bishop's University Archives (Sherbrooke)
    T.W.L. MacDermot fonds

Christian Medical College and Hospital Archives (Vellore)

General Synod Archives, Anglican Church of Canada
    Missionary Society of the Church of England in Canada (MSCC) fonds

Glenbow Archives (Calgary)
    James Gladstone family fonds

Harvard University Archives
    Nathan Keyfitz Papers

Library and Archives Canada
    Brascan Limited fonds
    Canadian International Development Agency Papers
    Department of External Affairs fonds
    Department of Indian Affairs and Northern Development Papers
    Department of National Health and Welfare Papers
    Francis Reginald Scott fonds
    Julia Grace Wales fonds
    Lester B. Pearson Papers
    Library of Parliament Papers
    P.K. (Patricia Kathleen) Page fonds
    W. Arthur Irwin Papers

McGill University Archives

Museu Villa-Lobos (Rio de Janeiro)

National Gallery of Canada Library and Archives
  National Gallery of Canada Papers

Presbyterian Historical Society
  RG 82 Presbyterian Church in the U.S.A. Board of Foreign Missions Secretaries' Files: China Missions

Provincial Archives of Saskatchewan Saskatchewan Archives Board

Rajkumari Amrit Kaur College of Nursing Library (New Delhi)

State Library of New South Wales
  Eleanor M. Hinder Papers

United Nations Archives and Records Administration
  Keenleyside files
  Technical Assistance Records

University of Regina Archives
  Bill Harding fonds

University of Toronto Archives and Records Management Services

World Health Organization Records and Archives

Wisconsin Historical Society Archives
  Julia Grace Wales Papers

Newspapers and Periodicals

A Manhã (Brazil)
A Noite (Brazil)
Careta (Brazil)
Correio da Manhã (Brazil)
Diário Carioca (Brazil)
Diário da Noite (Brazil)
Gazeta de Notícias (Brazil)
Globe and Mail
Guardian (United Kingdom)
Ha-Shilth-Sa (Canada)
Jornal do Brasil
Jornal do Commercio (Brazil)
Kainai News (Canada)
Lethbridge Herald
Maclean's
New York Times
Norwood News (United Kingdom)
Oakville Beaver
O Jornal (Brazil)
Ottawa Citizen
Ottawa Journal
Peterborough Examiner
Regina Leader-Post
Revista da Semana (Brazil)
Toronto Daily Star
Toronto Star
Tribal College (United States)
Última Hora (Brazil)
Voice of Women (Canada)
Vida Doméstica (Brazil)
Windspeaker (Canada)

Government and Institutional Publications

Canada
Canada. *An Opportunity for Global Leadership: Canada and the Women, Peace and Security Agenda. Report of the Standing Committee on Foreign Affairs and International Development.* October 2016. https://www.ourcommons.ca/Content/Committee/421/FAAE/Reports/RP8433298/faaerp03/faaerp03-e.pdf.

—. Department of Crown-Indigenous Relations and Northern Affairs Canada. *Crown-Indigenous Relations and Northern Affairs Canada: Departmental Plan 2020–21*. https://www.rcaanc-cirnac.gc.ca/eng/1581457623099/1581457696303.
—. Department of Foreign Affairs and International Trade. *Documents on Canadian External Relations*. Vol. 16, 1950. Edited by Greg Donaghy. Ottawa: Canadian Government Publishing, 1996.
—. Department of Foreign Affairs and International Trade. *Documents on Canadian External Relations*. Vol. 17, 1951. Edited by Greg Donaghy. Ottawa: Canadian Government Publishing, 1996.
—. Department of Foreign Affairs and International Trade. *Documents on Canadian External Relations*. Vol. 20, 1954. Edited by Greg Donaghy. Ottawa: Canadian Government Publishing, 1997.
—. Department of Foreign Affairs and International Trade. *Documents on Canadian External Relations*. Vol. 21, 1955. Edited by Greg Donaghy. Ottawa: Canadian Government Publishing, 1999.
—. Department of Foreign Affairs and International Trade. *Documents on Canadian External Relations*. Vol. 22, 1956–1957. Edited by Greg Donaghy. Ottawa: Canadian Government Publishing, 2001.
—. Department of Foreign Affairs and International Trade. *Documents on Canadian External Relations*. Vol. 23, 1956–1957. Edited by Greg Donaghy. Ottawa: Canadian Government Publishing, 2002.
—. Department of National Defence. "Statistics of Women in the Canadian Armed Forces." https://www.canada.ca/en/department-national-defence/services/women-in-the-forces/statistics.html.
Canadian International Development Agency. *CIDA's Policy on Gender Equality*. Hull: Minister of Public Works, 1999.
House of Commons Debates. Twenty-Fourth Parliament, Second Session, Vol. II.
MATCH International Centre. *An UnMATCHed Partnership. 25 Years of Working with Women*. Ottawa: author, 2001.
Montgomery, Ruth, and Curt Taylor Griffiths. "The Transformation of Policing and Growth of Private Industry." The Use of Private Security Services for Policing. Public Safety Canada. Last modified November 14, 2017, https://www.publicsafety.gc.ca/cnt/rsrcs/pblctns/archive-2015-r041/archive-index-en.aspx#01.
National Indian Brotherhood. *Indian Control of Indian Education*. Policy paper presented to the Minister of Indian Affairs and Northern Development. Ottawa: National Indian Brotherhood, 1972.
Sellick, Patricia. "The Impact of Conflict on Children in Afghanistan," 1998, UNICEF, Save the Children. http://repository.forcedmigration.org/show_metadata.jsp?pid=fmo:3225.
Union of British Columbia Indian Chiefs. "Minutes." 13th Annual General Assembly of the Union of BC Indian Chiefs, Vancouver, BC, October 28–30, 1981. http://constitution.ubcic.bc.ca/node/138.

China
Annual Report for the 99th Year of the Sun Yat Sen Memorial Canton Hospital, Lingnan University, 1933–1934. Canton, China: Canton Hospital, 1934.
Annual Report for the 100th Year of the Canton Hospital, Lingnan University, 1934–1935. Canton, China: Canton Hospital, 1935.
Annual Report of the David Gregg Hospital for Women and Children, Hackett Medical College for Women, Turner Training School for Nurses, Yau Tsai School of Pharmacy, 1931. Canton, China: Hackett Medical College, 1931.

Annual Report of the Hackett Medical College for Women and Affiliated Institutions. Canton, China: Hackett Medical College, 1933.
Annual Report of the Hackett Medical College for Women and Affiliated Institutions: Hospital Number, January 1, 1933 to June 30, 1934. Canton, China: Hackett Medical College, 1934.
Annual Report of the Sun Yat Sen Memorial Canton Hospital for the Year 1931–1932. Canton, China: Canton Hospital, 1932.
David Gregg Hospital for Women and Children, Hackett Medical College for Women, Turner Training School for Nurses: Bulletin, April, 1929. Canton, China: Hackett Medical College, 1929.
Hackett Medical College for Women, Turner Training School for Nurses: Catalogue 1925–1926. Canton, China: Hackett Medical College, 1926.
Hackett Medical College for Women, Turner Training School for Nurses: Catalogue 1928–1929. Canton, China: Hackett Medical College, 1929.
Hackett Medical College for Women, Turner Training School for Nurses: Catalogue, June, 1930. Canton, China: Hackett Medical College, 1929.
Hackett Medical College for Women, Turner Training School for Nurses, David Gregg Hospital for Women and Children: Bulletin 1924–1925. Canton, China: Hackett Medical College, 1925.
Report of the Canton Hospital for the Years 1924–1930. Canton, China: Canton Hospital, 1930.
Report of the Sun Yat Sen Memorial Canton Hospital for the Year 1930–1931. Canton, China: Canton Hospital, 1931.
Report of the Sun Yat Sen Memorial Canton Hospital for the Year 1931–1932. Canton, China: Canton Hospital, 1932.

India

Report of the Health Survey and Development Committee. *Volume 1: A Survey of the State of the Public Health and of the Existing Health Organisation.* Calcutta: Government of India Press, 1946.
Trained Nurses' Association of India. *History and Trends in Nursing in India.* New Delhi: The Trained Nurses' Association of India, 2001.

United Nations

Nairobi+21: Commemorating the 3rd World Conference of Women. Compiled by African Woman and Child Feature Service, with support from Heinrich Böll Foundation – Regional Office for East and Horn of Africa, 2007. https://ke.boell.org/sites/default/files/nairobi_21_-_commemorating_the_3rd_un_world_conference_on_women.pdf.
UN General Assembly. Resolution 61/295, United Nations Declaration on the Rights of Indigenous Peoples. A/RES/61/295, September 13, 2007.
UN Women. "World Conferences on Women." https://www.unwomen.org/en/how-we-work/intergovernmental-support/world-conferences-on-women.
United Nations Intellectual History Project, Interview with Margaret Joan Anstee, December 14, 2000.
World Council of Indigenous Peoples. "Four-Year Report (1977–1981)."

Other Sources

Abraham, Jacob, K.V. Mathai, Vedantam Rajshekhar, and Raj K. Narayan. "Jacob Chandy: Pioneering Neurosurgeon of India." *Neurosurgery* 67 (2010): 566–76.
Abraham, Meera. *Religion, Caste, and Gender: Missionaries and Nursing History in South Asia.* Bangalore, India: BI Publications, 1996.

Alexander, Kristine. "Canadian Girls, Imperial Girls, Global Girls: Race, Nation, and Transnationalism in the Interwar Girl Guide Movement." In *Within and Without the Nation: Canadian History as Transnational History*, edited by Karen Dubinsky, Adele Perry, and Henry Yu, 276–92. Toronto: University of Toronto Press, 2015.

—. *Guiding Modern Girls: Girlhood, Empire, and Internationalism in the 1920s and 1930s*. Vancouver: UBC Press, 2017.

Allen, Gemma. "The Rise of the Ambassadress: English Ambassadorial Wives and Early Modern Diplomatic Culture." *The Historical Journal* 62, 3 (2019): 617–38.

Alonso, Harriet Hyman. "Nobel Peace Laureates: Jane Addams and Emily Greene Balch; Two Women of the Women's International League for Peace and Freedom." *Journal of Women's History* 7, 2 (1995): 6–26.

Amrith, Sunil, and Glenda Sluga. "New Histories of the United Nations." *Journal of World History* 19, 3 (2008): 251–74.

Anstee, Margaret Joan. *Never Learn to Type: A Woman at the United Nations*. London: Wiley, 2004.

Armstrong-Reid, Susan. *Lyle Creeman: The Frontiers of Global Nursing*. Toronto: University of Toronto Press, 2014.

Azzi, Stephen, and Richard Foot. "Canada and the War in Afghanistan." In *The Canadian Encyclopedia*. Historica Canada. Article published June 4, 2009; last modified February 5, 2021. https://www.thecanadianencyclopedia.ca/en/article/international-campaign-against-terrorism-in-afghanistan.

Bailey, Suzanne. "Ethics, Aesthetics, Modernism, and the Primitive in P.K. Page's *Brazilian Journal*." *Mosaic* 46, 1 (2013): 53–75.

Ball, Christine. "The History of the Voice of Women/La Voix des Femmes: The Early Years, 1960–1963." PhD diss., University of Toronto, 1994.

—. "Towards a Feminine Perspective on Peace." *Peace Research* 23, 4 (1991): 57–66.

Ballantyne, Lereine. *Dr. Jessie MacBean and the Work at the Hackett Medical College, Canton, China*. Toronto: Women's Missionary Society of the Presbyterian Church in Canada, 1934.

Barbosa, Rosana. *Brazil and Canada: Economic, Political, and Migratory Ties, 1820s to 1970s*. London: Lexington Books, 2017.

Barker, Christine Ross. Foreword to *My Mother*, by Ruth Buchanan. Toronto: Women's Missionary Society of the Presbyterian Church of Canada, 1938.

Barker, Joanne. "Gender, Sovereignty, and the Discourse of Rights in Native Women's Activism." *Meridians* 7, 1 (2006): 127–61.

Bashevkin, Sylvia. "Numerical and Policy Representation on the World Stage: Women Foreign Policy Leaders in Western Industrialized Systems." *International Political Science Review* 35 (4): 409–29.

Bastien, Frédéric. *The Battle of London: Trudeau, Thatcher, and the Fight for Canada's Constitution*. Translated by J. Homel. Toronto: Dundurn Press, 2014.

Bean, Mary Jean Woodward. *Julia Grace Wales: Canada's Hidden Heroine and the Quest for Peace, 1914–1918*. Ottawa: Borealis Press, 2005.

Bedford, Kate. *Developing Partnerships: Gender, Sexuality, and the Reformed World Bank* Minneapolis: University of Minnesota Press, 2009.

Belisle, Donica. *Purchasing Power: Women and the Rise of Canadian Consumer Culture*. Toronto: University of Toronto Press, 2020.

Belisle, Donica, with Kiera Mitchell. "Mary Quayle Innis: Faculty Wives' Contributions and the Making of Academic Celebrity." *Canadian Historical Review* 99, 3 (2018): 456–86.

Bellenoit, Hayden J.A. *Missionary Education and Empire in Late Colonial India, 1860–1920*. London: Pickering and Chatto, 2007.
Bergbusch, Eric, and Michael D. Stevenson. "Howard Green, Public Opinion and the Politics of Disarmament." In *Architects and Innovators: Building the Department of Foreign Affairs and International Trade, 1909–2009*, edited by Greg Donaghy and Kim Richard Nossal, 196–206. Montreal/Kingston: McGill-Queen's University Press, 2009.
Bhatti, Ranbir S., N. Janakiramaiah, and S.M. Channabasavanna. "Family Psychiatric Ward Treatment in India." *Family Process* 19, 2 (1980): 193–200.
Bickers, Robert. *The Scramble for China: Foreign Devils in the Qing Empire, 1832–1914*. London: Penguin Books, 2016.
Boutilier, Beverley. "Educating for Peace and Cooperation: The Women's International League for Peace and Freedom in Canada, 1919–1929." Master's thesis, Carleton University, 1988.
Bradbury, Bettina. "'In England a Man Can Do as He Likes with His Property': Migration, Family Fortunes, and the Law in Nineteenth Century Quebec and the Cape Colony." In *Within and Without the Nation: Canadian History as Transnational History*, edited by Karen Dubinsky, Adele Perry, and Henry Yu, 145–67. University of Toronto Press, 2015.
Brookfield, Tarah. *Cold War Comforts: Canadian Women, Child Safety, and Global Insecurity*. Waterloo, ON: Wilfrid Laurier University Press, 2012.
Brouwer, Ruth Compton. *Canada's Global Villagers: CUSO in Development, 1961–68*. Vancouver: UBC Press, 2013.
–. "Canadian Presbyterians and India Missions, 1877–1914: The Policy and Politics of 'Women's Work for Women.'" In *North American Foreign Missions, 1810–1914: Theology, Theory, and Policy*, edited by Wilbert R. Shank, 192–217. Grand Rapids, MI: Wm. B. Eerdmans, 2004.
–. "From Missionaries to NGOs." In *Canada and the Third World: Overlapping Histories*, edited by Karen Dubinsky, Sean Mill, and Scott Rutherford, 120–54. Toronto: University of Toronto Press, 2016.
–. "Ironic Interventions: CUSO Volunteers in India's Family Planning Campaign, 1960s–1970s." *Social History* 43, 86 (November 2010): 279–313.
–. *Modern Women Modernizing Men: The Changing Missions of Three Professional Women in Asia and Africa, 1902–69*. Vancouver: UBC Press, 2002.
–. *New Women for God: Canadian Presbyterian Women and Indian Missions, 1876–1914*. Toronto: University of Toronto Press, 1990.
–. "When Missions Became Development: Ironies of 'NGOization' in Mainstream Canadian Churches in the 1960s." *The Canadian Historical Review* 91, 4 (2010): 661–93.
Brown, Ashley. "Swinging for the State Department: American Women Tennis Players in Diplomatic Goodwill Tours, 1941–59," *Journal of Sport History* 42, 3 (Fall 2015): 289–309.
Brownstone, Meyer. "The Douglas-Lloyd Governments: Innovation and Bureaucratic Adaptation." In *Essays on the Left*, edited by Laurier LaPierre et al. Toronto: McClelland and Stewart, 1971.
Bu, Liping. "Educational Exchange and Cultural Diplomacy in the Cold War." *Journal of American Studies* 33, 3 (1999): 393–415. doi.org/10.1017/S0021875899006167.
Buchanan, Edith. *A Study Guide in the Nursing Arts*. New Delhi: College of Nursing, 1953.
Buchanan, Ruth. *My Mother*. Toronto: Women's Missionary Society of the Presbyterian Church of Canada, 1938.
Buckner, Phillip, ed., *Canada and the End of Empire*. Vancouver: UBC Press, 2005.
Burns, E.L.M. "Toward the Cessation of Nuclear Tests." In *Canadian Foreign Policy 1955–1965: Selected Speeches and Documents*, edited by Arthur E. Blanchette, 61–62. Toronto: McClelland and Stewart, 1977.

Cadbury, George W. "Planning in Saskatchewan." In *Essays on the Left*, edited by Laurier LaPierre et al. Toronto: McClelland and Stewart, 1971.

–. "Saskatchewan: Democratic Social Ownership." *Public Affairs* (1948): 273–77.

Cadieux, Marcel. *The Canadian Diplomat: An Essay in Definition*. Toronto: University of Toronto Press, 1963.

Campbell, Cathy, and Marie Smallface-Marule. "The History and Future of Niitsitapi." *Alberta Teachers Association Magazine* 82, 4 (Summer 2002). https://www.teachers.ab.ca/News Room/ata magazine/Volume 82/Number 4/Articles/Pages/The History and Future of Niitsitapi.aspx.

Campbell, Isabel. "Pearson's Promises and the NATO Nuclear Dilemma." In *Mike's World: Lester B. Pearson and Canadian External Affairs*, edited by Asa McKercher and Galen Roger Perras, 275–96. Vancouver: UBC Press, 2017.

Campbell, Lara, Michael Dawson, and Catherine Gidney, eds. *Worth Fighting For: Canada's Tradition of War Resistance from 1812 to the War on Terror*. Toronto: Between the Lines, 2015.

Campbell-Miller, Jill. "Encounter and Apprenticeship: The Colombo Plan and Canadian Aid in India, 1950–1960." In *A Samaritan State Revisited: Historical Perspectives on Canadian Foreign Aid*, edited by Greg Donaghy and David Webster, 27–52. Calgary, AB: University of Calgary Press, 2019.

Campbell Windle, Victoria. "'We of the New Left': A Gender History of the Student Union for Peace Action from the Anti-Nuclear Movement to Women's Liberation," PhD diss., University of Waterloo, 2017, http://hdl.handle.net/10012/12406.

Carlson, Nellie, Kathleen Steinhauer, and Linda Goyette. *Disinherited Generations: Our Struggle to Reclaim Treaty Rights for First Nations Women and Their Descendants*. Edmonton: University of Alberta Press, 2013.

Carr, Graham. "'No Political Significance of Any Kind': Glenn Gould's Tour of the Soviet Union and the Culture of the Cold War." *Canadian Historical Review* 95, 1 (2014): 1–29.

Carstairs, Catherine. "Food, Fear, and the Environment in the Long Sixties." In *Debating Dissent: Canada and the Sixties*, edited by Lara Campbell, Dominique Clément, and Gregory S. Kealey, 29–46. Toronto: University of Toronto Press, 2012.

Carter, Sarah. *Imperial Plots: Women, Land, and the Spadework of British Colonialism on the Canadian Prairies*. Winnipeg: University of Manitoba Press, 2016.

Carty, Robert, Virginia Smith, and the Latin American Working Group. *Perpetuating Poverty: The Political Economy of Canadian Foreign Aid*. Toronto: Between the Lines, 1981.

Cassidy, Jennifer A., ed. *Gender and Diplomacy*. London: Routledge, 2017.

Cavell, Janice. "Like Any Good Wife: Gender and Perceptions of Canadian Foreign Policy, 1945–75." *International Journal* 63, 2 (June 2008): 385–403.

Chadda, Rakesh Kumar, Bichitra Nanda Patra, and Nitin Gupta. "Recent Developments in Community Mental Health: Relevance and Relationship with the Mental Health Care Bill." *Indian Journal of Social Psychiatry* 31, 2 (2015): 153–60. doi:10.4103/0971–9962.173296.

Charles, Helen, S.D. Manoranjitham, and K.S. Jacob. "Stigma and Explanatory Models among People with Schizophrenia and Their Relatives in Vellore, South India." *International Journal of Social Psychiatry* 53, 4 (2007): 325–32. doi: 10.1177/0020764006074538.

Cheung, Yuet-Wah. *Missionary Medicine in China: A Study of Two Canadian Protestant Missions in China before 1937*. Lanham, MD: University Press of America, 1988.

Chin, Carol C. "Beneficent Imperialists: American Women Missionaries in China at the Turn of the Twentieth Century." *Diplomatic History* 27, 3 (2003): 327–52.

China Interrupted: Japanese Internment and the Reshaping of a Canadian Missionary Community. Waterloo, ON: Wilfrid Laurier University Press, 2016.

Chironda, Andriata. "Narrators, Navigators and Negotiators: Foreign Service Officer Life Stories from Canada's Africa Refugee Resettlement Program, 1970 to 1990," PhD diss., Carleton University, 2020.
Clark, Alice. "A Study Guide in Nursing for Indian Nursing Students." *The American Journal of Nursing* 54, 5 (1954): 637.
Clark, Tova. *Compartments*. Newcastle, ON: Penumbra Press, 2005.
Connelly, Matthew. *Fatal Misconception: The Struggle to Control World Population*. Cambridge, MA: Harvard University Press, 2009.
Conroy-Krutz, Emily. *Christian Imperialism: Converting the World in the Early American Republic*. Ithaca, NY: Cornell University Press, 2015.
Cook, Peter. "Onontio Gives Birth: How the French in Canada Became Fathers to Their Indigenous Allies, 1645–73." *Canadian Historical Review* 96, 2 (2015): 165–93.
Cook, Sharon Anne. *"Through Sunshine and Shadow": The Woman's Christian Temperance Union, Evangelicalism, and Reform in Ontario, 1874–1930*. Montreal/Kingston: McGill-Queen's University Press, 1995.
Cooper, Andrew Fenton, ed. *Canadian Culture: International Dimension*. Toronto: Centre on Foreign Policy and Federalism, University of Waterloo/Canadian Institute of International Affairs, 1985.
Cooper, Dana. *Informal Ambassadors: American Women, Transatlantic Marriages, and Anglo-American Relations, 1865–1945*. Kent, OH: Kent State University Press, 2014.
Costin, L. "Feminism, Pacifism, Internationalism and the 1915 International Congress of Women." *Women's Studies International Forum* 5, 3–4 (1982): 301–15.
Court, John P.M. "Historical Synopsis: The Department of Psychiatry at the University of Toronto." Rev. April 2011. https://www.psychiatry.utoronto.ca/file/1181/download?token=wZLevETF.
Crawford, Vicki. "African American Women in the Mississippi Freedom Democratic Party." In *Sisters in the Struggle: African American Women in the Civil Rights Movement*, edited by Bettye Collier-Thomas and V.P. Franklin, 121–38. New York: New York University Press, 2001.
Crossen, Jonathan. "Another Wave of Anti-Colonialism: The Origins of Indigenous Internationalism." *Canadian Journal of History* 52, 3 (2017): 533–59. doi:10.3138/cjh.ach.52.3.06.
–. "Decolonization, Indigenous Internationalism, and the World Council of Indigenous Peoples." PhD diss., University of Waterloo, 2014.
Crum, Steven. "Almost Invisible: The Brotherhood of North American Indians (1911) and the League of North American Indians (1935)." *Wicazo Sa Review* 21, 1 (2006): 43–59. doi:10.1353/wic.2006.0003.
Curtis, Bruce. "'The Most Splendid Pageant Ever Seen': Grandeur, Condescension, and the Domestic in Lord Durham's Political Theatre." *Canadian Historical Review* 89, 1 (2008): 55–88.
Dalby, Simon. "Gender and Critical Geopolitics; Reading Security Discourse in the New World Disorder." *Environment and Planning D: Society and Space* 12, 5 (October 1994): 595–612. doi:10.1068/d120595.
David, Mirela. "Female Gynecologists and Their Birth Control Clinics: Eugenics in Practice in 1920s–1930s China." *Canadian Bulletin for the History of Medicine* 35, 1 (2018): 32–62.
Davis, Darién J. *Avoiding the Dark: Race and the Forging of a National Culture in Modern Brazil*. Aldershot, UK/Brookfield, VT: Ashgate, 1999.
De Costa, Ravi. "Identity, Authority, and the Moral Worlds of Indigenous Petitions." *Comparative Studies in Society and History* 48, 3 (2006): 669–98. doi:10.1017/S0010417506000260.
Degen, Marie Louise. *The History of the Woman's Peace Party*. New York: Garland, 1972.

DeLaat, Sonya. "Pictures in Development: The Canadian International Development Agency's Photo Library." In *A Samaritan State Revisited: Historical Perspectives on Canadian Foreign Aid*, edited by Greg Donaghy and David Webster, 223–44. Calgary, AB: University of Calgary Press, 2019.

DeRoche, Andy. "KK, the Godfather, and the Duke: Maintaining Positive Relations between Zambia and the USA in spite of Nixon's Other Priorities." *Safundi: The Journal of South African and American Studies* 12, 1 (2011): 97–121.

Deslauriers, Jean, and Denis Goulet. "The Medical Life of Henry Norman Bethune." *Canadian Respiratory Journal* 22, 6 (2015): e32–e42.

Diefenbaker, J.G. *One Canada: Memoirs of John G. Diefenbaker*. Vol 3, *The Tumultuous Years, 1962–1967*. Toronto: Macmillan, 1977.

Djwa, Sandra. *Journey with No Maps: A Life of P.K. Page*. Montreal/Kingston: McGill-Queen's University Press, 2012.

–. "P.K. Page: Discovering a Modern Sensibility." In *Wider Boundaries of Daring: The Modernist Impulse in Canadian Women's Poetry*, edited by Di Brandt and Barbara Godard, 75–96. Waterloo, ON: Wilfrid Laurier University Press, 2009.

Dodd, Dianne. "Canadian Historic Sites and Plaques: Heroines, Trailblazers, the Famous Five," *CRM: The Journal of Heritage Stewardship* 6, 2 (2009): 29–66.

Donaghy, Greg, and David Webster. *A Samaritan State Revisited: Historical Perspectives on Canadian Foreign Aid*. Calgary, AB: University of Calgary Press, 2019.

Drees, Laurie Meijer. *The Indian Association of Alberta: A History of Political Action*. Vancouver: UBC Press, 2002.

–. "Indian Hospitals and Aboriginal Nurses: Canada and Alaska." *Canadian Bulletin of Medical History* 27, 1 (2010): 139–61.

Dubinsky, Karen, Adele Perry, and Henry Yu, eds. *Within and Without the Nation: Canadian History as Transnational History*. Toronto: University of Toronto Press, 2015.

Dubinsky, Karen, Sean Mills, and Scott Rutherford, eds. *Canada and the Third World: Overlapping Histories*. Toronto: University of Toronto Press, 2016.

DuBois, Ellen Carol. "Women's Movements." In *The Palgrave Dictionary of Transnational History*, edited by Akira Iriye and Pierre-Yves Saunier, 1114–21. Basingstoke, UK: Palgrave Macmillan, 2009.

Dustan, Leanne. "Convention on the Political Rights of Women." In *Encyclopedia of Women and American Politics*, edited by Lynne E. Ford, 131. New York: Facts on File, 2008.

Early, Frances. "Canadian Women and the International Arena in the 1960s: The Voice of Women/La voix des femmes and the Opposition to the Vietnam War." In *The Sixties: Passion, Politics, and Style*, edited by Dimitry Anastakis, 25–42. Montreal/Kingston: McGill-Queen's University Press, 2014.

–. "'A Grandly Subversive Time': The Halifax Branch of the Voice of Women in the 1960s." In *Mothers of the Municipality: Women, Work, and Social Policy in Post–1945 Halifax*, edited by Judith Fingard and Janet Guildford, 253–80. Toronto: University of Toronto Press, 2005.

–. "Re-imaging War: The Voice of Women, the Canadian Aid for Vietnam Civilians, and the Knitting Project for Vietnamese Children, 1966–1976." *Peace and Change* 34, 2 (2009): 148–63.

Egan, Michael. *Barry Commoner and the Science of Survival: The Remaking of American Environmentalism*. Cambridge, MA: MIT Press, 2007.

Enloe, Cynthia. *Bananas, Beaches, and Bases: Making Feminist Sense of International Politics*. 2nd ed. Berkeley: University of California Press, 2014.

–. *Curious Feminist: Searching for Women in a New Age of Empire.* Berkeley: University of California Press, 2004.

Epp, Marlene. *Refugees in Canada: A Brief History.* Immigration and Ethnicity in Canada Series 35. Ottawa, ON: Canadian Historical Association, 2017. https://cha-shc.ca/_uploads/5c374fb005cf0.pdf.

Epstein, Alexandra. "International Feminism and Empire-Building between the Wars: The Case of Viola Smith." *Women's History Review* 17, 5 (2008): 699–719.

Erlandsson, Susanna. "Off the Record: Margaret Van Kleffens and the Gendered History of the Dutch World War II Diplomacy." *International Feminist Journal of Politics* 21, 1 (2019): 35–37.

Evans, Gary. *In the National Interest: A Chronicle of the National Film Board of Canada from 1949 to 1989.* Toronto: University of Toronto Press, 1991.

Fillion, Eric. "Experiments in Cultural Diplomacy: Music as Mediation in Canadian-Brazilian Relations (1940s–1960s)." PhD diss., Concordia University, 2019.

Fitzgerald, Rosemary. "Making and Moulding of the Indian Empire: Recasting Nurses in Colonial India." In *Rhetoric and Reality: Gender and the Colonial Experience in South Asia,* edited by Avril A. Powell and Siobhan Lambert-Hurley, 185–222. Oxford: Oxford University Press, 2006.

–. "Rescue and Redemption: The Rise of Female Medical Missions in Colonial India during the Late Nineteenth and Early Twentieth Centuries." In *Nursing History and the Politics of Welfare,* edited by Anne Marie Rafferty, Jane Robinson, and Ruth Elka, 64–79. London: Routledge, 1997.

Flynn, Karen. *Moving Beyond Borders: A History of Black Caribbean and Caribbean Women in the Diaspora.* Toronto: University of Toronto Press, 2011.

–. "'She Cannot Be Confined to Her Own Region': Nursing and Nurses in the Caribbean, Canada, and the UK." In *Within and Without the Nation: Canadian History as Transnational History,* edited by Karen Dubinsky, Adele Perry, and Henry Yu, 228–49. Toronto: University of Toronto Press, 2015.

Foot, Rosemary. "Where Are the Women? The Gender Dimension in the Study of International Relations." *Diplomatic History* 14, 4 (1990): 615–22.

Furth, Charlotte. "Concepts of Pregnancy, Childbirth, and Infancy in Ch'ing Dynasty China." *Journal of Asian Studies* 46, 1 (1987): 7–35.

Gagan, Rosemary R. *A Sensitive Independence: Canadian Methodist Women Missionaries in Canada and the Orient, 1881–1925.* Montreal: McGill-Queen's University Press, 1992.

Gass, Katrina, and Helen Kay. "Chrystal Macmillan, 1872–1937." In *These Dangerous Women.* London, UK: Women's International League for Peace and Freedom/The Clapham Film Unit. http://www.wilpf.org.uk/wp-content/uploads/2015/05/Macmillan-Chrystal.pdf.

George, Reena. *One Step at a Time: The Birth of the Christian Medical College, Vellore.* New Delhi: Roli Books, 2018.

Ghosh, Suresh Chandra. *The History of Education in Modern India, 1757–1986.* New Delhi: Orient Longman, 1995.

Girouard, Kim. "Médicaliser au féminin: quand la médecine occidentale rencontre la maternité en Chine du Sud, 1879–1938." PhD diss., Université de Montréal/École Normale Supérieure de Lyon, 2017.

Glassford, Sarah. *Mobilizing Mercy: A History of the Canadian Red Cross.* Montreal/Kingston: McGill-Queen's University Press, 2017.

Godard, Barbara. "Kinds of Osmosis." *Journal of Canadian Studies* 38, 1 (2004): 65–75.

Goedde, Petra. *The Politics of Peace: A Global Cold War History.* Oxford: Oxford University Press, 2019.

Gorman, Dan. "Race, the Commonwealth, and the United Nations: From Imperialism to Internationalism in Canada, 1940–1960." In *Dominion of Race: Rethinking Canada's International History*, edited by Laura Madokoro, Francine McKenzie, and David Meren, 139–59. Vancouver: UBC Press, 2017.

Gotlieb, Sondra. *Wife of ... An Irreverent Account of Life in Washington*. Halifax, NS: Formac, 1987.

Granatstein, J.L., and R. Bothwell. *Pirouette: Pierre Trudeau and Canadian Foreign Policy*. Toronto: University of Toronto Press, 1991.

—. *Trudeau's World: Insiders Reflect on Foreign Policy, Trade, and Defence, 1968–84*. Vancouver: UBC Press, 2006.

Grant, Agnes. "Feminism and Aboriginal Culture: One Woman's View." *Canadian Women Studies/Cahiers de la femme* 14, 2 (1994), 56–57.

Grypma, Sonya. *Healing Henan: Canadian Nurses at the North China Mission, 1888–1947*. Vancouver: UBC Press, 2008.

Hall, Michèle Rackham. *The Art of P.K. Irwin: Observer, Other, Gemini*. Erin, ON: The Porcupine's Quill, 2016.

Hammond-Callaghan, Marie. "Bridging and Breaching Cold War Divides: Transnational Peace Building, State Surveillance, and the Voice of Women." In *Worth Fighting For: Canada's Tradition of War Resistance from 1812 to the War on Terror*, edited by Lara Campbell, Michael Dawson, and Catherine Gidney, 135–45. Toronto: Between the Lines, 2015.

Hannant, Larry, ed. *The Politics of Passion: Norman Bethune's Writing and Arts*. Toronto: University of Toronto Press, 1998.

Hansson, Kailey. "Dancing into Hearts and Minds: Canadian Ballet Exchanges with the Communist World, 1956–76." In *Undiplomatic History: The New Study of Canada and the World*, edited by Asa McKercher and Philip Van Huizen, 233–52. Montreal/Kingston: McGill-Queen's University Press, 2019.

Hantel-Fraser, Christine. *No Fixed Address: Life in the Foreign Service*. Toronto: University of Toronto Press, 1993.

Hardiman, David. "Introduction." In *Healing Bodies, Saving Souls: Medical Missions in Asia and Africa*, edited by David Hardiman, 5–58. Amsterdam/New York: Rodopi B.V., 2006.

—. *Missionaries and Their Medicine: A Christian Modernity for Tribal India*. Manchester, UK: Manchester University Press, 2008.

Harding, Beatrice. *Around the World in 80 Years*. Regina, SK: self-published, 2004.

Hardy, Rae. *Distaff Diplomacy, or, My Elegant Life as a Diplomat's Wife*. Victoria, BC: Trafford on demand, 2001.

Hatch, John. *Two African Statesmen: Kaunda of Zambia and Nyerere of Tanzania*. London: Secker and Warburg, 1976.

Healey, Madelaine. *Indian Sisters: A History of Nursing and the State, 1907–2007*. London: Routledge, 2013.

—. "'Regarded, Paid, and Housed as Menials': Nursing in Colonial India, 1900–1948." *South Asian History and Culture* 2, 1 (2010): 55–75.

Heaps, Denise Adele. "P.K. Page's *Brazilian Journal*: Language Shock." *Biography* 19, 4 (1996): 355–70.

Heidt, Daniel. "'I Think That Would Be the End of Canada': Howard Green, the Nuclear Test Ban, and Interest-Based Foreign Policy, 1946–1963." *American Review of Canadian Studies* 42, 3 (2012): 343–69.

Heinrich, Larissa N. *The Afterlife of Images: Translating the Pathological Body between China and the West*. Durham, NC: Duke University Press, 2008.

Helfferich, Merritt. "WINHEC Formed at WIPCE." *Sharing Our Pathways* 7, 4 (2002).

Hilliker, John, and Donald Barry. *Canada's Department of External Affairs*. Vol. 2, *Coming of Age, 1946–1968*. Montreal/Kingston: McGill-Queen's University Press/Institute of Public Administration of Canada, 1995.

Hilliker, John, Mary Halloran, and Greg Donaghy. *Canada's Department of External Affairs*. Vol. 3, *Innovation and Adaptation, 1968–1984*. Toronto: University of Toronto Press/Institute of Public Administration of Canada, 2017.

Hoganson, Kristen. *Consumers' Imperium: The Global Production of American Domesticity, 1865–1920*. Chapel Hill: University of North Carolina Press, 2006.

—. "What's Gender Got to Do with It? Gender History as Foreign Relations History." In *Explaining the History of American Foreign Relations*, edited by Michael J. Hogan and Thomas G. Paterson, 304–22. 2nd ed. Cambridge: Cambridge University Press, 2004.

Hollinger, David A. *Protestants Abroad: How Missionaries Tried to Change the World but Changed America*. Princeton, NJ: Princeton University Press, 2017.

Humalajoki, Reetta "'Yours in Indian Unity': Moderate National Indigenous Organisations and the U.S.-Canada Border in the Red Power Era." *Comparative American Studies* 17:2 (2020), 183–98.

Hunter, Jane. *The Gospel of Gentility: American Women Missionaries in Turn-of-the-Century China*. New Haven, CT: Yale University Press, 1984.

Hutchinson, Braden. "Fighting the War at Home: Voice of Women and War Toy Activism in Postwar Canada." In *Worth Fighting For: Canada's Tradition of War Resistance from 1812 to the War on Terror*, edited by Lara Campbell, Michael Dawson, and Catherine Gidney, 147–58. Toronto: Between the Lines, 2015.

Ignatieff, George. *The Making of a Peacemonger: The Memoirs of George Ignatieff*. Toronto: University of Toronto Press, 1985.

Inwood, G.J. *Continentalizing Canada: The Politics and Legacy of the MacDonald Commission*. Toronto: University of Toronto Press, 2005.

Iriye, Akira. "Culture and Power: International Relations as Intercultural Relations." *Diplomatic History* 3, 2 (1979): 115–28.

—. *Cultural Internationalism and World Order*. Baltimore: John Hopkins University Press, 1997.

Ishiguro, Laura. "'How I Wish I Might Be Near': Distance and the Epistolary Family in Late-Nineteenth-Century Condolence Letters." In *Within and Without the Nation: Canadian History as Transnational History*, edited by Karen Dubinsky, Adele Perry, and Henry Yu, 212–27. Toronto: University of Toronto Press, 2015.

—. *Nothing to Write Home About: British Family Correspondence and the Settler Colonial Everyday in British Columbia*. Vancouver: UBC Press, 2019.

James, Carolyn, and Glenda Sluga, eds. *Women, Diplomacy and International Politics since 1500*. London: Routledge, 2016.

Janovicek, Nancy, and Carmen Nielson. "Introduction: Feminist Conversations." In *Reading Canadian Women's and Gender History*, edited by Nancy Janovicek and Carmen Nielson, 3–22. Toronto: University of Toronto Press, 2019.

Jessup, Lynda, and Sarah E.K. Smith. "Introduction: Curating Cultural Diplomacy." *Journal of Curatorial Studies* 5, 3 (2016): 283–88.

Johnston, Andrew M. "The Disappearance of Emily G. Balch, Social Scientist." *The Journal of the Gilded Age and Progressive Era*, 13, 2 (2014): 166–99.

—. "Jeanne Halbwachs, International Feminist Pacifism, and France's Société d'Études Documentaires et Critiques Sur La Guerre." *Peace and Change* 41, 1 (January 2016): 22–37.

Kaur, Rajkumari Amrit. Foreword to *A Study Guide in the Nursing Arts*, by Edith Buchanan. New Delhi: College of Nursing, 1953.

Keeble, Edna, and Heather Smith. *(Re)Defining Traditions: Gender and Canadian Foreign Policy*. Halifax, NS: Fernwood, 1999.

Khrushchev, Nikita Sergeevich. *Memoirs of Nikita Khrushchev*, edited by Sergei Khrushchev. Translated by George Shriver and Stephen Shenfield. Vol. 3, *Statesman (1953–1964)*. University Park: Pennsylvania State University Press, 2007.

King, Thomas. "Borders." In *One Good Story, That One: Stories*, 131–48. Minneapolis: University of Minnesota Press, 1993.

Kinnear, Mary. *Woman of the World: Mary McGeachy and International Cooperation*. Toronto: University of Toronto Press, 2004.

Lackenbauer, P. Whitney. "Race, Gender and International 'Relations': African Americans and Aboriginal People on the Margins of Canada's North, 1942–48." In *Dominion of Race: Rethinking Canada's International History*, edited by Laura Madokoro, Francine McKenzie, and David Meren, 112–38. Vancouver: UBC Press, 2017.

Ladner, Kiera. "An Indigenous Paradox: Both Monumental Achievement and Monumental Defeat." In *Patriation and Its Consequences: Constitution Making in Canada*, edited by Lois Harder and Steve Patten, 267–89. Vancouver: UBC Press, 2015.

Langford, Will. "Friendship Centres in Canada, 1959–1977." *The American Indian Quarterly* 40, 1 (2016): 1–37.

–. "International Development and the State in Question: Liberal Internationalism, the New Left, and Canadian University Service Overseas in Tanzania, 1963–1977." In *Undiplomatic History: The New Study of Canada and the World*, edited by Asa McKercher and Philip Van Huizen, 184–205. Montreal/Kingston: McGill-Queen's University Press, 2019.

Larmour, Jean. "The Douglas Government's Changing Emphasis on Public, Private and Co-operative Development in Saskatchewan, 1955–1961." In *Building the Co-operative Commonwealth: Essays on the Democratic Socialist Tradition in Canada*, edited by J. William Brennan, 161–80. Regina, SK: Canadian Plains Research Centre, 1984.

Levine, Robert M. *Father of the Poor? Vargas and His Era*. Cambridge: Cambridge University Press, 1998.

Lewis, Norman. *Golden Earth: Travels in Burma*. London: Eland Books, 1952.

Liberian Information Service. *Liberia: Story of Progress*. Monrovia: Liberian Information Service, n.d.

Lin, Yin-Tang, Thomas David, and Davide Rodogno. "Fellowship Programs for Public Health Development: The Rockefeller Foundation, UNRRA, and the WHO (1920s–1970s)." In *Global Exchanges: Scholarships and Transnational Circulations in the Modern World*, edited by Ludovic Tournès and Giles Scott-Smith, 140–55. New York: Berghahn, 2018.

Loewen, Candace. "Making Ourselves Heard: 'Voice of Women' and the Peace Movement in the Early Sixties." In *Framing Our Past: Canadian Women's History in the Twentieth Century*, edited by Sharon Anne Cook, Lorna R. McLean, and Kate O'Rourke, 248–51. Montreal/Kingston: McGill-Queen's University Press, 2001.

Love, Hattie F. "Chinese Women in Medicine." *China Christian Advocate* (April 1917): 9–10.

MacIsaac, Julie. "Legacy of Trail Blazer Includes Indigenous-Based Studies." *Alberta Sweetgrass* 22, 3 (2015).

Mackenzie, David. *Arthur Irwin: A Biography*. Toronto: University of Toronto Press, 1993.

Maclaren, Robert I. "George Woodall Cadbury: The Fabian Catalyst in Saskatchewan's 'Good Public Administration.'" *Canadian Public Administration* 38, 3 (1995): 471–80.

Macpherson, Kay. "Thérèse Casgrain: A Voice for Women." *Broadside* 3, 3 (December 1981–January 1982): 6. Reprinted in *Inside Broadside: A Decade of Feminist Journalism*, edited by Philinda Masters. Toronto: Second Story Press, 2019.

Macpherson, Kay, and Meg Sears. "The Voice of Women: A History." In *Women in the Canadian Mosaic*, edited by Gwen Matheson, 71–89. Toronto: Peter Martin Associates, 1976.

Madokoro, Laura, and Francine McKenzie. "Introduction: Writing Race into Canada's International History." In *Dominion of Race: Rethinking Canada's International History*, edited by Laura Madokoro, Francine McKenzie, and David Meren, 3–24. Vancouver: UBC Press, 2017.

Manuel, George, and Michael Posluns. *The Fourth World: An Indian Reality*. Don Mills, ON: Collier-Macmillan, 1974.

Marion, Nicole. "Canada's Disarmers: The Complicated Struggle against Nuclear Weapons, 1959–1963." PhD diss., Carleton University, 2017.

Massey, Rise M. "The World Council of Indigenous Peoples: An Analysis of Political Protest." Master's thesis, University of British Columbia, 1986. https://open.library.ubc.ca/collections/ubctheses/831/items/1.0096996.

Mathew, Anadit J., Beulah Samuel, and K.S. Jacob. "Perceptions of Illness in Self and in Others among Patients with Bipolar Disorder." *International Journal of Social Psychiatry* 56, 5 (2010): 462–70. doi.org/10.1177/0020764009106621.

McCarthy, Helen. "Gendering Diplomatic History: Women in the British Diplomatic Service circa 1919–1972." In *Women, Diplomacy and International Politics since 1500*, edited by Carolyn James and Glenda Sluga, 167–81. London: Routledge, 2016.

–. "Women, Marriage and Work in the British Diplomatic Service." *Women's History Review* 23, 6 (2014): 853–73.

McCarthy, Helen, and J. Southern. "Women, Gender and Diplomacy: A Historical Survey." In *Gender and Diplomacy*, edited by Jennifer A. Cassidy, 15–31. London: Routledge, 2017.

McFarlane, Peter. *Brotherhood to Nationhood: George Manuel and the Making of the Modern Indian Movement*. Toronto: Between the Lines, 1993.

McGregor, Hannah. "Troping the Foreign in P.K. Page's 'Questions and Images.'" *University of Toronto Quarterly* 82, 2 (2013): 185–97.

McKenzie, Francine. "A New Vision for the Commonwealth: Diefenbaker's Commonwealth Tour of 1958." In *Reassessing the Rogue Tory: Canadian Foreign Relations in the Diefenbaker Era*, edited by Janice Cavell and Ryan Touhey, 25–44. Vancouver: UBC Press, 2018.

McKercher, Asa. *Camelot and Canada: Canadian-American Relations in the Kennedy Era*. Oxford: Oxford University Press, 2016.

McKercher, Asa, and Philip Van Huizen, eds., *Undiplomatic History: The New Study of Canada and the World*. Montreal/Kingston: McGill-Queen's University Press, 2019.

McLean, Lorna. "'The Necessity of Going': Julia Grace Wales's Transnational Life as a Peace Activist and a Scholar." In *Feminist History in Canada: New Essays on Women, Gender, Work, and Nation*, edited by Catherine Carstairs and Nancy Janovicek, 77–95. Vancouver: UBC Press, 2013.

McLean, Lorna, and Jamilee Baroud, "Democracy Needs Education: Performance, Peace and Pedagogy, Julia Grace Wales." *Paedagogica Historica: International Journal of the History of Education* 56, 4 (2019): 503–9. doi:10.1080/00309230.2019.1616783.

McMahon, Patricia I. *Essence of Indecision: Diefenbaker's Nuclear Policy, 1957–1963*. Montreal/Kingston: McGill-Queen's University Press, 2014.

McManus, Sheila. *The Line Which Separates Race, Gender, and the Making of the Alberta-Montana Borderlands*. Lincoln: University of Nebraska Press, 2005.

McNeilly, Kevin. "Toward a Poetic of Dislocation: Elizabeth Bishop and P.K. Page Writing 'Brazil.'" *Studies in Canadian Literature* 23, 2 (1998): 85–108.

Meckel, Richard A. *Save the Babies: American Public Health Reform and the Prevention of Infant Mortality, 1850–1929*. Baltimore: Johns Hopkins University Press, 1990.

Meren, David. "Conclusion: Race and the Future of Canadian International History." In *Dominion of Race: Rethinking Canada's International History*, edited by Laura Madokoro, Francine McKenzie, and David Meren, 284–300. Vancouver: UBC Press, 2017.

–. "Getting Over Tragedy: Some Further Thoughts on Canadian International History." *Canadian Historical Review* 96, 4 (2015): 590–93. doi:10.3138/chr.96413.

–. "The Tragedies of Canadian International History." *Canadian Historical Review* 96, 4 (2015): 534–66.

Miller, Christine, and Patricia Chuchryk. *Women of the First Nations: Power, Wisdom, and Strength*. Winnipeg: University of Manitoba Press, 1996.

Miller, Iva M. "A Health Campaign in South China." *China Medical Journal* 42, 3 (1928): 154–61.

Miller, J.R. *Compact, Contact, Covenant: Aboriginal Treaty-Making in Canada*. Toronto: University of Toronto Press, 2009.

Miller, Kailey. "'An Ancillary Weapon': Cultural Diplomacy and Nation-Building in Cold War Canada, 1945–1967." PhD diss., Queen's University, 2015.

Minden, Karen. *Bamboo Stone: The Evolution of a Chinese Medical Elite*. Toronto: University of Toronto Press, 2014.

Mitchell, Silvia Z. "Marriage Plots: Royal Women, Marriage Diplomacy and International Politics at the Spanish, French and Imperial Courts, 1665–1679." In *Women, Diplomacy and International Politics since 1500*, edited by Carolyn James and Glenda Sluga, 86–106. London: Routledge, 2016.

Montag, Mildred Louise, and Margaret Filson. *Nursing Arts*. 2nd ed. Philadelphia, PA: Saunders, 1953.

Morantz-Sanchez, Regina. *Sympathy and Science: Women Physicians in American Medicine*. Chapel Hill: University of North Carolina Press, 2000. First published 1985 by Oxford University Press.

Morgan, Rhiannon. *Transforming Law and Institution: Indigenous Peoples, the United Nations and Human Rights*. Burlington, VT: Ashgate, 2011.

Morra, Linda M. *Unarrested Archives: Case Studies in Twentieth-Century Canadian Women's Authorship*. Toronto: University of Toronto Press, 2014.

Morra, Linda M., and Jessica Schagerl. "Introduction: No Archive Is Neutral." In *Basements, Attics, Closets and Cyberspace: Explorations in Canadian Women's Archives*, edited by Linda M. Morra and Jessica Schagerl. Waterloo, ON: Wilfrid Laurier University Press, 2012.

Natesh, A.M. *Rural Broadcasting (Literacy): Zambia (Mission) December 1969–December 1972*. Serial no. 2825/RMO.RD/MC. Paris: UNESCO, 1972.

Nehring, Holger. "The Last Battle of the Cold War: Peace Movements and German Politics in the 1980s." In *The Euromissile Crisis and the End of the Cold War*, edited by Leopoldo Nuti, Frédéric Bozo, Marie-Pierre Rey, and Bernd Rother, 309–12. Washington, DC: Woodrow Wilson Center Press; Stanford, CA: Stanford University Press, 2015.

–. *Politics of Security: British and West German Protest Movements and the Early Cold War, 1945–1970*. Oxford: Oxford University Press, 2013.

Nicolson, Harold. *Diplomacy*. New York: Harcourt Brace, 1939.

Ninkovich, Frank A. *The Diplomacy of Ideas: U.S. Foreign Policy and Cultural Relations 1938–1950*. Cambridge University Press, 1981.

Oakley, Roy Elliot. "Opening the Waiwai *Ewto*: Indigenous Social and Spatial Relations in Guyana." PhD diss., University of Edinburgh, 2018.

"Obituary: Dr. (Ms.) Edith Buchanan." *Nursing Journal of India* 94, 11 (2003).

Page, P.K. *Brazilian Journal*. Toronto: Lester and Orpen Dennys, 1987.

–. "Questions and Images." *Canadian Literature* 41 (1969): 17–22.

Palmer, Bryan. *Canada's 1960s: The Ironies of Identity in a Rebellious Era*. Toronto: University of Toronto Press, 2009.

Papachristou, Judith. "American Women and Foreign Policy, 1898–1905: Exploring Gender in Diplomatic History." *Diplomatic History* 14, 4 (Fall 1990): 493–509.

Pearson, Landon. *Letters from Moscow*. Newcastle, ON: Penumbra Press, 2003.

Perlin, G.C. *The Tory Syndrome: Leadership Politics in the Progressive Conservative Party*. Montreal/Kingston: McGill-Queen's University Press, 2006.

Pierson, Ruth Roach. *Women and Peace: Theoretical, Historical and Practical Perspectives*. London, UK: Croom Helm, 1987.

Prietao, Laura R. "Introduction: Women and Missionary Encounters with Foreign Nationalism in the 1920s." *Diplomatic History* 43, 2 (2019): 237–45.

"Qingmo chuangye xing guangzhou xiguan xiaojie: Huang Yuying." [Western Guangzhou entrepreneur at the end of the Qing Dynasty: Miss Huang Yuying]. *Guangdong shizhi* 1 (1999): 5.

Quiring, David. *CCF Colonialism in Northern Saskatchewan*. Vancouver: UBC Press, 2005.

Ravndal, Ellen, and Edward Newman. "The International Civil Service." In *Oxford Handbook of Global Policy and Transnational Administration*, edited by Diane Stone and Kim Moloney, 165–81. Oxford: Oxford University Press, 2019.

Reardon, Betty A. *Women and Peace: Feminist Visions of Global Security*. New York: State University of New York Press, 1993.

Reddy, Sujani K. *Nursing and Empire: Gendered Labor and Migration from India to the United States*. Chapel Hill: The University of North Carolina Press, 2015.

Renshaw, Michelle. *Accommodating the Chinese: The American Hospital in China, 1880–1920*. New York/London: Routledge, 2005.

Ricci, Amanda. "Making Global Citizens? Canadian Women at the World Conference of the International Women's Year, Mexico City 1975." In *Undiplomatic History: The New Study of Canada and the World*, edited by Asa McKercher and Philip Van Huizen, 206–29. Montreal/Kingston: McGill-Queen's University Press, 2019.

Richards, John, and Larry Pratt. *Prairie Capitalism: Power and Influence in the New West*. Toronto: McClelland and Stewart, 1979.

Rosenberg, Emily S. "Consuming Women: Images of Americanization in the 'American Century.'" *Diplomatic History* 23, 3 (July 1999): 479–97.

–. "Gender." *The Journal of American History* 77, 1 (1990): 116–24.

Ross, Margaret Taylor. "A Child Welfare Clinic." *The China Medical Journal*, 41, 3 (1927): 250–54.

Rostkowski, Joëlle. "The Redman's Appeal for Justice: Deskaheh and the League of Nations." In *Indians and Europe: An Interdisciplinary Collection of Essays*, edited by Christian F. Feest, 435–54. Lincoln: University of Nebraska Press, 1989.

Roy, Patricia, and Greg Donaghy, eds. *Contradictory Impulses: Canada and Japan in the Twentieth Century*. Vancouver: UBC Press, 2008.

Rupp, Leila J. "Sexuality and Politics in the Early Twentieth Century: The Case of the International Women's Movement." *Feminist Studies* 23, 3 (1997): 577–605.

–. *Worlds of Women: The Making of an International Women's Movement*. Princeton, NJ: Princeton University Press, 1997.

Rutherford, Scott. "'We Have Bigotry All Right – but No Alabamas': Racism and Aboriginal Protest in Canada during the 1960s." *American Indian Quarterly* 41, 2 (2017): 158–79. doi:10.5250/amerindiquar.41.2.0158.

Said, Edward W. *Culture and Imperialism*. New York: Vintage Books, 1994.

Sampat-Mehta, Ramdeo. *The Day After: A Political Guide for the Third World*. Ottawa: Heron Pub. House, 1974.

Samuel, Reema, Paul Russell, Tapan Kumar Paraseth, Sharmila Ernest, and K.S. Jacob. "Development and Validation of the Vellore Occupational Therapy Evaluation Scale to Assess Functioning in People with Mental Illness." *International Journal of Social Psychiatry* 62, 7 (2016): 616–26.

Sanders, Douglas E. *The Formation of the World Council of Indigenous Peoples.* Copenhagen: International Work Group for Indigenous Affairs, 1977.

Scott, Joan Wallach. *Gender and the Politics of History.* New York: Columbia University Press, 1988.

Shannon, Michael K. *Losing Hearts and Minds: American-Iranian Relations and International Education during the Cold War.* Ithaca: Cornell University Press, 2017.

Sharer, Wendy. *Vote and Voice: Women's Organizations and Political Literacy, 1915–1930.* Carbondale: Southern Illinois University Press, 2004.

Sharpe, S. *The Gilded Ghetto, Women and Political Power in Canada.* Toronto: HarperCollins 1995.

Shemo, Connie Anne. *The Chinese Medical Ministries of Kang Cheng and Shi Meiyu, 1872–1937: On a Cross-Cultural Frontier of Gender, Race, and Nation.* Bethlehem, PA: Lehigh University Press, 2011.

Shorter, Edward. *Partnership for Excellence: Medicine at the University of Toronto and Academic Hospitals.* Toronto: University of Toronto Press, 2013.

Siu, Helen F., and Wing-hoi Chan. "Introduction." In *Merchant's Daughters: Women, Commerce, and Regional Culture in South China,* edited by Helen F. Siu, 1–22. Hong Kong: Hong Kong University Press, 2010.

Sjolander, Claire Turenne. "Margaret Meagher and the Role of Women in the Foreign Service: Groundbreaking or Housekeeping?" In *Architects and Innovators: Building the Department of Foreign Affairs and International Trade, 1909–2009,* edited by Greg Donaghy and Kim Richard Nossal, 223–36. Montreal/Kingston: McGill-Queen's University Press, 2009.

Sjolander Clare Turenne, Heather A. Smith, and Deborah Stienstra, eds. "Taking Up and Throwing Down the Gauntlet: Feminists, Gender, and Canadian Foreign Policy." In *Feminist Perspectives on Canadian Foreign Policy,* edited by Claire Turenne Sjolander, Heather A. Smith, and Deborah Stienstra, 1–11. Don Mills, ON: Oxford University Press, 2003.

–, eds. *Feminist Perspectives on Canadian Foreign Policy.* Don Mills, ON: Oxford University Press, 2003.

Skidmore, Thomas E. *Black into White: Race and Nationality in Brazilian Thought.* Durham, NC: Duke University Press, 1993.

–. *Brazil: Five Centuries of Change.* New York: Oxford University Press, 1999.

Sluga, Glenda. "Women, Feminisms and Twentieth-Century Internationalisms." In *Internationalisms: A Twentieth-Century History,* edited by Glenda Sluga and Patricia Clavin, 61–84. Cambridge: Cambridge University Press, 2017.

Smallface-Marule, Marie. "The Canadian Government's Termination Policy: From 1969 to the Present Day." In *One Century Later: Western Canadian Reserve Indians since Treaty 7,* edited by Ian A.L. Getty and Donald B. Smith, 103–16. Vancouver: UBC Press, 1978.

–. "Traditional Indian Government: Of the People, by the People, for the People." In *Pathways to Self-Determination: Canadian Indians and the Canadian State,* edited by Leroy Little Bear, Menno Boldt, and J. Anthony Long, 36–45. Toronto: University of Toronto Press, 1984.

–, ed. "First Nations, States of Canada and United Kingdom: Patriation of the Canadian Constitution." Lethbridge, AB: World Council of Indigenous Peoples, 1981.

Smith, Heather A. "Unlearning: A Messy and Complex Journey with Canadian Foreign Policy." *International Journal* 72, 2 (June 2017): 203–16.

Smith, Joseph. *A History of Brazil, 1500–2000: Politics, Economy, Society, Diplomacy.* London, UK: Pearson Education, 2002.

Smith, Sarah E.K. "Art and the Invention of North America, 1985–2012." PhD diss., Queen's University, 2013.

South and Meso-American Indian Information Center Women's Committee. *Daughters of Abya Yala: Native Women Regaining Control.* Summertown, TN: Book Publishing Co, 1994.

Starr, Paul. *The Social Transformation of American Medicine: The Rise of a Sovereign Profession and the Making of a Vast Industry.* 2nd ed. New York: Basic Books, 2017.

Stevenson, Michael D. "Howard Green, Disarmament, and Canadian-American Defence Relations, 1959–1963." In *The Nuclear North: Histories of Canada in the Atomic Age*, edited by Susan Colbourn and Timothy Andrews Sayle, 67–87. Vancouver: UBC Press, 2020.

–. "'Tossing A Match into Dry Hay': Nuclear Weapons and the Crisis in U.S.-Canadian Relations." *Journal of Cold War Studies* 16 (2014): 5–34.

Stewart, Roderick, and Jesùs Majada. *Bethune in Spain.* Montreal/Kingston: McGill-Queen's University Press, 2014.

Stewart, Roderick, and Sharon Stewart. *Phoenix: The Life of Norman Bethune.* Montreal/Kingston: McGill-Queen's University Press, 2011.

Stienstra, Deborah. "Can the Silence Be Broken? Gender and Canadian Foreign Policy." *International Journal* 50, 1 (1994–95): 103–27.

Stiles, Diane. "'The Person You Call I': Configurations of Identity in the Poetry of P.K. Page." PhD diss., University of British Columbia, 2001.

Stoler, Ann Laura. *Along the Archival Grain: Epistemic Anxieties and Colonial Common Sense.* Princeton, NJ: Princeton University Press, 2008.

–. *Carnal Knowledge and Imperial Power: Race and the Intimate in Colonial Rule.* Berkeley: University of California Press, 2010.

Strong-Boag, Veronica Jane. *Liberal Hearts and Coronets: The Lives and Times of Ishbel Marjoribanks Gordon and John Campbell Gordon, the Aberdeens.* Toronto: University of Toronto Press, 2015.

Stursberg, Peter. *Diefenbaker: Leadership Lost, 1962–1967.* Toronto: University of Toronto Press, 1976.

Thomas, Frédéric. "Taking the World without Changing Power." *Le Monde diplomatique.* English edition, April 2020, 7.

Tournès, Ludovic, and Giles Scott-Smith. "A World of Exchanges: Conceptualizing the History of International Scholarship Programs (Nineteenth to Twenty-First Centuries)." In *Global Exchanges: Scholarships and Transnational Circulations in the Modern World*, edited by Ludovic Tournès and Giles Scott-Smith, 1–29. New York: Berghahn, 2018.

Trehearne, Brian. *The Montreal Forties: Modernist Poetry in Transition.* Toronto: University of Toronto Press, 1999.

Tucker, Sara W. "A Mission for Change in China: The Hackett Women's Medical Center of Canton, China, 1900–1930." In *Women's Work for Women: Missionaries and Social Change in Asia*, edited by Leslie A. Flemming, 137–257. Boulder, CO: Westview Press, 1989.

Tunis, Barbara Logan. *In Caps and Gowns: The Story of the School for Graduate Nurses, McGill University, 1920–1964.* Montreal/Kingston: McGill-Queen's University Press, 1966.

Van Kirk, Sylvia. "The Role of Native Women in the Fur Trade Society of Western Canada, 1670–1830." *Frontiers: A Journal of Women Studies* 7, 3 (1984): 9–13.

Vellacott, Jo. "Feminism as if All People Mattered: Working to Remove the Causes of War, 1919–1929." *Contemporary European History* 10, 3 (2001): 375–94.

–. *From Liberal to Labour with Women's Suffrage: The Story of Catherine Marshall.* 2nd ed. Montreal/Kingston: McGill-Queen's University Press, 2016.

—. "A Place for Pacifism and Transnationalism in Feminist Theory: The Early Work of the Women's International League for Peace and Freedom." *Women's History Review* 1 (1993): 23–56.

Verghese, Abraham. "Family Participation in Mental Health Care – the Vellore Experiment." *Indian Journal of Psychiatry* 30, 2 (1988): 117–21.

—. "The History of the Mental Health Centre: Some Reminiscences." *The Alumni Journal of the Christian Medical College Vellore: Psychiatry Issue* (2007): 9.

Vik, Hanne Hagtvedt. "Indigenous Internationalism." In *Internationalisms: A Twentieth-Century History*, edited by Glenda Sluga and Patricia Clavin, 315–39. Cambridge: Cambridge University Press, 2016.

Vinen, R. *Thatcher's Britain: The Politics and Social Upheaval of the Thatcher Era*. London: Simon and Schuster, 2009.

Vucetic, Srdjan. *The Anglosphere: A Genealogy of a Racialized Identity in International Relations*. Stanford, CA: Stanford University Press, 2011.

Ware, Vron. *Beyond the Pale: White Women, Racism and History*. London: Verso, 1992.

Warsh, Cheryl Krasnick. *Prescribed Norms: Women and Health in Canada and the United States since 1800*. Toronto: University of Toronto Press, 2012.

Webster, David. "Modern Missionaries: Canadian Postwar Technical Assistance Advisors in Southeast Asia." *Journal of the Canadian Historical Association* 20, 2 (2009): 86–111.

—. "'Red Indians' in Geneva, 'Papuan Headhunters' in New York: Race, Mental Maps, and Two Global Appeals in the 1920s and 1960s." In *Dominion of Race: Rethinking Canada's International History*, edited by Laura Madokoro, Francine McKenzie, and David Meren, 254–83. Vancouver: UBC Press, 2017.

Weiers, Margaret K. *Envoys Extraordinary: Women of the Canadian Foreign Service*. Toronto: Dundurn Press, 1995.

Whitehead, Clive. "The Historiography of British Imperial Education Policy, Part I: India." *History of Education* 34, 3 (2005): 315–29.

Willemsen-Diaz, Augusto. "How Indigenous Peoples' Rights Reached the UN." In *Making the Declaration Work: The United Nations Declaration on the Rights of Indigenous Peoples*, edited by Clair Charters and Rodolpho Stavenhagen, 16–31. Copenhagen: International Work Group for Indigenous Affairs, 2009.

Williamson, Janice, and Deborah Gorham, eds. *Up and Doing: Canadian Women and Peace*. Toronto: Women's Press, 1989.

Wood, Molly M. "'Commanding Beauty' and 'Gentle Charm': American Women and Gender in the Early Twentieth-Century Foreign Service." *Diplomatic History* 31, 3 (2007): 505–30.

—. "Diplomatic Wives: The Politics of Domesticity and the 'Social Game' in the U.S. Foreign Service, 1905–1941." *Journal of Women's History* 17, 2 (2005): 142–65.

—. "Wives, Clerks, and 'Lady Diplomats': The Gendered Politics of Diplomacy and Representation in the U.S. Foreign Service, 1900–1940." *European Journal of American Studies* 10, 1 (2015): 1–12. doi.org/10.4000/ejas.10562.

Wood, Whitney. "Spreading the Gospel of Natural Birth: Canadian Contributions to an International Medical Movement, 1945–1960." In *Undiplomatic History: The New Study of Canada and the World*, edited by Asa McKercher and Philip Van Huizen, 137–60. Montreal/Kingston: McGill-Queen's University Press, 2019.

Xu, Guangqiu. *American Doctors in Canton: Modernization in China, 1835–1935*. New Brunswick, NJ: Transaction, 2011.

Yi-Li, Wu. *Reproducing Women: Medicine, Metaphor, and Childbirth in Late Imperial China*. Berkeley: University of California Press, 2010.

Young Mary M., and Susan J. Henders. "'Other Diplomacies' and World Order: Historical Insights from Canadian-Asian Relations." *Hague Journal of Diplomacy* 11 (2016): 351–82.

Zancarini-Fournel, Michelle. "Histoire des femmes, histoire du genre." In *Historiographies, Concepts et débats. 1*, edited by Christian Delacroix, François Dosse, Patrick Garcia, and Nicholas Offenstadt, 208–19. Paris: Gallimard, 2010.

Contributors

Stacey Barker is the historian for the Arts and Military History at the Canadian War Museum.

Jill Campbell-Miller was most recently a SSHRC/FRQSC postdoctoral fellow in the Department of History at Carleton University and is an adjunct professor in the Department of History at Saint Mary's University.

Joe Clark is a former Canadian prime minister, party leader, and cabinet minister.

Susan Colbourn is associate director of the Triangle Institute for Security Studies, based at Duke University's Sanford School of Public Policy.

Sharon Anne Cook is a professor emerita and Distinguished University Professor at the University of Ottawa. She teaches educational history in the Faculty of Education.

Jonathan Crossen is an associate professor at UiT The Arctic University of Norway.

Greg Donaghy was the director of the Bill Graham Centre for Contemporary International History at the University of Toronto and the former head of the Historical Section at Global Affairs Canada.

Eric Fillion is a SSHRC/FRQSC postdoctoral fellow in the Department of History at the University of Toronto.

Kim Girouard is Postdoctoral Research Fellow in History of Medicine, Department of Innovation in Medical Education, Faculty of Medicine, University of Ottawa.

Dominique Marshall is professor of Canadian history at Carleton University.

Steve Marti is an independent scholar who worked with the Historical Section at Global Affairs Canada and taught at Trent University.

Francine McKenzie is a professor in the Department of History at the University of Western Ontario.

Lorna McLean is professor emerita in the Faculty of Education at the University of Ottawa.

Patricia E. Roy is professor emerita of history at the University of Victoria.

David Webster is a history professor at Bishop's University.

Index

Note: Illustrations are indicated by an (i) appended to the page number

2SLGBTQQIA individuals and communities, 10, 13, 78–80

A Study Guide in Nursing Arts, 39, 44, 47–51
Ad Hoc Committee on Indian Women's Rights, 141
Addams, Jane, 93, 95–97, 99, 105, 106(i)–9, 111
  early life, 105
  founding of WILPF, 97
  International Committee of Women for Permanent Peace, 96, 107
  Nobel Peace Prize, 93, 105, 107
  personality, 99, 111
  settlement movement, 95, 105
  Woman's Peace Party, 95, 97, 107
  women's suffrage, 106
  work with WILPF, 107
Africa, 6, 11, 43, 64–65, 67, 73–77, 136, 138–42, 189–90, 215, 218
  See also individual country names
Alberta, 11, 124, 136–39, 144, 148–51, 164
Albright, Madeleine, 210
Alonso, Harriet, 93, 105, 107
American Presbyterian Mission, 22

Amrith, Sunil, 63
Anglican Church of Canada, 42, 55, 147, 223
Anstee, Margaret, 64–65, 73, 83
Armstrong-Reid, Susan, 57
Asia, 6, 24, 43, 54, 57, 64–65, 69, 71, 78, 80–82, 84, 189, 208
  See also individual country names
Atkey, Ron, 208
atomic testing
  See nuclear weapons testing
atomic weapons
  See nuclear weapons
Australia, 67, 78–80, 82, 142, 161, 164, 166, 170

Balch, Emily Greene, 93, 97, 98(i)–99, 101, 103, 105–7, 110–11, 213
  academic career, 97, 110–11
  founding of WILPF, 98
  International Congress of Women, 98
  Nobel Peace Prize, 93, 97, 99
  personal life, 99
  socialism, 97–98, 110
  work with WILPF, 99, 101, 103
Ballon, Ellen, 170

Banff School of Fine Arts, 137
Barlow, Betty, 73–74(i)
Bashevkin, Sylvia, 200
BC Women's Committee Against Radiation Hazards, 118
Belgium, 93, 96, 217
Bethune, Norman, 21–22, 34
Bhore, Sir Joseph, 43, 49
Bikini Atoll, 117
birth control
See family planning
Bothwell, Robert, 185, 196
Brazil, 12, 14, 161–77
Brebner, John Bartlett, 5
Britain, 6, 9–10, 12, 13, 26, 43, 66–68, 93, 95, 97–98, 100–1, 103, 113, 118, 121–24, 126, 146–47, 164, 170, 183–84, 190–200, 210
British Columbia, 65, 144–46
British Commonwealth of Nations, 43, 70, 142–43, 163, 189–90, 193
British empire, 24, 26, 33, 190
British Guiana, 75–76, 78
British North America Act, 183, 193–94
Broadbent, Ed, 197
Brookfield, Tarah, 8, 116
Brouwer, Ruth Compton, 8, 65
Buchanan, Edith, 9, 39, 40(i), 42, 44, 45(i), 46–49, 51, 57–58
A Study Guide in Nursing Arts, 47–51
early life, 44–45
nursing career, 45–47, 51
WHO Fellowship, 46
work at Delhi College of Nursing, 46–47
Burma, 65, 70, 80

Cadbury, Barbara, 10, 13–14, 66–69, 83–84
early life, 66–67
family planning work, 68–69
political career, 66–68
Cadbury, George, 67–68, 73, 81, 84
Cadieux, Marcel, 84
Calgary, 151, 164
Camp, Dalton, 188
Canadian Broadcasting Corporation (CBC), 127
Canadian Club, 196
Canadian Committee for the Control of Radiation Hazards, 118

Canadian Indian Youth Council, 138
Canadian International Development Agency (CIDA), 147–48, 218
Canadian Peace Research Institute (CPRI), 120
Canadian Presbyterian Church, 26, 39, 42, 44
Canadian Presbyterian Mission, 22–23, 27, 44
Canadian University Service Overseas (CUSO), 11, 139–40, 144
Cardinal, Harold, 138, 140
caring labour
See diplomatic wives
Casgrain, Thérèse, 122
Catley-Carlson, Margaret, 65
Ceylon, 66, 68–72
Chandy, Jacob, 54
Charette, Janice, 201
Charter of Rights and Freedoms, 193, 197, 199
Charteris, Lord, 195
Cheever, Helen, 99
Chin, Carol C., 27, 66
China, 9, 21–34, 42–43, 52, 66, 79–80, 120, 223
Chrétien, Jean, 142, 196, 198
Christian Medical College, Vellore, India, 40, 42, 51–57
Churchill, Winston, 190
Clark, Joe, 12, 147, 183, 205–11, 216
Clark, Lorne, 163
Clark, Tova, 163
class, 15, 41, 103, 105, 164, 167, 200, 216
Cold War, 8, 81, 116–20, 129, 165, 189
Collenette, David, 195
Colombo Plan, 43, 70–72, 189
colonialism, 6–7, 84, 135–36, 140, 142, 144, 149, 151
Combined Universities Campaign for Nuclear Disarmament, 118
Committee for Nuclear Information, 124
communism, 82, 107, 120, 141, 166–67
Connelly, Matthew, 69
constitution, Canada, 12, 146–47, 183, 185, 193–200, 215
notwithstanding clause, 198
repatriation of, 12, 146–47, 183, 185, 193–200, 215

Continuous Mediation without Armistice Peace Plan (Wisconsin Plan), 93, 104, 108–10, 215
Co-operative Commonwealth Federation (CCF), 67, 68, 73, 207
Creelman, Lyle, 57
Crown-Indigenous Relations and Northern Affairs Canada, 213
Cuban Missile Crisis, 123
cultural diplomacy, 12, 169–70, 173–74

Dalhousie University, 191–92
Daughters of the American Revolution, 99
Davey, Dorothy, 149
David Gregg Hospital for Women and Children, 28, 30, 33
Davis, Josephine, 119
de Boucherville, Corinne, 168–69, 171
decolonization, 136, 138–42, 146, 148–49
Dempsey, Lotta, 119
Department of External Affairs (Canada), 6–8, 12, 65, 68, 72, 117, 119, 121, 147, 164, 166, 170–75, 177, 183–84, 205–6, 209, 211, 216, 222
Department of Indian Affairs (Canada), 139
Department of Indian Affairs and Northern Development (Canada), 152
Department of National Defence (Canada), 212
  Elsie Initiative for Women in Peace Operations, 212
Désy, Jean, 168–70
Diefenbaker, John, 11, 118, 120–12, 188, 190, 210
diplomatic wives, 8, 10, 12–13, 63–68, 70–75, 79, 83–84, 112, 161–77, 185, 195, 213
  role of, 10, 64, 67–68, 70, 83–84, 112, 195
disarmament, 99, 106, 109, 118, 121–22
Dodd, Dianne, 111
Donaghy, Greg, 6, 222–24
Douglas, Tommy, 67
Dubinsky, Karen, 6
DuBois, Ellen Carol, 213

Edmonton, 124, 137–39, 141
education, 23, 25, 28, 31, 33–34, 39–58, 74, 137–39, 149–51, 164, 187–88, 207, 211, 214, 216
Eide, Asbjørn, 135
Eisenhower, Dwight D., 118, 122

England
  See Britain
Enloe, Cynthia, 4, 64, 66, 83, 163, 169
Erlandsson, Susanna, 10

Fairclough, Ellen, 210
family planning, 14, 66, 68–69, 217
Family Planning Federation of Canada, 69
femininity, 22, 83, 184, 192, 200
feminism, 3, 14–15, 95–97, 107, 111–12, 191–92, 200, 212, 217–18
First World War, 10–11, 30, 44, 93–94, 96, 98, 100, 103, 112
Flynn, Karen, 9
Foot, Michael, 195–96
Ford, Sir John, 197
France, 7, 13, 71, 118, 122, 129, 146, 173
Franklin, Dr. Ursula, 124–29
Freeland, Chrystia, 223
Fulton, Mary H., 22

gender and foreign policy, 21, 24, 29, 34, 63, 168, 176–77, 190–92, 200–1, 207–8, 213
  gender roles in, 8–9, 11–12, 14–15, 24, 30, 58, 111, 177, 185, 190–91, 200–1, 213–14
  scholarship, 3–4, 7, 10, 13, 23, 64, 79, 163, 184, 212
General, Deskaheh Levi, 135
Geneva, 96, 99–100, 102, 122
Germany, 93, 122, 126
Global Affairs Canada (GAC), ix, 3–4, 212–13, 222–23
  Feminist International Assistance Policy, 3, 212, 217, 218
Goodall, Joan, 65
Gotlieb, Allan, 199
Granatstein, J.G., 185, 196
Great Britain
  See Britain
Greece, 67
Green, Howard, 119, 121–23
Grosart, Allister, 206
Grypma, Sonya, 28
Guyana, 66, 75, 143

Hackett Medical College for Women, 9, 22–23, 27–34
Haggan, Reeves, 195–96
Halifax, 124

Hantel-Fraser, Christine, 8, 170
Hardiman, David, 26, 43
Harding, Beatrice, 10, 66, 72–75, 76(i)–77, 78, 83–84
    British Guiana, 75–78
    early life, 73
    Liberia, 73–75
Harding, Bill, 73, 74(i), 75–76, 77(i), 78, 84
Hardy, George, 163
Hardy, Rae, 163
Hays, Harry, 127
Healey, Denis, 196
Healey, Madelaine, 46, 51
health care, women's, 9, 22–23, 25–26, 29, 30–33, 52, 212, 214, 217, 223
Henders, Susan, 64
Henderson, Dorothy, 119
Henderson, Julia, 73
Hillman, Kirsten, 13, 201
Hinder, Eleanor, 10, 66, 78, 80–84
    early life, 79
    meets Viola Smith, 79–80
    personal life, 10, 78, 80
    United Nations Economic Commission for Asia and the Far East, 80
    UNRRA, 80
    United Nations Technical Assistance Administration, 80–83
historiography, 3–10, 13–15, 23–24, 41, 64, 79, 163, 184, 212
Hitschmanova, Lotta, 9
Hong Kong, 27, 80
Howe, C.D., 188
Hudon, Isabelle, 201
Hughes, Vivien, 8
humanitarian work, 9, 21–34

Ignatieff, George, 122
imperialism, 8–9, 23–27, 33, 41–44, 58, 65–66, 84, 96, 138–40, 146, 189–90
India, 9–10, 24, 39–57, 64, 78–79, 81–82, 139, 214, 223
Indian Act (Canada), 141
Indian Association of Alberta, 137–38
Indian independence, 9–10, 39, 41, 43–44, 46, 53, 55–57
Indian National Congress, 39, 43, 49–50
Indigenous activism, 11, 135–37, 149, 197–98, 214, 216

Indigenous diplomacy, 135–36
Indigenous education, Canada, 150
Indigenous internationalism, 11, 140, 142–43, 148–51
Indigenous peoples, 7, 11, 43, 75, 84, 135–52, 190, 197, 198, 213–14, 216–17
Indonesia, 66, 70–71, 84, 213
Innis, Harold, 67
Innis, Mary Quayle, 67
International Committee of Women for Permanent Peace, 96, 107
International Council of Indigenous Women, 149
International Council of Women, 184
international development, 9, 67, 71–75, 78, 80–84, 147–50, 189, 212–13, 215, 218
International Planned Parenthood Federation, 69, 73
International Woman Suffrage Alliance, 103
International Women's Congress, 95–96, 98, 103–4, 109
International Women's Relief Committee, 103
Iriye, Akira, 163
Irwin, Arthur, 12, 161–62, 164–68, 171–77

Jamaica, 66, 68–69, 84, 213
James, Carolyn, 185
Japan, 21, 26, 81, 117, 193, 223

Káínai Nation, 11, 136–38, 144, 149–51, 214
Keenleyside, Hugh, 65
Kesler, Ethel, 124
Keyfitz, Beatrice, 10, 66, 70–72, 83–84
    Ceylon, 71–72
    Indonesia, 70–71
Keyfitz, Nathan, 70–72, 84
Khrushchev, Nikita, 118, 122
Kidd, Phoebe Ross, 65
King, William Lyon Mackenzie, 188
Kirby, Michael, 196

LaDuke, Winona, 149
LaMarsh, Judy, 127–28
Latin America, 6, 43, 64, 81, 144, 146
    See also individual country names
Laurendeau, Ghislaine, 122
Lazarus, Dr. Hilda, 44

League of Nations (LON), 11, 67, 79, 93, 96–97, 100–3, 110–12, 135, 184, 218
League of Nations Union, 66–67
Leger, Jules, 72, 164, 167, 174
Lévesque, René, 198
Lewis, David, 67
Liberal Party of Canada, 119, 123, 127, 183, 188, 210, 212
Liberia, 73–77
Little Bear, Leroy, 144
Loiselle, Gilles, 196

MacBean, Jessie, 9, 14, 21–34, 214, 223
   education, 24
   missionary work, 26–33
MacCallum, Elizabeth, 64
MacDermot, Terrence, 67
MacDonald, Flora, 12–14, 147, 205–11, 216
MacGill, Elsie, 212
MacGuigan, Mark, 183, 196
Mackenzie, David, 166
Macmillan, Chrystal, 98, 103, 104(i)–5
Macphail, Agnes, 111
Madokoro, Laura, 5
Manitoba, 73, 145
Manley, Norman, 69
Manuel, George, 140–44, 146–47
Marion Barclay Hospital, 22, 32
marriage, 51, 64–65, 79, 140–41, 163, 175
Marshall, Catherine E., 99–103
Martin, Paul Sr., 222–24
Marule, Jacob, 140–41
MATCH International, 212
maternal feminism and maternalism, 11, 111–12, 192
McCarthy, Helen, 191
McClung, Nellie, 111
McGeachy, Mary, 184, 191
McGill University, 34, 45, 108, 118
McKercher, Asa, 5
McManus, Sheila, 136
Meagher, Margaret, 8, 184
medical education, women, 24–25, 28, 31–34, 39–58
Mehta, Hansa, 64
memoirs and autobiographical writing, 7–8, 51, 72–73, 163
Merne, David, 23
Mi'kai'sto Red Crow Community College, 149–51

Mills, Sean, 6
missionaries and missionary movement, 8–9, 13–14, 21–34, 39–58, 63, 66, 172, 214–16, 223
Montreal, 54, 65, 70, 108, 118, 121, 124, 165, 170, 173
Moon, Barbara, 126
Morgan, Marta, 13
Morra, Linda, 69
Murray, Lowell, 209

Nairobi Conference
   See World Conference on Women, 1985
National Action Plan on Women, Peace, and Security (Canada), 212
National Film Board of Canada (NFB), 161, 165–66
National Indian Brotherhood (Canada), 140–43, 149
National Indian Council (Canada), 137
National Peace Conference, 1915 (United States), 108
National Research Council of Canada (NRC), 124
National Union of Women's Suffrage Societies (Britain), 95, 100
Native Women's Association of Canada, 145, 149
Nehru, Jawaharlal, 39, 42, 50, 58, 81
New Democratic Party (NDP), 127, 187, 193, 197, 207, 210
New York City, 66, 80, 83,176, 187, 213
New Zealand, 129, 142
Nichols, Florence, 9, 14, 39–42, 44, 51–58
   early life, 52
   education, 52
   missionary work, 52–57
Niitsitapi (Blackfoot Confederacy), 136–37, 150
Nobel Peace Prize, 93, 97, 99, 105, 107, 120
Non-Aligned Movement, 139, 143
North Atlantic Treaty Organization (NATO), 116, 193
Nova Scotia, 44, 124, 207–8
nuclear weapons, 11, 116–30, 189
   anti-nuclear movement, 116–19, 129–30
   BOMARC missiles, 116, 123
nuclear weapons testing, 11, 116–17, 120–22, 124, 127–29
   Castle Bravo test, 117

252   INDEX

Limited Test Ban Treaty, 124, 127–29
nursing and nurses, 8–10, 28, 30–32, 39–58, 65, 150
  education, 47–49
Nyerere, Julius, 139, 142, 149

Ontario, 24, 125, 186, 193
Ontario Women's Medical College, 24
Organization of American States, 167
Ottawa, 13, 70–71, 83, 117–19, 121–23, 126–28, 140–41, 144, 146, 148, 164–66, 171, 190, 195–98, 206, 222–24
Owen, David, 73, 78

pacifism, 96–97, 100, 111–13
Page, P.K., 12–14, 161, 162(i)–77, 216
  Australia, 164, 166
  Brazil, 166–77
  Brazilian Journal, 161–63, 171, 175–76
  early life, 164–65
Paris Summit (1960), 118
Pavitt, Laurie, 196
peace movements, 8, 10–11, 14, 93–113, 116–30, 213, 215, 216
Pearson, Lester, 119, 123, 127, 166, 189, 209
Pearson, Maryon, 120
Penfield, Wilder, 54
Pethick-Lawrence, Emmeline, 97, 106
Philippines, 75
Piikáni, 136
Planned Parenthood Association of Toronto, 69
Planned Parenthood Federation, 68–69
Prairie Farm Rehabilitation Administration, 73
Progressive Conservative Party, 11–12, 183, 186–89, 206–7, 210–11
prosopography, 13, 63
Powers, Francis Gary, 118

Quebec, 108, 122, 172, 196, 198, 215

racism, 81, 26, 28, 71, 137–39, 145, 151, 167
radiation, 117–18, 121, 123, 125–27
Rajkumari Amrit Kaur College of Nursing
  See University of Delhi College of Nursing
Ramond-Hirsch, Cor, 98
Red Cross, 8, 75
Red Scare, 98, 107

refugees, 99, 102–3, 208
Regina, 67–68, 72–75, 78
religious institutions, 22, 26–27, 39, 42, 44, 55, 147, 223
Robertson, Norman, 166, 174
Roosevelt, Franklin D., 73
Roosevelt, Teddy, 106
Roy, Ghislaine, 122
Royal Commission on the Status of Women in Canada, 192, 218
Russia
  See Soviet Union
Rutherford, Scott, 6

Said, Edward, 163
Sara, Maret, 149
Saskatchewan, 66–68, 73–75
Schwimmer, Rosika, 97–98, 106
Scott, F.R., 65, 70, 165
Scott, Joan, 63
Scott, Marian Dale, 65
Scudder, Dr. Ida, 42, 44, 52
Settee, Priscilla, 149
settlement movement, 95, 99, 105, 107
  Hull House, 105, 107
sexism, 12, 14, 25, 52, 151, 190, 192
Sheepshanks, Mary, 102–3
Shore, Peter, 195
Siksiká, 136
Sino-Japanese War (1894–95), 26
Sjolander, Claire Turenne, 3, 8, 184
Sluga, Glenda, 63, 185
Smallface-Marule, Marie, 11, 14, 136–52, 214, 216, 218
  CUSO, 139–41
  early life, 136–38
  education, 137–38
  Indian Act, 141
  Mi'kai'sto Red Crow Community College, 149–51
  National Indian Brotherhood, 140–43
  University of Lethbridge, 148–49
  World Council of Indigenous Peoples, 143–48
Smith, Heather, 3
Smith, Sidney, 171
Smith, Viola, 78–83
social gospel movement, 28
socialism, 42, 50, 67, 73, 97, 100, 139–40, 142, 187

South Africa, 67, 140–41, 190
Southern, James, 191
Soviet Union, 66, 78–79, 81–84, 118, 121–24, 165, 213
Spanish Civil War, 99
Stanfield, Robert, 186, 206, 209
Steel, David, 195
Steinhauer, Kathleen, 141
Stienstra, Deborah, 3–4
Stoler, Anne Laura, 68
Stowe, Dr. Emily, 24
strontium, 90, 124–25, 128–29
Suez crisis, 190, 209
suffrage movement, 95–97, 99–107, 111
Sweden, 122, 140, 153, 184

Tanzania, 139, 140, 142
Tauli-Corpuz, Victoria, 149
Taylor, Florence, 57
Thatcher, Margaret, 184, 191–92, 194, 196–99
Toronto, 22, 24, 44–46, 52–54, 69, 80, 119, 124, 126, 129, 138, 167, 186
Toronto Committee for Disarmament, 119
Treaty of Versailles (1919), 27, 96
Trudeau, Justin, 212
Trudeau, Pierre Elliott, 146–47, 183–85, 193–99
Tucker, Helen, 119
Turkey, 64
Turner Training School for Nurses, 28, 31

Union of British Columbia Indian Chiefs, 145
Unitarian Service Committee Canada, 9
United Nations (UN), 43, 46, 63, 65–66, 68, 73–74, 80–82, 84, 99, 110, 113, 120–21, 137, 139, 143, 145–47, 149, 176, 184, 187, 189, 213, 218
  Charter, 146
  Conference on the Human Environment, 143
  Declaration of the Rights of Indigenous Peoples, 135, 149
  development advisors, 63–64, 71
  Development Program, 78
  General Assembly, 121, 135, 142
  Technical Assistance Administration, 68, 78, 80–81
  Technical Assistance Resident Representatives (TARR), 64, 70, 75, 213
United Nations Economic and Social Council, 135, 218
United Nations Educational, Scientific, and Cultural Organization (UNESCO), 139, 145
United Nations International Children's Emergency Fund (UNICEF), 189
United Nations Permanent Forum on Indigenous Issues, 213
United Nations Relief and Rehabilitation Program (UNNRA), 8, 80, 184
United States, 4–7, 10, 13, 25–26, 28, 32, 54, 68, 73, 79, 80–82, 93, 95, 97, 99, 103, 105, 107–10, 113, 116–18, 121–24, 126, 136, 165, 168, 170, 199, 210, 222
Universal Declaration of Human Rights (1948), 63
University of Alberta, 11, 137–38
University of Calgary, 151
University of Delhi College of Nursing, 39–40, 42, 46
University of Lethbridge, 144, 149–50
University of Manitoba, 73, 145
University of Regina, 72–73
University of Toronto, 24, 44–46, 52, 124, 126, 129, 186

Van Huizen, Philip, 5
Vancouver, 65, 121, 124
Vellacott, Jo, 95–96, 101
Vietnam War, 116
Voice of Women/la Voix des Femmes (VOW), 11, 14, 116–30
  baby teeth collecting, 116–17, 124, 125, 129

Wadds, Jean Casselman, 12, 14, 101, 183–201, 210, 215
  and gender, 190–92, 200
  image, 192–93
Wales, Julia Grace, 14, 93–94(i), 104–5, 108–12, 215
war in Afghanistan (2001–14), 214
Weiers, Margaret, 8
Whitton, Charlotte, 190
Wilson, Woodrow, 14, 94–95, 108, 110
  Fourteen Points, 94, 96, 110
Windle, Victoria Campbell, 215

Winnipeg, 124
Wisconsin Peace Society, 108
Woman's Christian Temperance Union (Canada), 95
Woman's Peace Party, 95–96, 98, 107
women diplomats, 3, 7–10, 12–13, 64–65, 163, 184, 191, 205, 209, 213–15
  marriage bar, 64–65
women physicians, 22–26, 28–30, 32, 34, 42, 52, 223
women's archival record, lack of, 44, 57, 66, 68–70, 72, 83
Women's International League for Peace and Freedom (WILPF), 10, 14, 93–113, 118, 120
Women's Social and Political Union (Britain), 96

Wood, Molly, 68
Working Group on Indigenous Populations, 135
World Conference on Women, 1985, 218
World Council of Indigenous Peoples, 11, 143–48
World Health Organization (WHO), 46–47, 51, 57
World's Woman's Christian Temperance Union, 95

Young, Mary, 64

Zambia, 11, 139–41, 148, 214
Zancarini-Fournel, Michelle, 216